# SUCCESSFUL PROJECT MANAGERS

## Leading Your Team to Success

JEFFREY K. PINTO
O. P. KHARBANDA

 VAN NOSTRAND REINHOLD
I(T)P A Division of International Thomson Publishing Inc.

New York • Albany • Bonn • Boston • Detroit • London • Madrid • Melbourne
Mexico City • Paris • San Francisco • Singapore • Tokyo • Toronto

Printed in the United States of America
For more information, contact:

Van Nostrand Reinhold
115 Fifth Avenue
New York, NY 10003

International Thomson Publishing GmbH
Königswinterer Strasse 418
53227 Bonn
Germany

International Thomson Publishing Europe
Berkshire House 168-173
High Holborn
London WCIV 7AA
England

International Thomson Publishing Asia
221 Henderson Road #05-10
Henderson Building
Singapore 0315

Thomas Nelson Australia
102 Dodds Street
South Melbourne, 3205
Victoria, Australia

International Thomson Publishing Japan
Hirakawacho Kyowa Building, 3F
2-2-1 Hirakawacho
Chiyoda-ku, 102 Tokyo
Japan

Nelson Canada
1120 Birchmount Road
Scarborough, Ontario
Canada M1K 5G4

International Thomson Editores
Campos Eliseos 385, Piso 7
Col. Polanco
11560 Mexico D.F. Mexico

1 2 3 4 5 6 7 8 9 10 QEBFF 02 01 00 99 98 97 96 95

Library of Congress Cataloging-in-Publication Data
Pinto, Jeffrey K.
    Successful project managers : leading your team to success / Jeffrey K. Pinto. O.P.
    Kharbanda.
        p.      cm.

    Includes bibliographical references and index.
    ISBN 0-442-01952-1
    1. Industrial project management.   I. Kharbanda, Om Prakash.   II. Title.
HD69.P75P55   1995                      94-49394
658.4'04—dc20                           CIP

•••••••••

# *Contents*

## PART 3 TEAMS ACHIEVE WONDERS

## PART 4 SOME SUCCESS AND FAILURE STORIES

## PART 5 WHERE DO WE GO FROM HERE?

•  •  •  •  •  •  •  •  •

# *Preface*

*The last thing one settles in writing a book is what one should put in first.*

—Pascal

In today's fast-paced business environment, projects can be viewed as critical stepping stones for organizational growth and productivity. Indeed, we see projects everywhere in areas as diverse as accounting, advertising, banking, law, medicine, and even the United Nations. In this book, we are primarily concerned with projects in industry. A project, defined as a nonroutine, nonrepetitive, one-time undertaking, with its own specific time and cost targets, presents an ongoing and formidable challenge to any manager. In the frenetic pace of the modern business world, project management as a discipline has truly come of age. There has been an explosion in the literature on project management in practically all its aspects, except one—namely, the one person who can make or break a project, the project manager/leader. It is an effort to fill this serious gap that our book was written.

Project managers are truly the heart and soul of a project. They are in a position of tremendous responsibility, one usually characterized by serious limiting constraints. Within the organization's hierarchy, they rarely hold any real formal authority, they have minimal power or status, they command a team of temporary subordinates who maintain loyalty to their functional departments, and they are expected to successfully bring their projects to fruition while keeping a tight rein on budgets and schedules. When viewed in this perspective, is it any wonder that successful project managers are valuable commodities?

In spite of the importance that project managers have to project success, we know surprisingly little about the skill sets they need to be effective. The irony of this lack of a broad-based knowledge about project managers is that project management, far more than traditional functional management, is fundamentally leader-intensive. Although leadership is vital throughout all aspects of any business undertaking, it is impossible to overestimate its importance in project management. Competent project leaders have a tremendous capacity to impact on team building, generating enthusiasm and motivation, efficient time management, and accurate target setting.

The project manager may be likened to a captain of a ship or commander of an aircraft. While at sea or in the air, quick and decisive action is imperative. Action must often be taken on the spur of the moment, even with incomplete data and information. Further, the crew must implement these decisions without any question or delay (of course, if time permits, a good project manager will try to arrive at a consensus decision with the project team), or disaster will result. The project manager can also be likened to the conductor of an orchestra producing high-quality music only if all the musicians play in unison, following the lead of the conductor. The conductor succeeds only because of direct and instant communication with all members of the orchestra. The project manager needs exactly such a relationship with his or her team. They must develop a level of trust and comfort with each other that allows them to forego interpersonal difficulties and agendas in the single-minded pursuit of project goals.

The above metaphors demonstrate the reality of project management. As more and more researchers and consultants are coming to understand (and seasoned project managers have known for years!), in spite of its technical aspects, project management is still essentially a "people management" process. The skills that separate successful project managers from those who are unsuccessful are rarely technical: They are almost always human skills. And by this term, we mean the ability to understand team building, leadership, motivation, time management, meeting skills, managing diverse personalities, power and politics, and stakeholder management. *These* are the qualities of successful project managers.

Unfortunately, for most project managers, these skills are rarely taught beforehand. In fact, within most organizations, including those currently practicing project management, a comprehensive skill set for project managers is rarely taught at all. At a recent national meeting of the U.S. Project Management Institute, a noted consultant presented a paper entitled "A Survival Guide for the Accidental Project Manager," in which he argued that most of the skills learned by project managers develop *after* they have been put in charge of a project! Clearly, the implication of such an approach in those companies that employ this practice is the risk of serious difficulties. We owe more to our projects and our people than to continue to perpetuate these ad hoc procedures that cast novice project managers adrift in a sea of difficulties embracing the full range of technical, human, planning, and budgetary problems. With this book, we hope to make the project management function less mysterious, especially for newly appointed project managers, who until now have been relying largely on on-the-job training and the occasional helpful advice of senior managers. Briefly, our aims are:

- To help project managers, particularly first-timers, do a better job of managing their projects.

- Provide them with the necessary skills by offering a pragmatic, comprehensive, and *managerially based* guide to the challenges of project management in modern organizations.

Our approach is a combination of theory and practice, thanks to a team comprising an American academician and an Indian practitioner, both with wide-ranging consulting and training experience. It seeks to establish a foundation with some important guiding principles from the fields of organizational behavior and project management and to then put the problems confronting project managers within their proper context. For example, it is necessary that first-time project managers understand concepts such as organizational stakeholder analysis in order to identify who the key actors are within their company who can help or hinder their efforts. Further, as project managers progress, they also begin to realize that the act of attempting to satisfy one stakeholder is likely to upset another, illustrating one salient feature of project management: It often is a balancing act, with the project manager attempting to keep all balls in play at the same time.

Successful project managers are *kingpins,* but not kings. They dare not order their people around in an autocratic fashion, for that approach would be a sure road to disaster. They are the boss, but in a loosely defined way. Indeed, within most organizations, they may not even have the authority to conduct performance appraisals of or offer rewards to their team members. As a result, their management style must be one of persuasion and influence. In their personal backgrounds, project managers are likely to be engineers or specialists in certain technical fields. However, one of the first lessons they must learn in their present roles is to "forget" their technical knowledge, opting for the role of a "generalist," learning instead to rely on their team member specialists.

A truly effective manager today has to do more than just manage. He or she must also be able to lead the team. We maintain that although leaders can and must manage, a manger cannot necessarily lead as well. This is now simply a play on words: The "managing" function of yesteryear is now yielding to the "leading" function, tomorrow's role for managers. Because of the key role that effective leadership does play, nowhere is this distinction more profoundly felt than in the realm of project management. The project manager must aspire to the more rigorous and demanding title of "project leader." It is by exerting personal qualities of leadership in their own work and through interaction with their teams that project leaders make their presence felt.

This then conveys the essence of our approach. Although our range of interests, backgrounds, and locations added materially to the difficulties of completing this project, we feel they nevertheless contributed substantially to both its scope and flavor. In this book, we have been able to include several real-life case studies of successful project managers and their projects from around the world. Each of these stories solidifies our message about the fundamental role that project managers play, through their own efforts and those of their team, in project success. Just as the majority of practicing project managers have acquired their skills, we too have learned "the hard way," and we now bring to you some of these lessons, in the hope that after reading this book, a new generation of project managers will find itself far better equipped to deal with the rigors of their designated profession.

November 1, 1994

Dr. Jeffrey K. Pinto
*Erie, Pennsylvania*

Dr. O. P. Kharbanda
*Bombay, India*

●●●●●●●●●

*To Mary Beth and Sudershan,*
*our "silent partners"*

Part *1*

# *Setting the Scene*

*A*t the center of the project management challenge lies the context in which project managers must operate. Their relationship to the rest of the organization, to a temporary project team, and to a variety of stakeholders all offer unique challenges for the effective management of projects. In this section, we will explore some of the important contextual factors that make project management such a challenge and differentiate its practices from more traditional managerial roles. In the first chapter, we offer some important definitions and lay the groundwork for the relationship of project-based work to the standard functional structure, distinguishing between the types of duties that characterize the two environments.

The second chapter, on project stakeholders, will demonstrate the peculiar challenge that project managers face, in attempting to address and satisfy the various project stakeholders. We will argue that the various demands of these stakeholders are often in conflict with each other and put the project manager in a difficult position of trying to find a middle ground for satisfying this seemingly insoluble problem.

The third chapter explores an extremely important contextual factor: the nature of power and politics in project management. Many project managers suffer from being expected to perform their duties efficiently and effectively without being given the commensurate power to achieve project goals. As a result, this chapter will offer a framework for better understanding the political nature of organizations and how project managers can make use of political tactics to gain the resources necessary for project success. Written in a pragmatic style, this chapter offers some practical suggestions for project managers seeking to attain the resources necessary to accomplish their goals.

The fourth chapter in this section examines past research on the critical factors in successful project implementation. We will argue that although technical skills and knowledge are important, research clearly demonstrates that the most important determinants of project success lie in the successful management of the behavioral, "people" issues. In this chapter, we will address these studies, focusing on the important factors that were uncovered, and consider methods for project managers to better manage the human side of the project, proven to have the greatest impact on successful project outcomes.

# 1

## Introduction: The Challenge of Managing Projects

*The road is a long one from the projection of a thing to its accomplishment.*

—MOLIÈRE

IN AN INCREASINGLY interwoven and fast-paced corporate world, projects have become the "engines of growth" for most companies. Whether the company regularly employs project teams or creates them as ad hoc "skunkworks" to address immediate crises or market opportunities, the use of projects and cross-functional teams continues to proliferate. Wherever we look these days, we can find teams of people working on projects, headed up by a project manager. Indeed, the use of project management is now a worldwide phenomenon, operating in companies across the United States, Canada, Europe, South America, Asia, and the Pacific Rim. This substantial increase in the use of project teams represents a mixed blessing for most companies. Research and anecdotal evidence demonstrate the tremendous flexibility and improved time to market that project-based work allows modern corporations. However, many companies starting to use project teams for the first time are discovering that these teams are often only as good as the individuals who are managing them. Indeed, there are few management or corporate activities that are as "leader-intensive" as the project management process (Posner, 1989). A competent project manager can have a tremendous impact on project success, serving as a catalyst for the most important project activities, including team building, generating motivation and enthusiasm, efficient time management, accurate target setting, and so on.

It has been said that effective project managers are the kingpin, but not the king. Because of limits on the real power they wield, they dare not order their people around in an autocratic fashion, for that approach would be a sure road to disaster. They are the bosses, it is true, but often in a loosely defined way. Indeed, within most organizations, they may have neither the authority to conduct performance appraisals nor offer incentives and rewards to their subordinates. As a result, their management styles must be those of persuasion and influence, rather than coercion and command. In many modern corporations, project managers are likely to be engineers or even specialists in certain fields. However, in their present roles it is best for them to "forget" their technical affiliation and instead learn to rely on team members for guidance, advice, and expertise.

Because of these and other limitations on the flexibility and power of project managers, project management has rightly been termed the "accidental profession" by more than one writer (Davis, 1984; Frame, 1987; Graham, 1992). The diverse challenges, high pressure to perform, and myriad responsibilities that face project managers ensure that within most organizations, a sufficient number of competent project managers are likely to remain in short supply. Although it is true that the rewards for successful project management can sometimes be great, visibility, status, and promotions often accrue only to those who are managing programs that have significant strategic value to the organization. The vast majority of project managers toil in relative obscurity, working to bring their projects to completion with limited support and little recognition or acknowledgment for jobs well done.

Unfortunately and perhaps ironically, it is due to the very popularity of project management techniques that many organizations are facing their most severe challenges as they often belatedly discover that they simply do not have sufficient numbers of the sorts of competent project managers who are often the key driving force behind successful product or service development. Senior managers in many companies readily acknowledge the ad hoc manner in which most project managers acquire their skills, but are unsure how to better develop and provide for a supply of well-trained project leaders for the future (Thamhain, 1991). These companies are caught in a classic double bind: They perceive the need to rely on project management techniques for long-term success and yet they are unsure of ways in which to "grow" skilled project managers.

Few if any of those who are currently running projects possess any formal project management training beyond learning some of the rudimentary skills and basic activities of project scheduling and control. In fact, if the reader were to sample a cross section of project managers within any large corporation, he or she would quickly discover an important truth: Project management represents one of the purest examples of on-the-job training in existence today. In other words, most project managers *are* project managers simply by virtue of the fact that they have been selected by their superiors to run a project. Having been so assigned, they are often thrown into the fray to sink or swim as they are able. Those who learn quickly will most likely succeed; those who do not will founder. Hence, the term "accidental project manager" has been coined to illustrate the nature of the managerial problem in performing well in an important role whose only "training" is often a trial by fire.

This book has been written in order to shed some light on some of the myriad demands, opportunities, travails, challenges, and vexations that are part of becoming a better project manager. It is important that we make an early distinction between project management—a set of techniques used to bring projects to completion—and project managers—those who have been tasked with overseeing a project, this being one of the most difficult duties any organization can offer to its members. Our purpose is not to write another book about the techniques of project management. There are a number of excellent texts and resource manuals currently in print that deal with the wide range of project management activities. Rather, we sought to write a book for the project manager. Books of this sort have been and remain surprisingly underdeveloped. To illustrate and support this contention, we searched through the CD-ROM for business periodicals index for the last 10 years (1984–1993) and input some key words to determine their popularity in terms of articles and books that have been written on these subjects. Specifically, we entered the terms "manager," "management," "project," "project management," and finally, "project manager." The results were illuminating:

| Term | Number of Entries |
| --- | --- |
| Manager | 2054 |
| Management | 2440 |
| Project | 2836 |
| Project management | 539 |
| Project manager | 23 |

The above figures lend themselves to making the obvious conclusion: Although much has been and continues to be written in the areas of projects, managers, and management in general, there is a dearth of material related most particularly to the project manager. Given the linchpin role that project managers play in the successful implementation of projects, this lack of literature underscores the state of much of our project management theory: It is aimed far more at processes and techniques than at key individuals and their roles. We would argue that the above data are not, in fact, terribly surprising. We simply do not know enough about the roles that project managers play and the depth of their personal involvement with and responsibility for projects.

Our goal is to offer a practical work that identifies some of the most important aspects of the duties project managers must perform, set within a realistic analysis of the organizational context in which project managers must operate. As such, we will be examining a number of questions, issues, and topics that project managers must acknowledge and come to terms with if they are to succeed. For example, who are the various project stakeholders and what is their impact on project success? How must project managers use political behavior and negotiation in order to compensate for the frequently low status of their projects? In dealing with top management, how might informal influence tactics work when power will not? Exactly what are the various duties and skills necessary to become a proficient project manager?

Questions such as these continue to trouble the accidental project managers who inhabit our corporations. As they try to pick up some of the important, informal keys to project management success, they are often forced to learn the hard way (i.e., what did *not* work). As you can imagine, this practice is expensive to the company in time and resources and tremendously frustrating to these newly designated project managers. It is true that all of us learn a great many lessons in life through having first failed. However, to use this argument as a basis for continuing to approve of these "learning the hard way" practices, even tacitly, is simply disingenuous. It is the equivalent of a tour guide withholding a road map in order to force tourists to learn the streets of New York by driving around lost for several hours (or days!). After numerous stops, starts, detours, and much blundering about, the tourists may eventually get where they are going. However, once having arrived, they will not likely be in a position to either remember their path for future trips or advise other travelers on the best routes to follow.

We originally conceived of this book to serve as a guide for both experienced and aspiring project managers. In formulating the various topics and chapters in the work, we purposely selected many of those managerial and organizational concerns that are often ill-defined and "fuzzy," but can have a tremendous impact on the successful implementation of projects. For example, it does not take long for many project managers to discover exactly how far their personal power and status will take them in interacting with the rest of the organization. Hence, an understanding of influence tactics and political behavior is absolutely essential for project managers to succeed. Unfortunately, novice project managers are rarely clued into this important bit of information until it is too late (e.g., they have appealed through formal channels for extra resources and been denied). Likewise, it is often not until a project manager has managed to offend a key member of the top management staff or an important constituent that he or she becomes aware of the importance of understanding the various types of project stakeholders and their divergent demands.

It is important that the reader understand that we are firm supporters of the use of project teams in organizations. On balance, project management success stories have been impressive. However, they cannot overshadow the fact that at the other end of the spectrum, many projects across a large number of organizations regularly operate well over budget and behind schedule, turning out goods and services that either do not work very well or are not what customers sought in the first place. As project management consultants as well as writers, we have both had ample opportunities to observe at close range companies that are paying an expensive price for poor project management. Some of the most systemic and troubling problems that we see stem from the same sources: 1) an unclear understanding of what project management will do and will not do for the company, and 2) placing too high expectations for project success on managers who have received poor or nonexistent training in their new duties.

The examples are numerous:

- A long-distance telephone company whose chief executive officer became so enamored of the concept of high-profile project teams, or "skunkworks," he assigned that title to the few most highly visible, strategically important projects. Once having established this priority system, the company began to neglect or deemphasize every other project that did not have the skunkworks label. Quickly, both senior and middle management in departments across the organization came to realize that the only way to get their pet projects the resources necessary to succeed was to redesignate *all* new projects as skunkworks. In short order, the company, which had originally developed four high-profile projects in 1990 found, by 1992, that literally dozens of projects were now considered high-priority skunkworks programs—whether they deserved the label or not. Consequently, because *every* project became a high-profile project, the firm could not actually identify *any* high-profile projects. In trying to decide how to apportion resources among the wide variety of skunkworks projects, top management was unsure how to separate the wheat from the chaff, making a number of questionable funding decisions because of poor control processes and the mixed signals that they had unintentionally sent out.

- A large computer hardware manufacturer has been dominated by the members of the hardware engineering department to such an extent that practically all new product ideas originate internally, within the department. Funding and early development decisions are often made with minimal or no communication and information exchange with the marketing organization. In many instances, by the time marketing (cynically referred to as simply "order takers" by the engineering department) is brought on board, it is presented with a *fait accompli:* a finished product that it is instructed to sell. Marketing has had little input in the development process, offered no advice, and forwarded no industry demands or customer requirements. Rather, it is given a piece of equipment that it is told will suit the needs of the "public." Understandably, many members of the marketing department have become so disillusioned by the obvious lack of respect with which they are held throughout the rest of the company that they no longer offer unsolicited advice and rarely attend new product meetings, even when asked.

- A medium-sized manufacturing organization made it a policy to reward and punish project managers on the basis of their ability to bring projects in on time and under budget. These project managers were never held to any requirement that the project be accepted by its clients or become commercially successful. In fact, once the project had been "completed," the project manager was rewarded and immediately assigned to new duties, sometimes without ever interacting directly with a customer. Project managers quickly learned that their rewards were simply tied to satisfying the cost accountants and began to willfully cut corners and make trade-off decisions that seriously undermined new product quality. After several disastrous new product introductions, the company has finally begun to reassess its reward system, making it clear to project managers that rewards are contingent on not only satisfying internal processes and controls, but through providing a product that customers are willing to buy.

- Projects at a large, multinational corporation are routinely assigned to new managers who often have less than one year of experience with the company. They are instructed to form their project teams and begin the development process without any formal training or channels of communication to important clients and functional groups. In fact, all that the company provides is project management software for their personal computers (again, with no formal training on how to use it) and the phone number of a senior manager who has had some past project management experience. These neophyte project leaders are advised to contact the senior manager only in the case of emergencies. Not surprisingly, the company estimates that fewer than 25% of these projects, regardless of their importance, are ever successfully concluded. At the same time, the company seems loath to establish any form of formal training or mentoring program with experienced project managers.

This sort of on-the-job training in project management is pervasive. It is also pernicious. Senior managers who when confronted with the faulty nature of their firm's project management training simply shrug their shoulders and respond "that's how I learned" do their companies a grave disservice. Further, such casual approaches to a vital practice serve to undercut the potential for expanded use of project-based work in a number of companies. Rather than reexamine their central core philosophies and project management training programs, many companies are inclined to simply dismiss project management as a fad that failed to live up to its potential.

Although it is not our purpose nor is it necessary to offer a defense of project management, it is important that readers, particularly those who may have found themselves skeptical about project management in the past, acknowledge that project management's track record for success is far too strong to be dismissed as simply the latest management fad. Project management does work. How, then, are managers from companies across the globe to make the most of the potential that projects offer for enhanced time to market, increased organizational flexibility, improved coordination and communication across functional boundaries, and better-quality products produced with greater efficiency? This book will explore some of the important techniques and concerns that project managers must incorporate into their roles and activities if they and their projects are to achieve the level of productivity and enhanced performance that effective project management truly offers.

## SOME IMPORTANT TERMS AND CONCEPTS

Before we can develop a comprehensive discussion of the roles and duties of project managers, it is important to establish a baseline consisting of some of the most important terms and concepts that underpin the project management process. Most of us understand implicitly what terms such as "project" or "life cycle" mean. However, we must devote some time and attention to reexamining and formally defining these and other important terms so that the reader will have a common body of basic knowledge of the key terms and properties of projects. As we continue to use terms such as "project management" throughout the course of this book, we will be employing a meaning that will remain clear to all readers.

## WHAT IS A PROJECT?

Although we see or read about impressive examples of projects every day, actually defining a project is sometimes not easy. The recently opened English Channel Tunnel (or "Chunnel"), the successful bid for the 1994 Summer Olympic Games by the city of Atlanta, the great pyramids of Giza, and the Panama Canal are all famous examples of projects. On a less grand scale, the completion of a team project at school, writing a termpaper, decorating the house for a Christmas party or visit from family, or a weekly shopping trip to the grocery store are all examples of projects that we engage in on a daily, almost routine, basis. Although vastly different in form, time frame, and goals to be accomplished, each of the above examples, whether great or modest, shares some common properties that define the nature and character of most projects.

In order to be meaningful, we need to consider definitions general enough to include a range of organizational activities that comprise "project functions." At the same time, the definition should be narrow enough so that we are able to focus specifically on those organizational activities that both managers and writers can agree are "project-oriented." Let us consider two excellent definitions of projects that seem to satisfy the dual requirements of specificity and inclusiveness. The first, by Steiner, suggests:

> A project is an organization of people dedicated to a specific purpose or objective. Projects generally involve large, expensive, unique, or high risk undertakings which have to be completed by a certain date, for a certain amount of money, within some expected level of performance. At a minimum, all projects need to have well defined objectives and sufficient resources to carry out all the required tasks.

The second definition, offered by Cleland and Kerzner, includes the following characteristics:

> [A project is] a combination of human and nonhuman resources pulled together in a temporary organization to achieve a specified purpose.

With these and other definitions, it is possible to isolate some of the important characteristics underlying projects. Specifically, most writers on project management point to four common dimensions of projects:

- They are constrained by a finite budget and time frame to completion; that is, they typically have a specific budget allocated to them as well as a defined start and completion date.

- They comprise a set of complex and interrelated activities that require effective coordination.

- They are directed toward the attainment of a clearly defined goal or set of goals.

- To some degree, each project is unique.

These features form the core that distinguishes project-based work from other forms of organizational activity. Because they are significant and underscore the inherent challenge in managing projects, it is important that we examine each of these characteristics in more detail.

## *Finite Budget and Schedule Constraints*

Unlike the typical ongoing operations that occur within "line" or functional units of most corporations, projects are set up with two very important bounds on their activities: a specified time period for completion and limited budget. Projects are temporary undertakings, intended to solve a specific problem (more on this later). They are not intended to supplant the regular functional operations of the organization, but rather operate until they have achieved their intended goals. Once these goals have been completed, the project ends. Certainly, we should note that budget and time constraints are estimates, based on the best available (and sometimes naively optimistic) information that the organization has. As a result, it is not uncommon to build in a margin for error to allow for unforeseen expenses or time slippages. The key to understanding the nature of project work as opposed to, say, an assembly line production run is that, unlike the production line that can continue on into the indefinite future, projects are temporary. They fulfill their goals, in accordance with time and money limits, and disband.

### *Complex and Interrelated Activities*

Projects typically comprise a degree of complexity that is not found to the same degree within other functional departments, often due to the cross-functional nature of the activities. For example, in developing a new product, a project team may be staffed with members from a wide variety of functional backgrounds: marketing, production, finance, human resources, and so forth. This cross-disciplinary nature of much of project-based work adds another order of magnitude to the usual levels of complexity found within any individual department.

Unfortunately, the complexity and interrelatedness of projects have an unwelcome side effect: conflict. Sources of conflict abound within projects due to the unique properties that they possess as well as the multiple goals and attitudes of different members of the project team. Not only are projects forced to compete with functional units for their share of a variety of scarce resources, but even within the project team, the almost ubiquitous nature of conflict is clearly demonstrated. Members of the project team regularly experience these sources of tension and must seek a balance between dual allegiances to their functional bosses and project manager. As one well-known project management textbook noted, "Project management is no place for the timid" (Meredith and Mantel, 1989).

Another example of the complex and interrelated nature of projects derives from the multiple activities that are carried out, often simultaneously, by different members of the project team. This interrelatedness is typified by the scheduling techniques of PERT and Gantt charting that demonstrate the sometimes bewildering array of interdependent activities performed by a project team. If tasks are not performed in their correct order and within the time allotted to them, the entire project can be jeopardized. Consequently, the project manager's job here is twofold: First, to establish a coherent working relationship among a number of team members from diverse functional backgrounds and second, to create a scheduling and control system that permits the greatest level of efficiency of project activities.

## *Clearly Defined Goals*

Projects are usually created with specific purposes or a narrowly determined set of purposes in mind. Indeed, the worst sorts of projects are those that are established with vaguely defined or fuzzy mandates permitting a wide range of interpretations among members of the project team and parent organization. Projects of this sort are usually doomed to spin along out of control as goals are continually interpreted and reassessed while the budget grows and the estimated completion date slips further and further into the future.

One of the most important bits of advice that we habitually offer to organizations establishing project teams is to narrow their focus: Make the goals clear and concise. Indeed, it is usually better to create two separate project teams, each with a smaller set of clearly defined goals, than load excessively vague or expansive goals on a single project. The more well-defined the goals, the clearer the indications, both internally and externally, that the project team is succeeding. Some of the chief causes of projects continuing well past the point of serving any reasonable purpose are a lack of initial goals, changing goals, or goals that were so poorly elucidated they provided no help to the project team.

## *Uniqueness*

Projects are usually "one-shot" propositions, that is, they are non-recurring and typically established to address a particular problem or market opportunity. Their very uniqueness is the characteristic that underscores the challenge of project management: The learning curve from one project to the next is, at best, tenuous. Once a manager has become part of a functional department concerned, for example, with the production of brand X, that manager will likely continue facing a series of duties and even problems that can be somewhat anticipated due to past experience with similar products being manufactured using similar techniques. Past experience (either their own or others) and learning curves will allow that manager to begin to anticipate likely problem areas and points of potential difficulty in the production process. We are able to gain a measure of comfort with the company's manufacturing activities due to our familiarity with how the process has always operated.

The world of project managers is very different. Because we are faced with a unique problem or opportunity, the "rules" for how the project should be configured and run have not been developed. In effect, we have to learn some lessons as we progress. In learning these lessons and exploring virgin territory, project managers encounter the sort of risks and uncertainty that typify project-based work. It is, however, important to note that a project's "uniqueness" may vary to a considerable degree from company to company and project to project. For example, a project team for a computer software manufacturer preparing the fourth modification and reissue of a well-known product will have the experiences of the original development team and the first three modification teams to draw on in setting work schedules and coordinating activities. Certainly, recent demands for new features and changes to hardware technology have to be taken into consideration and represent a source of uniqueness, but the basic project shares common characteristics that limit the risk inherent in new product development.

## WHAT IS PROJECT MANAGEMENT?

Given the nature and idiosyncrasies of projects as they have been explicated, how are we to define project management? Simply put, project management is the dynamic process of leading, coordinating, planning, and controlling a diverse and complex set of processes and people in the pursuit of achieving project objectives. The reader can quickly see that this definition encompasses a number of distinct and often intimidating challenges. The successful management of projects is simultaneously a human and technical challenge, requiring a far-sighted strategic outlook coupled with the flexibility to react to conflicts and trouble areas as they arise on a daily basis. The project managers who are ultimately successful at their profession must learn to deal with and anticipate the constraints on their project team and personal freedom of action while consistently maintaining their eyes on the ultimate prize.

But what is the ultimate objective for project managers? What are the determinants of a successful project and how do they differ from projects that we may rightfully consider to have failed? Our initial definition of projects offers some important clues as to how we should evaluate project team performance. Ask any seasoned project manager and he or she will usually tell you that a successful project is one that has come in *on time, under budget, and performs as expected (conforms to specifications)*. In fact, this definition is so common, it is usually referred to as the triple constraint of project management: the combined demands for accomplishing our project goals while maintaining firm control on our time and other pertinent resources.

In the last few years, we have seen a reassessment of this traditional model for project success. The old triple constraint is rapidly being replaced by a new model, invoking a fourth hurdle for project success: client satisfaction. Client satisfaction refers to the idea that a project is only as successful as it satisfies the needs of its intended user. As a result, client satisfaction places a new and important constraint on project managers who have often thus far been evaluated through "internal" measures of success: budget, schedule, and performance. With the inclusion of client satisfaction as a fourth constraint, project managers must now devote additional time and attention to maintaining close ties with and satisfying the demands of external clients. Figure 1.1 illustrates the inclusive nature of project success through adding the fourth success measure.

Among the implications of this new "quadruple" constraint is its effect on traditional project management roles. As we will see in a later chapter, concern for the client, although extremely important, necessitates that project managers adopt an outward focus in their efforts. In effect, they must now become not only managers of project activities, but also sales representatives for the company to the client base. The product they have to sell is their project.

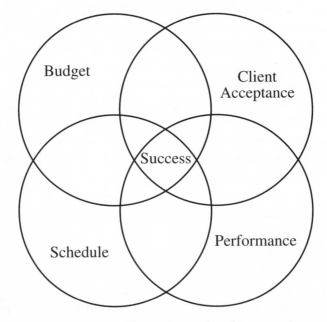

FIGURE 1.1. Project success: The new quadruple constraint.

Therefore, if they are to facilitate acceptance of the project and, hence, its success, they have to learn how to engage in these marketing duties effectively.

When we begin to view project management as a technique for implementing overall corporate strategy, it is clear that the importance of project management and, hence, project managers cannot be underestimated (Bryson and Bromiley, 1993; Lord, 1993). Project management becomes a framework for monitoring corporate progress as it further provides a basis on which the skillful manager can control the implementation process. No wonder, then, that there is a growing interest in the project manager's role within the corporation.

## THE PROJECT LIFE CYCLE

One common means to help managers conceptualize the work and budgetary requirements of a project is to employ the project life cycle. The concept of life cycles is very familiar to most of us; we are all aware of product life cycles, used to explain the sales life and demand for new products; organizational life cycles, used to predict the rise and demise of corporations; and so forth. Likewise, most projects pass through a similar form of life cycle that project managers find extremely useful for predicting resource needs, material and staffing requirements, and budget considerations.

Figure 1.2 shows an example of a project life cycle. This representation of a life cycle is based on the four-stage model suggested by Adams and Barndt (1988) and King and Cleland (1988). In their model, the project life cycle has been divided into four distinct stages or phases, including:

*Conceptualization.* The initial project stage. During a project's conceptualization, the initial goals and objectives of the project are set, as well as possible means to achieve these goals. Project managers begin to make some personnel selections as they seek to staff their project teams. During the conceptualization phase of the project, actual resource outlay is low, as preliminary assessments are conducted.

*Planning.* During the planning stage, the project manager is busy conducting preliminary capability studies, assessing the goals of the project in light of resource and time commitments. As part of this process, project managers will develop initial schedules and work breakdown, as well as assign specific tasks to their team members. Further, they will make clear to the team how both the concurrent and consecutive tasks are structured so that team members are able to understand how their individual roles fit into the overall project development picture. Note in Figure 1.2 how the commitment of resources has begun to "ramp up" at a more rapid pace, as increasing levels of money and other resources are committed to the project.

*Execution.* The third stage involves performing the actual "work" of the project. Materials, people, and other necessary resources are procured and brought on line as they are needed. The

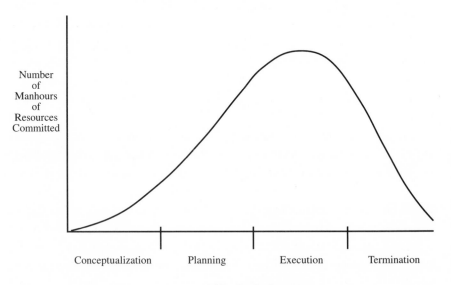

Life Cycle Stages

FIGURE 1.2. Project life cycle.

various subroutines and other assigned tasks are being carried out in the proper sequence and the performance capabilities of the project are verified. During the execution stage, the project team is operating at maximum strength, with full resources brought into play. It is during this stage that the majority of the budget is spent and the project developed.

*Termination.* The final stage of a project is called termination. Although the term suggests that the project is simply finished, in reality, it is during a project's termination that a number of important tasks are performed. One of the most significant is the transfer of the project to its ultimate intended user, the client. It is hoped that, as part of the project development process, the project team has kept the client closely informed of the performance characteristics of the project and addressed any of its concerns in order to smooth the actual transfer process. Further, the project manager begins to release back project resources to the parent organization and reassigns project team personnel to other duties, either in their former functional roles or to other project teams.

## HOW ARE MOST PROJECT TEAMS STRUCTURED AND STAFFED?

One of the most intriguing and challenging aspects of project management lies in the relationship of project teams to the rest of the parent organization. With the exception of companies that are set up with matrix or project structures, the majority of organizations using project management techniques employ some form of a standard functional structure. As Figure 1.3 shows, within the classic functional structure, departments are organized in accordance with functional roles: for example, marketing, finance, R&D, production, and so forth. Most activities and operations occur within these functional groupings. Further, as we intimated earlier, these functional duties are often on-going and act as necessary parts of the organization's activities. For example, the manager of new

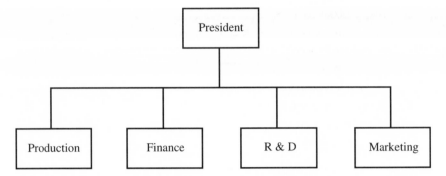

FIGURE 1.3. Simplified functional organizational design.

business development within the marketing department of a firm doing business with the federal government would be concerned with determining what programs our company will bid, what price we can offer, and the sort of product attributes we can reasonably deliver as part of those bids. In essence, no matter what program they are bidding on, this activity comprises the manager's full-time job and will continue on indefinitely, as long as he or she works for the company and it remains in business.

When project teams are added to an organization, the structural rules change dramatically. Figure 1.4 demonstrates the same simplified functional structure in which project teams have been overlaid. Note the inclusion of dotted lines from the functional departments of finance, R&D, marketing, and production. The implication of these lines is that when project teams are formed in most organizations that possess functional structures, they are staffed on an ad hoc basis from members of the various departments. These personnel are assigned to project teams through one of several ways: Their services are expressly requested by a project manager who values their competence, they are "exiled" to the project team by a functional boss who is dissatisfied with their work, or they are assigned simply because they are available. The key, however, is that the nature of these assignments, like the projects themselves, is temporary. Personnel who staff the vast majority of project teams serve on those teams while maintaining links back to their functional departments. In fact, it is quite com-

mon for these individuals to split their time between their project
and functional duties. Not surprisingly, this arrangement can lead
to a great deal of internal conflict within each member of the project team as that person seeks to create a workable balance between
the competing demands of functional and project team superiors.

The temporary nature of projects, coupled with the very real
limitations on their power and discretion that most project managers face, constitutes the core challenge of managing projects effectively. Table 1.1 gives a comparative breakdown of some of the
important distinctions between project-based work and more common functional activities. It is clear that the very issues that characterize projects as distinct from functional work also illustrate the
added complexity and difficulties they create for project managers.
For example, within a functional department, it is common to find
people with a more homogenous background; that is, the finance
department is staffed with finance people, the marketing department is made up of marketers, and so on. On the other hand,
most projects are constructed from special, cross-functional teams.
These teams are composed of representatives from each of the
relevant functional departments and they each bring their own
attitudes, time frames, learning, past experiences, and biases to the
team. Creating a cohesive and potent team out of this level of
heterogeneity presents a challenge for even the most seasoned and
skilled project managers.

Likewise, functional activities are intended to reinforce the organizational status quo, the standard operating procedures that
are clearly documented in most companies. Project management
work is different: As Figure 1.4 demonstrates, project teams operate at the periphery of the organization, redirecting human, technical, and monetary resources away from the functional areas for
their own needs. Rarely are there manuals written on how these
project teams are expected to operate. Rather, much of project
management involves "violating" such sacred rules as the manner
in which members of different functional departments are expected to communicate, the way additional resources are secured,
close interaction with clients by all members of the project team,
and so forth. It is in violating these standard operating procedures

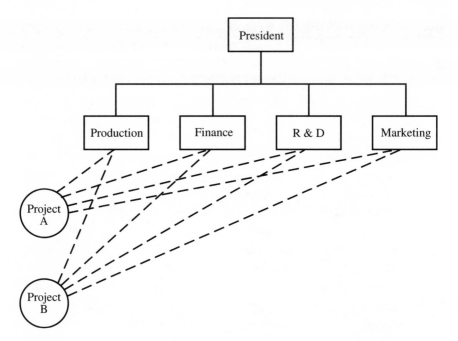

FIGURE 1.4. Functional organizational design with project teams.

that project teams are most effective, operating in a flexible and responsive manner to a variety of both internal technical and external client demands.

In the following chapters, we will continue to explore in depth the nature of the limits on project managers, the challenges these limits create, and the opportunities they offer. Successful project managers accept these challenges and learn to manage well in spite of them. It is for the purpose of helping to create a new generation of effective project managers that this book was written. It is hoped that through exploring the various roles of project managers and addressing the challenges and opportunities they constantly face, we will offer a new and refreshing approach to better understanding the task of project management.

**TABLE 1.1. Differences Between
Department and Project Management**

| *Department* | *Project* |
| --- | --- |
| Repeat process or product | New process or product |
| Several objectives | One objective |
| On-going | One shot, limited life |
| People are homogenous | More heterogenous |
| Well-established systems in place to integrate efforts | Systems must be created to integrate efforts |
| Higher certainty of performance, cost, schedule | Higher uncertainty of performance, cost, schedule |
| Part of line organization | Outside of line organization |
| Bastions of established practice | Violates established practice |
| Supports status quo | Upsets status quo |

*Source: R. J. Graham (1992).*

## THE ORGANIZATION OF THIS BOOK

The above discussion is intended to achieve two objectives:

- To highlight the importance of paying attention to the leadership "problem" in project management. There are few organizational activities that depend to such a degree on the efforts and skills of motivated, highly trained leaders as does project management.

- To create a backdrop for understanding the project management role within modern corporations. Projects are crucial mechanisms for the effective introduction of new products and services. Unfortunately, until organizations become more familiar with project management and the importance of well-trained project managers, project management will never be given the opportunity to live up to its potential.

The specific organization of this book revolves around two general issues: the organizational context of project management and the key roles and responsibilities that project managers are required to accept. In the five parts of this book, we will discuss issues such as the use of power versus influence, project stakeholder analysis, motivating project teams, conflict resolution, and much more. The second part will cover some of the specific demands and roles that project managers must undertake. What are the characteristics of effective project managers? What are the sorts of skills that can go far toward helping them perform successfully? Third, we will explore the role of these project managers as leaders. Readers and first-time project managers need to understand that project management is leader-intensive, but requires that teambuilding be carefully performed and meticulously cultivated. The fourth part of the book will focus on some success stories and real-world examples that can help project managers understand appropriate and inappropriate behaviors on the job. These cases are intended to drive home and reinforce the theory and practical advice offered in the first three parts. Finally, Part 5 will take a look at future trends in the field of project management, making it clear that project management is an activity whose time has come. Managers need to be aware that more, not less, of their time in future activities is likely to be devoted to project management work and they must begin to prepare accordingly.

With these goals in mind, let us consider our own conceptualization stage to be behind us and proceed with our project in the following pages. We hope that the reader finds it a trip well worth taking.

# 2

## Stakeholder Analysis and Project Management

THE PROCESS OF stakeholder analysis is helpful to the degree that it compels firms to acknowledge the potentially wide-ranging effect that their actions can have, both intended and unintended, on various stakeholder groups (Mendelow, 1986). For example, the strategic decision to close an unproductive manufacturing facility may make good "business" sense in terms of cost versus benefits that the company derives from the manufacturing site. However, the decision to close the plant has the potential to unleash a torrent of stakeholder complaints in the form of protests from local unions, workers, community leaders in the town affected by the closing, political and legal challenges, environmental concerns, and so forth. The prudent company will often consider the impact of stakeholder reaction as it weighs the sum total of likely effects from its strategic decision.

Just as stakeholder analysis is instructive for understanding the impact of major strategic decisions, we are also able to employ stakeholder analysis for our discussion of project management. That is, within the project environment, there is also a very real concern for the impact that various project stakeholders can have on the project development process. This relationship is essentially reciprocal in that the project team's activities can also impact the external stakeholder groups (Gaddis, 1959). For example, the project's clients, as a group, once committed to a new project's development, have an active stake in that project being completed on time and living up to its performance capability claims. The client stakeholder group can impact project team operations in a number of ways, the most common of which are agitating for faster development, working closely with the team to ease project transfer problems, and influencing top management in the parent organization to continue supporting the project. On the other hand, the project team can reciprocate this support through actions that show their willingness to closely cooperate with the client and smooth transition of the project to its intended user groups.

The key point for project managers to bear in mind is that project stakeholder analysis solidifies the fact that in addition to considering all the managerial activities involved in project development, project managers need to be aware of the ways in which attaining the project's goals can impact a host of external stakeholders outside of their authority. Further, project managers must develop an appreciation for the ways in which these stakeholder groups, some of which have considerable power and influence, can affect the viability of their projects. For example, there is an old saying in project management that states, "Never get the accountant mad." The obvious logic behind this dictum is that cost accountants can make the project manager's life easy or very difficult, depending on how closely they choose to monitor and control project expenditures.

In this chapter, we will explore the concept of stakeholder analysis as it forms a backdrop for project development and implementation. Stakeholders, while having varying levels of power and influence over the project, nevertheless have the potential to exert a number of significant demands on project managers and their teams. We will see that this problem is compounded by the fact

Past organizational research and, indeed, common sense tell us that organizations and even managers within those companies cannot operate in ways that ignore the external effects of their decisions. Put another way, no manager makes decisions exclusive of consideration of how those decisions will affect external groups (Dill, 1958). One way to understand the relationship of project managers and their projects vis à vis the rest of the organization is through employing stakeholder analysis. Stakeholder analysis is a useful tool for demonstrating some of the seemingly unresolvable conflicts that occur through the planned creation and introduction of any new project. An organizational "stakeholder" refers to any individual or group that has an active stake in the activities of an organization (Wheelen and Hunger, 1992). Consequently, when a company makes strategic decisions, they often will have major implications for a number of stakeholder groups—for example, environmental watchdog groups, stockholders, government regulatory bodies, and so forth. Stakeholders can impact on and are impacted by organizational actions to varying degrees (Wiener and Brown, 1986). In some cases, a corporation must take serious heed of the potential influence that some stakeholder groups are capable of wielding. In other situations, a stakeholder group may have relatively little power to influence a company's activities.

that the nature of these various demands quite often places them in direct conflict with each other. That is, in responding to the concerns of one stakeholder, project managers often unwittingly find themselves having offended or angered another stakeholder with an entirely different agenda and set of expectations. The challenge for project managers is to find a way to balance these various demands in order to maintain supportive and constructive relationships with each important stakeholder group.

## IDENTIFYING PROJECT STAKEHOLDERS

For any project, there are usually several distinct project stakeholder groups (see Figure 2.1). Internal stakeholders are a vital

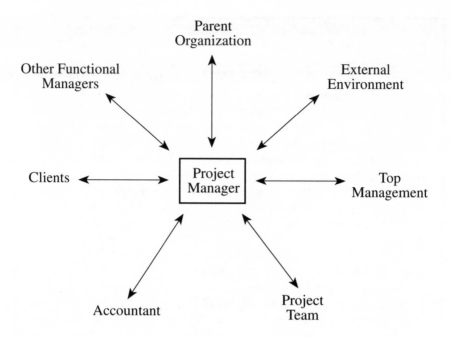

FIGURE 2.1.  Project stakeholders.

component in any stakeholder analysis and their impact is usually felt in relatively positive ways; that is, although serving as limiting and controlling influences, most internal stakeholders *do* want to see the project developed successfully. On the other hand, many external stakeholder groups operate in manners that are hostile to project development. For example, consider the case in which a European city is seeking to upgrade its subway system, adding new lines and improving facilities. There is a strong potential for those who are interested in preserving antiquities to actively resist the completion of such a project if they perceive that the tunnel digging could be destroying valuable artifacts. Cleland (1988) refers to these types of external stakeholders as "intervenor" groups and demonstrates that they have the potential to pose a major threat to the successful completion of projects.

    Among the set of project stakeholders that project managers must consider are included:

*Internal*

- Top management
- Accountant
- Other functional managers
- Project team members

*External*

- Clients
- Competitors
- Suppliers
- Environmental, political, consumer, and other "intervenor" groups

Let us briefly consider the demands that these stakeholder groups commonly place on project managers. Although we will start with top management, it is also important to note that "top management," as a single entity, may be too simplistic a classification for this stakeholder group. A valid argument could be made that within top management there are obviously differing degrees of enthusiasm for and commitment to the development of a particular project. Likewise, any environmental intervenor groups are likely to be composed of a number of different factions, with their own agendas and priorities. In other words, a good deal of conflict and differences of opinion will be discovered within any generalized group. Nevertheless, this approach is useful because it demonstrates the inherent nature of conflict and other pressures arising from project development as it exists *between* stakeholder groups, rather than *within* any group.

**1.** *Top management.* The top management group in most organizations holds a great deal of control over project managers and is in the position to regulate their freedom of action. Top management is, after all, the body that authorizes the development of the project through the initial "go-ahead" decision, sanctions additional resource transfers as they are needed by the project team, and supports and protects the project managers and their teams from other organizational pressures. The top management group has, as some of its key concerns, the requirement that the project be timely (the project needs to be out the door quickly), cost-efficient (it does not want to pay more for the work than it has to), and minimally disruptive to the rest of the functional organization.

**2. *Accountant.*** The accountant's *raison d'être* is maintaining cost efficiency from the project team. Accountants support and actively monitor project budgets and, as such, are often perceived as the enemy by project managers. We suggest that this perception, while convenient, is wrong-minded. Accountants perform an important administrative service for the project manager and team in keeping an eye on costs and expenditures, and canny project managers will work to make an ally of accountants rather than simply assume that they serve in adversarial capacities.

**3. *Functional managers.*** The functional managers who occupy line positions within the traditional chain of command represent an important stakeholder group that project managers must learn to acknowledge. As we noted in Chapter 1, most projects are staffed by individuals who are essentially on loan from their functional departments. In fact, in many cases, project team members may only have part-time appointments to the team, while their functional managers expect 20 hours of work out of them per week in performing their functional responsibilities. This situation serves to create a good deal of confusion and seriously divided loyalties among team members, particularly when their only performance evaluation is conducted by the functional manager rather than the project manager. In terms of simple self-survival, team members are likely to maintain closer allegiance to their functional group than the project team.

Project managers need to appreciate the power of the organization's functional managers as a stakeholder group. Functional managers, like the accountants, are not usually out to actively torpedo project development. Rather, they have loyalty to their functional roles operating within the traditional organizational hierarchy. Nevertheless, as a formidable stakeholder group, functional managers need to be treated with due consideration by project managers.

**4. *Project team members.*** The project team obviously has a tremendous stake in the project's outcome. As we noted above, although they may have a divided sense of loyalty between the project and their functional group, in many companies these team members volunteered to serve on the project and are, it is hoped, receiving the sorts of challenging work assignments and opportunities for growth that will motivate them to perform effectively. Just as the top management group and accountants have their priorities, the project team's concerns focus on the need for as much time as the project manager can secure for them. Top management seeks deadlines: Project teams prefer to avoid them. Further, the project team wants the client to "lock in" to project specifications as early as possible. It is much easier for project team members to operate within this environment if they are reasonably sure that the client will not be changing its mind and asking for new features or additions to the project downstream.

**5. *Clients.*** Clients are concerned with receiving the project as quickly as they can possibly get it from the team. As long as costs are not passed on to the client, they are not overly interested in how much expense was involved in the project's development. On the other hand, they seek the right to make suggestions and request alterations in the project's features and operating characteristics for as long as the project manager and team are willing to listen. These groups feel, with some justification, that a project is only as good as it is acceptable and used by them. As a result, they demand a certain flexibility and willingness from the project team to make themselves amenable to specification changes.

**6. *Competitors.*** Competitors can be an important stakeholder in that they are materially affected by the successful implementation of a new project. Likewise, should a rival company bring a new product to market first, the project team's parent organization could be forced to alter, delay, or even abandon its project. In assessing competitors as a project stakeholder group, project managers should try and uncover what information is available concerning the status of potential rival projects being developed within competing firms. Further, when possible, the lessons learned by competitors can be an important and useful source of information for a project manager who is initiating a similar project in another company. If a number of severe implementation problems occurred within the first organization's project launch, that information could offer valuable lessons to the other project organization in terms of what activities or steps to avoid in its own situation.

**7. *Suppliers.*** Suppliers refers to any group that provides the raw materials or other resources that the project team needs in order to complete its project. If the project requires a significant supply of externally purchased components, it behooves the project manager to take every step possible to ensure that steady deliveries will continue. For example, in large-scale construction projects, project managers must daily face and satisfy an enormous number of supplier demands. Part of the project manager's job in this type of project is to make certain that the project team will continue to have the raw material resources to continue project development.

**8. *Intervenor groups.*** Any environmental, political, social, community-activist, or consumer groups that can have a positive or (more likely) detrimental effect on the project's development and successful launch are referred to as "intervenor groups" (Cleland, 1988). That is, they have the capacity to intervene in the project development and force their concerns to be included in the equation for project implementation. There are some classic examples of intervenor groups curtailing major construction projects, particularly within the nuclear power plant construction industry. As federal, state, and even local regulators decide to involve themselves in these construction projects, they have at their disposal the legal system as a method for tying up or even curtailing projects. Prudent project managers need to make a realistic assessment of the nature of their projects and the likelihood that one intervenor group or another may make an effort to impose its will on the development process. In fact, in some of the better-known project success stories, the construction project manager devoted a great deal of time early in the process to make a stakeholder management assessment of the potential intervenor groups, plotting out strategies for finding the most effective and cost-efficient ways of dealing with them.

## MANAGING STAKEHOLDERS

The simplified management process consists of planning, organizing, directing, motivating, and controlling the resources necessary to deal with the various internal and external stakeholder groups. Figure 2.2 shows a model suggested by Cleland (1988) that illustrates the nature of the management process within the framework of stakeholder analysis and management. Cleland suggests that these various stakeholder management functions are interlocked and repetitive; that is, this cycle is recurring. As we identify and adapt to stakeholder threats, we develop plans to better manage the challenges they pose. In the process of developing and implementing these plans, we are likely to uncover new stakeholders whose demands must also be considered. Further, as the environment changes or the project enters a new stage of its life cycle, we may be required to cycle through the stakeholder management model again to verify that our old management strategies are still effective. If, on the other hand, we deem that new circumstances make it necessary to alter those strategies, project managers must work through this stakeholder management model anew to update the relevant information.

FIGURE 2.2. Project stakeholder management process (Cleland, 1988).

## STAKEHOLDER CONFLICT

In addition to the above discussion of the various project stakeholder groups and their demands on the project team, we can
also illustrate the essential conflict in project development and
implementation through the use of stakeholder analysis. For the
sake of our discussion, let us assume a project has been undertaken
in a company to implement a new information system. Further,
there are four identifiable stakeholder groups: top management,
the accountant, the clients, and the manager's own implementation
team. As we suggested previously, top management has given the

initial go-ahead to acquire and install the system. Likewise, the accountant provides the control and support for the implementation effort, ensuring that budgets are maintained and the project is coming in near projected levels. The clients are the most obvious stakeholder as they are the intended recipients of the new system. Finally, if we assume an implementation team is working together to implement the information system, this team itself has a stakeholder interest in the implementation, particularly if it is receiving some type of evaluation for its efforts.

To demonstrate the nature of conflict among stakeholder groups, we will focus on three criteria under which the implementation project effort will be evaluated: schedule, budget, and performance specifications. Schedule refers to the projected time frame to complete the installation and get the system on-line. Budget refers to the implementation team's adherence to initial budget figures for the information system implementation. Finally, performance specifications involve the assessment that the project is up and running, while performing the range of tasks for which it was acquired. Certainly, additional evaluative criteria can and should be employed—for example, whether the system will be used by the client group. However, for simplicity's sake, these three success measures serve to illustrate the nature of the underlying conflict in any project implementation.

Figure 2.3 shows the four identified stakeholders and three success criteria that have been selected. The arrows are used to illustrate the emphasis placed on each of these criteria by the stakeholders. For example, consider the case of stakeholder preferences as differences between clients and the implementation team. It is obvious that in terms of evaluation criteria such as schedule and budget, there are significant differences in attitude: The clients want the system delivered as soon as possible for as cheap a final price as possible. On the other hand, the implementation team would like large budgets and longer installation schedules because that takes the pressure off the team in terms of bringing the system on-line. Further, the criterion of performance specifications will vary with stakeholder group. Clients want the opportunity to alter the system, customize it, or add as many technical capabilities as

| | Cost | Schedule | Performance Specs. |
|---|---|---|---|
| Top Management | ↓ | ↓ | — |
| Accountant | ↓ | — | — |
| Client | ↓ | ↓ | ↑ |
| Implementation Team | ↑ | ↑ | ↓ |

FIGURE 2.3. Stakeholders' conflicting demands.

is possible. The implementation team is much more comfortable with a simple system that has few technical surprises (and therefore, less likelihood of long debugging procedures) and is not changed or modified once it has been acquired.

Figure 2.3 presents a compelling case for the underlying conflict of most project implementation efforts. It also serves to illustrate one inescapable conclusion: In order to rationalize and resolve the diverse goals and priorities of the various stakeholders, a considerable amount of bargaining and negotiation is called for. As the reader will discover, bargaining and negotiation are two of the primary defining elements of organizational politics. Clearly, political behavior is required in successful implementation efforts. If we take as our starting point the conclusion that a successful project manager is *not* one who will satisfy all stakeholder parties, it becomes clear that implementation success is instead predicated on that project manager's ability to successfully bargain and negotiate with the various stakeholders in order to maintain a balance between their needs and the realities of the project implementation process.

Project implementation becomes a process that depends on the project manager's clever and effective exercise of political skills. Indeed, we would argue that the trick is not keeping every stakeholder happy. Figure 2.3 demonstrates that such an outcome is not possible. When the client is happy with the number of specification changes the project manager is willing to make, the team is likely to be upset by the manager's unwillingness to freeze specifications. Likewise, when the team is satisfied with the amount of time that the project manager has scheduled for the development process, the manager is likely to begin to hear complaints from top management about lagging schedules. As a result, rather than seek general happiness from each stakeholder group, we often suggest in training sessions that the true goal of project managers should be to keep everyone minimally annoyed! If everyone is minimally upset with the project manager's compliance with various components of the project (time, budget, and specifications), it is likely that this project manager has found a way to strike an effective balance among the various competing demands.

## CONCLUSIONS

The management of project stakeholders represents a challenge that most project managers are only now beginning to acknowledge. Part of the reason for this, we suspect, is that little is known about the nature of the various project stakeholders: who they are, what their separate agendas are, and how to understand the nature of project stakeholder trade-offs. In this chapter, we have sought to offer a framework for understanding some of the most well-known project stakeholder groups, arguing that the stakeholder management process is cyclical, requiring that project managers continually update and reassess the nature of the stakeholder groups and their potential impact on the project's likelihood for successful implementation. Finally, we demonstrated a model that illustrates the compelling nature of project stakeholder trade-offs. That is, different stakeholder groups have different priorities that project managers must acknowledge. Behind this acknowledgment is the tacit understanding that it is manifestly impossible to "maximize" satisfaction levels among all project stakeholders. Rather, insightful project managers must learn to find a delicate balance of trade-offs among these various stakeholder groups, seeking to satisfy all groups only to the degree possible. It is our hope that this chapter has triggered a better understanding of the importance of project stakeholder management in corporations. The second step depends on the project manager's willingness to internalize these concepts and seek to manage not only the project's development, but stakeholder concerns as well.

# 3

# The Politics of Project Management *

*Politics is the conduct of public affairs for private advantage.*

—BIERCE

FEW TOPICS GENERATE as much heat and passionate feelings as a discussion of political behavior. Most organizational personnel are quick to condemn politics and their chief practitioners—company "politicians"—as predatory and counter to the interests of the overall organization. In fact, in our personal experience, it is generally impossible to find individuals with even minimal organizational experience who have not had some bad experiences with office politics in their careers. In spite of most managers' familiarity and experiences with organizational politics,

---

* Portions of this chapter were adapted from J. K. Pinto (1994), *Successful Information System Implementation: The Human Side,* Drexel Hill, PA: PMI Publications.

surprisingly little is known about the concept and its true impact on individuals within organizations.

One of the areas where politics is better understood—particularly its impact—is in the process of developing and implementing projects in organizations. A phenomenal amount of anecdotal and case study information exists that strongly reinforces the importance of understanding and *effectively utilizing* organizational politics as a tool in successful project implementation. Indeed, one could pose the argument with some validity that without an understanding of the role that power and politics play in project management, the likelihood of managing the successful development of a project will be significantly diminished.

The purpose of this chapter is to explore one of the more profound and, in many ways, fascinating factors in successfully implementing new projects: the roles of organizational power and politics. We will examine, in some detail, the bases of a project manager's personal power and the concept of organizational politics from the project management perspective, developing some of the more well-acknowledged themes that pervade the topic. In order to gain an understanding of the role that politics plays in the successful implementation of projects, it is important to highlight the various definitions of politics that are usually employed. We will argue that no matter what definitions of politics the reader uses, the end result is that political behavior is used as a method for dealing with basic organizational conflicts. Unfortunately, although the practice of politics is often used to deal with conflict, the irony is that political behavior itself usually becomes a contributing cause of additional organizational conflict (Butler, 1973). This chapter will present a comprehensive overview of the power bases of project managers as well as a political framework for organizations, demonstrating the inherent nature of conflict in attempting to implement projects in the face of a variety of project stakeholders, and explaining in detail the types of activities that project managers can engage in to promote the likelihood of successful development and implementation of their projects. Finally, we will offer some suggestions to project managers on how to effectively operate within the political arena of organizations, not to achieve predatory and self-serving ends, but in an effort to smooth the process by which their systems are adopted.

## POWER AND THE PROJECT MANAGER

The topic of power in organizations is endlessly fascinating. We all see how power is used on a daily basis to get things accomplished. Indeed, without the mechanism of power, one wonders how any organization would move at all. Power has been defined in many different ways. For our purposes, we define power as *the ability to get someone to do something that that person would not ordinarily do otherwise.* Power gives project managers access to the scarce resources that are so necessary to effective project development: qualified personnel, additional money or physical resources, and so forth. Because power is so important to project and, indeed, corporate success, it is important that we see how and what forms of power can be most readily utilized by project managers.

When one examines the sorts of options that project managers are able to use in furthering their goals—the successful development of projects—it is both useful and instructive to consider their alternatives in terms of three modes of power: *authority, status,* and *influence.* This authority, status, and influence model has been proposed by our colleague, Bob Graham (1989), as a way to make clear the methods by which project managers can achieve their desired ends. The model is valuable because it illustrates clearly one of the key problems that most project managers have in attempting to develop and implement their projects in corporations.

Much has been written on the sorts of power that individuals have. One of the best known studies of power argued that each of us has available two distinct types of power: power that derives from our personality (personal power) and power that comes from the position or title we hold (French and Raven, 1959). For our purposes, let us define authority as this latter type of power: one that accrues from the position we occupy in the organization (positional power). In other words, the positional power base derives solely from the position that managers occupy in the corporate hierarchy. In effect, if one individual sits higher on the organizational chart than another member of the project team, that person is said to have some degree of positional power over that person. Unfortunately, the nature of positional, or formal, power is extremely problematic within project management situations due to the temporary and "detached" nature of most projects vis à vis the rest of the formal organizational structure (Goodman, 1967). As we noted in Chapter 1, project teams sit "outside" the normal vertical hierarchy, usually employing personnel who are on loan from their functional departments. As a result, project managers have a much more tenuous degree of positional power within the organization. Other than the nominal control they have over their own team, they do not have a corporate-wide base of positional power through which they can acquire resources, issue directives, or enforce their will. As a result, authority, as a power base, is not one that project managers can rely on with any degree of certainty in most organizations.

Likewise, the second mode of power, status, is often problematic for most project managers. Status implies that the project manager, due to the nature, importance, or visibility of his or her project, can exert power and control over others in the corporate hierarchy as needed. Unfortunately, although some projects and project managers do, indeed, possess an enormous degree of status due to the importance of their projects (e.g., the project manager for the Boeing 757 program or the English Channel "Chunnel"), the vast majority of project managers toil in relative obscurity, working to bring their projects to fruition while receiving little public recognition for their work. Although it would be nice to think that most project managers can rely on status as a form of power and control over resources to enhance their project's likelihood of success, the reality is that very few projects or project managers can depend on their status as a persuasive form of power.

This, then, leads us to the final form of power or control that project managers may possess: influence. Influence is a form of power that is usually highly individualized. That is, some individuals are better able to use influence to achieve their desired ends than others (Cialdini, 1993). One of the best examples of influence is the power an individual possesses because he or she has a dynamic personality or personal charisma that attracts others. For example, well-known athletes are popular choices for endorsing new products because of the personal charisma and "referent" appeal that they hold with the public. Other examples of influence include informational or expert power. To illustrate, if only one member of the project team has the programming or computer skills that are vital to the successful completion of the project, that person, regardless of title or managerial level within the organization, has a solid base of influence in relation to other members of the project team.

The key point to bear in mind about influence is that it is often an informal method of power and control (Thamhain and Gemmill, 1974). Project managers who use influence well in furthering the goals of their project usually work behind the scenes, negotiating, cutting deals, or collecting and offering IOUs. Influence, as a power tactic, is most readily used when managers have no formal positional authority on which to rely. Hence, they are forced to use less formal means to achieve their desired ends. Influence is most widely seen as a power tactic in situations in which there is no obvious difference in authority levels among organizational members. To use a political example, a president who is unsure of his degree of formal power and ability to force his legislative agenda through a recalcitrant Congress is likely to spend a great deal of time making back-channel deals and negotiating compromises. Dictators have no need to resort to using influence.

What is the implication of the authority, status, and influence model? Graham notes that the nature of project management work, the manner in which project managers and their teams are selected, and the relationship of projects to the formal organizational hierarchy force project managers to rely to far greater degrees on their ability to cultivate and effectively use influence as a negotiating and power tactic than either of the other two forms of power. Formal, broad-based authority rarely exists for project managers to use in furthering their project's ends. Likewise, although some projects and/or project managers have the status to gain the resources they need, it is much less likely that the typical project manager, particularly younger members of the organization, will have enough status to effect any sort of change they desire. On the other hand, any project manager can learn to develop the skills to use influence as a power tactic. The key is realizing that influence is a form of corporate political behavior that can be utilized for the benefit of the project and, ultimately, the organization. In order to better understand the relationship between the use of informal influence tactics and political behavior, we need to explore in some detail exactly what organizational politics implies.

## WHAT IS ORGANIZATIONAL POLITICAL BEHAVIOR?

Probably no topic stirs up as many sharply voiced opinions and general disagreement as the notion of corporate politics. Writers and researchers usually find that they cannot even agree on a uniform definition of politics, let alone acknowledge the role of politics in organizational life. When one sifts through the material on power and politics, a number of definitions are suggested, often with varying degrees of usefulness. Among the definitions of politics that are currently extant, some important patterns can be discerned that help establish a framework for understanding the concept. For example, one colleague has referred to politics as self-interested behavior with guile. Another definition suggests that politics "involves those activities taken within an organization to acquire, develop, and use power to get one's way" (Pfeffer, 1981). Henry Mintzberg, another well-known researcher in organization theory, suggests that politics encompasses modern organizations, referring to them (organizations) as "system(s) captured by conflict" (Mintzberg, 1983). Yet another definition of politics offers the characterization that political behavior is inherently competitive and focused on satisfying self-interests (Mayes and Allen, 1977). These and other definitions of the "negative school" generally characterize political behavior as essentially malevolent, conflict-laden, self-aggrandizing, and unhealthy. The basic attitude can be summed up by the following arguments. They suggest that politics is:

**1. *Behavior designed to benefit the individual or group at the organization's expense.*** This idea suggests that political behavior is entirely self-serving, predicated on getting ahead in spite of the possible side effects to the organization as a whole. For example, a manager who continually violates production safety codes in order to increase efficiency and speed of operations may, in the short term, reap the benefits of achieving higher production quotas. However, should workers be injured due to relaxed safety standards, both the company and manager could be liable for substantial legal action. The short-term benefits of these acts are usually simply outweighed by long-term ethical and legal difficulties.

**2. *The displacement of legitimate power.*** "Legitimate" power is defined as the power that accrues to an individual due to his or her position within the organization (French and Raven, 1959). For example, bosses who simply rely on the position that they occupy as a basis for giving orders are said to make use of legitimate power. Politics has the capacity to displace legitimate power through mechanizations designed to circumvent the conventional authority structure of the organization. For example, consider a situation in which a three-person chain of command exists: Sue is at the top, Bob is her subordinate, and Allen is Bob's subordinate. Allen would be exercising a political approach if he habitually found ways to "end-run" Bob's authority by going directly to Sue to mediate disagreements, solve problems, or offer advice. Allen could pick any of a number of ways to cultivate Sue's help, from joining the same civic organizations, church, country club, etc., in an effort to create a personal relationship with Sue. Allen is banking on this relationship as a bulwark against Bob being able to use his legitimate authority. Allen has attempted to displace this authority through political behavior.

**3. *The use of means not sanctioned by the organization to attain sanctioned ends, or the use of sanctioned means to obtain***

***unsanctioned ends.*** This proposition has two elements: First, it suggests that political behavior might actually be used in the interests of the organization. Unfortunately, this behavior would be widely perceived as unethical or immoral. Recently, for example, the Chairman and CEO of Bath Iron Works, a major shipbuilding company with extensive defense department contracts, resigned in disgrace following the disclosure that he had illegally accepted and made use of photocopied Department of Defense documents of a sensitive and secret nature that gave his firm an unfair advantage in bidding for new contracts. Obviously, it was in the interests of his company to win those contracts. Equally obvious, however, was his violation of the law (using unsanctioned means) in gaining this competitive advantage and, following his resignation, his company was forced to pay a substantial fine for his actions.

The second aspect of this proposition suggests that political behavior may involve using acceptable means to obtain unacceptable ends. Again, the issue here has to do with the degree to which political actors are willing to "bend" moral or ethical codes in order to gain an advantage. There are many actions in which an individual or organization can engage that are legal but may be highly questionable from an ethical perspective. To illustrate, Johns-Manville Corporation received a great deal of bad press some years ago when, following the ban on the use of asbestos in the United States, it began selling its stockpiles overseas to countries that did not have comprehensive health and welfare policies.

Note that the underlying commonalty among each of the arguments listed above is the notion that political behavior is, at its core, unhealthy, counter to organizational goals, and essentially predatory. Writers who have taken this view have argued with some heat that the sooner politics is removed from the organizational arena, the better organizations will be in terms of their operations and personal relationships. In more recent years, another school of thought has developed to counter the "negative" school. This second school of thought on organizational politics, while not denying the potential for abusing the use of politics through self-serving behavior and subsequently damaging organizational relationships, tends to take a more neutral view of the process, arguing rather, that politics and political activity are simply a natural part of organizations and must be acknowledged as no different, in essence, than a firm's culture or organizational structure. This argument suggests that politics can be neither characterized as good or bad but rather, as natural and, as such, counters previous arguments by suggesting that efforts or calls to eliminate politics are naive. Politics, this school of thought contends, "exists" and must be learned and applied, preferably in a nonaggressive manner (Beeman and Sharkey, 1987; Allen et al., 1979; Markus, 1981, 1983; Markus and Pfeffer, 1981).

There are five propositions that underscore the neutral or "natural" view of organizational politics. These propositions follow a logical sequencing as they develop the argument for understanding the "true" nature of politics.

## Proposition 1

**Most important decisions in organizations involve the allocation of scarce resources.**

This statement lays the groundwork under which the context for decision making is established. When decisions need to be made, particularly in the context of group decisions, they are often triggered by some problem or concern. For example, suppose that the operations of a city planning department are fragmented and haphazard. A committee would be tasked with ways of reworking operating policies or finding alternatives for how operations are conducted. The decision it arrives at and, indeed, the decision process itself, are almost always bounded by a number of contingency factors. For example, a short time frame for making the recommendations, a limited operating budget, or the concerns and prerogatives of senior managers may all form a boundary around which the decision must be made. One of the most compelling boundaries is the notion of scarce resources. It goes without saying that most organizations, both public and private, have limited resources with which to carry out their tasks. There are only so many good jobs to go around. There is only so much money that can be spent. The list is endless. Consequently, any attempts to arrive at the optimal decision in dealing with a perceived problem are necessarily constrained by the limits of scarce resources.

It is possible to take this proposition one step further and suggest that not only are most decisions constrained by scarce resources, but also the majority of important decisions made within organizations involve, to one degree or another, the allocation or distribution of these scarce resources among a number of competing demands. Departmental budgets are submitted in order to divide organizational resources in as equitable a manner as possible. Deciding whether or not to develop and implement a project involves the implicit trade-off between the decision to invest in that project and other demands that could be met through the money that was budgeted to initiate the project's development. Consequently, these points give credence to the argument that decision making (particularly important decisions) is in some way bound to the prioritization and distribution of organizational resources.

## Proposition 2

---

**The decision process often involves bargaining, negotiation, and jockeying for position.**

It is likely to come as no surprise to the majority of readers, particularly those who are currently employed in organizations, that the manner by which many decisions are made is often based less on purely logical decision-making processes than a variety of intervening criteria. Certainly, as James March and Herbert Simon noted over 35 years ago, individuals strive for logic in their decision processes. However, for a variety of reasons, we are often more likely to be influenced by and make use of a variety of extra or additional criteria in arriving at decisions (March and Simon, 1958). One process that is common within organizations where scarce resources are the rule is to make use of bargaining or negotiation behavior. Bargaining follows one of the most common approaches to dealing with conditions of scarce resources: Individuals and department heads make "deals," or compromises between the variety of competing desires and organizational reality. Since all parties cannot, by definition, attain everything they seek (due to scarce resources), in order to gain as much advantage as possible, individuals who may be in competitive relationships are forced to compromise or negotiate to gain as much as possible.

## Proposition 3

**Organizations are coalitions composed of a variety of self-interested groups.**

It is important to understand that when we refer to an "organization," it may be a convenient short-hand to use the term in a monolithic sense; that is, an organization can and will act as a single, purposeful entity. In reality, the term "organization" gives meaning to the reality behind this misperception. In both the public and private arenas, organizations are composed of a variety of groups: labor versus management, finance versus marketing, and so forth. These groups, which must be viewed as essentially self-interested, are the sum total of what comprises an organization. We are sure that this proposition will, on the surface, raise some objections; for example, the notion that these groups are basically self-interested implies that they are willing to put their own concerns before the "legitimate" goals and concerns of the organization. Some may object to this characterization, as it implies that these groups will seek their own goals even at the expense of what is best for the organization generally. In reality, although the different interest groups in the organization generally do buy into the overall corporate goals, they do so to varying degrees and rarely are they willing to ascribe to all the firm's objectives. The reasons for this reluctance to totally subordinate their own goals for corporate-wide objectives can be understood from a discussion of Proposition 4 below.

## Proposition 4

**Groups differ in terms of goals, values, attitudes, time frames, and so forth.**

In 1967, a landmark research study was conducted by Paul Lawrence and Jay Lorsch (1967, 1969) that sought to investigate the manner in which roles and attitudes differ among various subgroups in organizations. They uncovered and introduced a phenomenon that they referred to as organizational differentiation. The concept of differentiation was used to describe the fact that as individuals enter the organization through joining a functional group such as accounting or marketing, they develop a set of values and goals that are in accord with that functional group; that is, they begin to ascribe to subgroup values and attitudes rather than strictly organization-wide goals. The reasons for this phenomenon are obvious: It is in their functional reference group (marketing, finance, R&D, etc.) that individuals are staffed, given task assignments, evaluated, and rewarded. Hence, their allegiance becomes focused on their immediate work group.

The second important finding of Lawrence and Lorsch was that these functional groups usually differ in terms of a number of important criteria, including goals, time frames, values, and so forth. To illustrate, consider the situation that is often found in organizations having separate R&D and marketing departments. Marketing is primarily concerned with making sales to customers; in fact, the reward systems (bonuses, promotions, and incentives) for those who work in marketing departments are usually geared toward sales volume achieved. Given reward systems that value sales volume, it is easy to understand the emphasis that marketing personnel place on short-term profitability and "making their numbers." Compare this value system to that of a typical R&D department where incentives are related to creativity, innovation, and technological development. These activities cannot be regulated in any way that is similar to the approaches used in marketing. Further, the time frames of R&D personnel are often more long-term, aimed at achieving technological development regardless of how long that may take. Naturally, the short-term, sales volume goals of marketing not only differ from R&D's long-term focus, but often they actually conflict; that is, in order for marketing personnel to achieve their goals, members of R&D may have to sacrifice theirs.

Here, in a nutshell, is the basic contradiction uncovered by Lawrence and Lorsch that pervades most organizations. Subgroups within organizations differ due to differences in a variety of criteria: time frames, goals, attitudes, values, and so forth. The result of this change in goal criteria is why these groups must, to some degree, be characterized as self-interested; that is, they feel most keenly the need to achieve their own departmental goals first. These differences are important because they shape the types of dynamics that almost always characterize the modern organization. These dynamics can be best described through the final proposition.

## Proposition 5

---

**Because of scarce resources and enduring differences, power and conflict are central to organizational life.**

---

This final proposition forms the underlying rationale behind the political model of organizational life. Because of the essential differences and contradictions that exist within organizations, conflict is not simply a side-effect of organizational members' interaction; it is a natural and self-perpetuating state. Likewise, political behavior cannot be characterized as malevolent and deviant, but must be seen as a natural consequence of the interaction between organizational subsystems. This "natural" view of politics refuses to condemn the use of political tactics among organizational members, as it views these behaviors as an expected side effect of company life.

## POLITICAL TACTICS

Although we have examined the basic theories that underlie a discussion of political behavior, it is important to consider some of the more common political tactics that occur in organizations. These tactics, as we shall see, comprise both negative and natural aspects of politics as some are inherently self-serving and predatory, whereas others are aimed at expanding power or influencing decision processes. In either case, the focus is on attempting to gain a measure of power within the organization. The difference usually is in how this power, once acquired, is used by organizational members.

Although there are a wide variety of political tactics used to varying degrees within organizations (Mintzberg, 1983), we have chosen to focus on some of the more well-known activities. Among the more common tactics and political behaviors employed are acts to 1) expand networks and build coalitions, 2) control decision processes, and 3) develop and project expertise. Expanding networks and building coalitions is one of the most common political behaviors seen in organizations. People who understand and use politics well realize that the best way to get what they need is to never force the issue to a head; rather, they are much more likely to network with powerful members of the organization who are able to help them achieve their desired goals. Politicians have two reasons for avoiding open fights. First, they realize that when an issue comes to a head publicly, it forces them to defend their actions and views publicly. Politicians, as many of us can attest, prefer to remain in the background while maintaining congenial relations with all, as it is in such an atmosphere that they are able to achieve their ends more effectively. The second reason why they prefer to avoid open conflict is that political actors are perfectly willing to target any member of the organization as a potential ally for future actions. Consequently, the last thing that good politicians want is open conflict with another member of the organization, as it virtually guarantees that a potential source for future favors and advantages has been eliminated.

A far better method for achieving ends involves the politician working to create and continually expand a network of allies and acquaintances who can be called on to help when needed. It is through networking and developing a wide-spread coalition that politicians are better able to call in favors or influence decisions involving allocating scarce resources. In discussing the process of coalition building with a manager at a company with whom one of the authors was consulting, he made the powerful statement that, "Around here, most important decisions have already been made before the meeting begins." What he was suggesting was that through networking, a politically savvy individual will have already influenced the key decision makers to such a degree that the "meeting" to make the decision is often moot.

Controlling decision processes is the politician's effort to constrain the bounds of a decision in such a way that the decision finally made is in accordance with the politician's wishes. There are several ways to control decision-making processes, some of which are unethical, whereas others may be considered perfectly legitimate. For example, consider the situation in which a city planning department is planning to purchase a computer system and a member of the department has been tasked with gathering information about various PC-based alternatives. Suppose further that this individual had a vested financial interest in the selection of one specific vendor. An unethical approach to controlling the decision process would be to present only that selected information which would validate the politician's choice of computer vendor. In other words, information is held or used selectively in order to guide a decision in a desired direction.

The other method for controlling the decision process is to find ways to influence the meeting agenda or decision-making approaches. For example, suppose that the head of the R&D department at a corporation wished to propose the development of a new, high-technology project. The project's initial investment cost will be $250,000 and the approval for such a project must come from the key members of upper management. There are several tactics that could be employed in order to attempt to influence the decision process. To illustrate, "sowing" questions with two or three confederates in the audience during the project proposal to be asked at key points in the presentation will give the manager the chance to demonstrate knowledge of the system, as well as impress the council members with his or her "spontaneous" expertise. Further, using the meeting agenda as an influence tool can be very effective. This process consists of burying a particular issue of concern far down the list of agenda items where it is likely to be quickly dealt with by tired or bored committee members.

The final political tactic is that of developing and projecting expertise. Simply put, the argument is that if others perceive an individual as being an expert on a particular topic, that individual is deferred to and given control. It is important to remember that "expertise" is a perceptual issue. In other words, whether or not an individual truly does have expertise in a particular field is immaterial. What is important is that others *believe* that he or she has expertise. Consequently, a well-known political tactic is to enhance legitimacy and expertise as a method for status. Being the only member of a department to be proficient with the organization's computer equipment, for example, guarantees that member a measure of status and power.

An analysis of four mega projects illustrates the force for good or ill that real and imagined experts can wield. Two of the projects refer to civil aircraft development (Concorde and Airbus) and two are space agencies (ESRO and ELDO). The two successful projects (Airbus and ESRO) were found to be comparable in terms of their organizational features, whereas the two less successful (an understatement for "disasters") were similar with respect to their organizational design. In the first two, professional engineers having real expertise were in charge; they had the power to implement decisions and emerged as champions. In the case of the two project failures, top management was seen as more highly involved in internal politics and projected imagined "expertise." Two quotations regarding the Concorde debacle aptly sum up the analysis, particularly in relation to the success of Airbus (May, 1979):

> "Concorde was an entirely political aeroplane: the plane was to show that we were good Europeans."

> "After Concorde, an engineer's dream built by politicians, comes Airbus, a businessman's dream built by engineers."

Obviously, where engineers succeeded, politicians and illusory "experts" failed. We are certain that in the successful projects, the respective project managers were fully in charge, with decentralized decision-making authority and an absence of constraining bureaucracy. In the absence of strategic vision, leadership, positive incentives, and rapid decision-making processes, as in the cases of Concorde and ELDO, they are bound to fail (Koenig and Thietart, 1988).

## APPROACHES TO ORGANIZATIONAL POLITICS

In presenting both the "negative" and "natural" sides of the debate on the nature of corporate politics, it is important to point out that readers need to draw their own conclusions about the role of politics in organizational life. We would suggest that there are usually three distinct positions regarding political behavior taken by individuals as they enter organizational service for the first time: Two of these positions are equally inappropriate but for entirely different reasons (see Table 3.1). The first approach can be best termed the "naive" attitude regarding politics. Naive individuals view politics as unappealing at the outset and make a firm resolution never to engage in any type of behavior that could be construed as political. Their goal is, in effect, to remain above the

**TABLE 3.1. Characteristics of Political Behaviors**

| Characteristics | Naive | Sensible | Sharks |
|---|---|---|---|
| Underlying attitude: "Politics is . . ." | Unpleasant. | Necessary. | An opportunity. |
| Intent | Avoid at all costs. | Used to further department's goals. | Self-serving and predatory. |
| Techniques | Tell it like it is. | Network, expand connections, use system to give and receive favors. | Manipulation, use of fraud and deceit when necessary. |
| Favorite tactics | None, the truth will win out. | Negotiation, bargaining. | Bullying, misuse of information, cultivate and use "friends" and other contacts. |

fray, not allowing politics in any form to influence their conduct. The second and exact opposite approach is undertaken by individuals who enter organizations with the express purpose of using politics and aggressive manipulation to reach the top. We tend to regard these people as "sharks." Although actually few in number, this type readily embraces political behavior in its most virulent form. Their loyalty is entirely to themselves and their own objectives. Work with them and one is likely to be used and manipulated; get between them and their goal and their behavior becomes utterly amoral. The only cause these individuals espouse is their own. As we stated initially, we regard both the naive and shark as equally and unprofitably wrong-minded about politics. Their attitudes underscore the awareness of the third type of organizational actor: the "politically sensible."

Politically sensible individuals enter organizations with few illusions about how many decisions are made. They understand, either intuitively or through their own past experiences and mistakes, that politics is simply another side, albeit an unattractive one, of the behavior in which one must engage in order to succeed in modern organizations. Although not shunning politics, neither do they embrace their practice. Rather, the politically sensible is apt to state that this behavior is at times necessary because "that is the way the game is played." It is also important to point out that politically sensible individuals generally do not play politics of a predatory nature, as in the case of the sharks who are seeking to advance their own careers in any manner that is expedient. Politically sensible individuals use politics as a way of making contacts, cutting deals, and gaining power and resources for their departments or projects in order to further corporate, rather than entirely personal, ends.

Everyone must make up their own minds regarding the efficacy and morality of engaging in corporate politics. We suspect that interviewing successful project managers will show the reader, as it has clearly demonstrated to the authors, that it is almost impossible to be successful in organizational systems without a basic understanding of and willingness to employ organizational politics. Whatever the position one adopts, research on the topic has led to some important conclusions about politics. A recent large-scale study of senior- and mid-level managers offered a number of interesting conclusions about the use of politics in organizations:

1. Although unable to agree whether or not politics is a natural process, most managers regard politics in a negative manner and view political behavior as unprofitably consuming organizational time and resources.

2. Managers believe that political behavior is common to all organizations.

3. The majority of managers believe that political behavior is more prevalent among upper managers than those at lower levels in organizations.

4. Political behavior is much more common in certain decision domains, such as structural change or new system implementation, than other types of organizational activities, such as handling employee grievances (Gandz and Murray, 1980).

The fourth conclusion is particularly relevant to our discussion of politics. The reason why political behavior is more common under certain conditions such as new system introduction is that these types of organizational changes signal the potential for a significant shift in power relationships. Any form of organizational change has the potential to alter the power landscape. The reason, as Hickson and his colleagues have noted, is that one important determinant of power is the notion of *centrality* (Hickson et al., 1971). Centrality refers to how involved with, or central to the main activities of an organization, a particular individual or department is. The more central to the organization's mission, the greater the power held by that department. The initiation and implementation of a new project have the potential to remove the power of centrality from departments and transfer it to another location—the project team. As in our earlier example, if a project is developed under the auspices of one department, other functional areas may view that development with suspicion because it shifts the spotlight from their own activities to a project team sitting outside of their jurisdiction. Any action or move toward change initiated by members of an organization that has the potential to alter the nature of current power relationships provides a tremendous impetus for political activity.

Why is the study of politics so important for successful project implementation? The short answer is that the implementation process itself is often highly politicized, as different managers and departments view the development and implementation of a project as a potentially useful base of power. In other words, any shift in the current operational status quo, resulting from the introduction of a new project within a corporation, will inevitably affect how operations and activities are conducted. Once there is a threatened shift in status, departments and managers who perceive themselves as losing power because of the output of the project are apt to do whatever is necessary to discourage or subvert its use. For example, consider a situation in which a city planning department has contracted to install an MIS that has the technical ability to perform a wide variety of tasks, including infrastructure tracking and repair. These duties were originally handled by the city engineering department. However, as a result of the new MIS, the city planners have the capacity to track and schedule road and bridge repair themselves. Under this scenario, one would expect the city engineers to do everything they can to either halt use of the MIS or severely limit it in such a way that it will not interfere with activities they view as their personal responsibility. For example, they might push through a procedural resolution that requires all infrastructure repair planning be done through their office, in spite of the existence of the MIS. The essence of this argument is this: *With responsibility comes power.* If the computer system reallocates operational responsibilities, it thereby redefines the power structure. There are few changes as threatening to organizational members as a redivision of power. Hence, those with a vested interest in the old system will actively resist any efforts to introduce new or innovative changes.

## MANAGERIAL IMPLICATIONS: WHAT DO WE DO?

An understanding of the political side of organizations and the often intensely political nature of system implementation gives rise to the concomitant need to develop appropriate attitudes and strategies that help project managers operate effectively within the system. What are some of the steps that project managers can take to become politically astute, if this approach is so necessary to effective project implementation?

## 1. Understand and Acknowledge the Political Nature of Most Organizations

In dealing with individuals suffering from a variety of dysfunctional illnesses, therapists and counselors of all types have long taken as their starting point the importance of the patients' acknowledgment that they have a problem. Positive results cannot be achieved in a state of continued denial. Although it is not our purpose to suggest that this analogy holds completely true with organizational politics, the underlying point is still important: Denial of the political nature of organizations does not make that phenomenon any less potent. Organizations in both the public and private sectors are inherently politicized for the reasons that have been previously discussed (Dill and Pearson, 1984). We realize that, in offering this view, we run the risk of offending some readers who are uncomfortable with the idea of politics and believe that somehow, through the combined efforts of all organizational actors, it is possible to eradicate the political nature of companies or governmental agencies. We must disagree as also will, we believe, the majority of managers in organizations today. Politics is too deeply rooted within organizational operations to be treated as some aberrant form of bacteria or diseased tissue that can be excised from the organization's body.

The first implication argues that before managers are able to learn to utilize politics in a manner that is supportive of project implementation, they must first acknowledge 1) its existence, and 2) its impact on project success. Once we have created a collective basis of understanding regarding the political nature of organizations, it is possible to begin to develop some action steps that will aid in project implementation.

## 2. Learn to Cultivate "Appropriate" Political Tactics

This principle reinforces the earlier argument that although politics exists, the manner in which organizational actors use politics is the determinant of whether or not the political arena is a healthy or unhealthy one. We have tried to assert, as is shown in Table 3.1, that there are appropriate and inappropriate methods for using politics. Since the purpose of all political behavior is to develop and keep power, we believe that both the politically naive and shark personalities are equally misguided and, perhaps surprisingly, *equally* damaging to the likelihood of project implementation success. A project manager who, either through naiveté or stubbornness, refuses to exploit the political arena is destined to be not nearly as effective in introducing the project as a project team leader who knows how to use politics effectively. On the other hand, project managers who are so politicized as to appear predatory and aggressive to their colleagues are doomed to create an atmosphere of such distrust and personal animus that there is also little chance for successful project adoption.

Pursuing the middle ground of political sensibility is the key to project implementation success. The process of developing and applying appropriate political tactics means using politics as it can be used most effectively: as a basis for negotiation and bargaining. As Table 3.1 pointed out, politically sensible managers understand that initiating any sort of organizational disruption or change due to developing a new project is bound to reshuffle the distribution of power within the organization. That effect is likely to make many departments and managers very nervous as they begin to wonder how the future power relationships will be rearranged. "Politically sensible" implies being politically sensitive to the concerns (real or imagined) of powerful stakeholder groups. Legitimate or not, their concerns about the new project are real and must be addressed. Appropriate political tactics and behavior include making alliances with powerful members of other stakeholder departments, networking, negotiating mutually acceptable solutions to seemingly insoluble problems, and recognizing that most organizational activities are predicated on the give and take of negotiation and compromise (Talbott, 1994). It is through these uses of political behavior that managers of project implementation efforts put themselves in the position to most effectively influence the successful introduction of their systems.

In a recent article on project management and the nature of power, Lovell (1993) makes a similar point in arguing that effective project managers must work to maintain constructive political alliances with power senior management and influential department managers. He further notes that the persuasive skills and political acumen of a seasoned project manager will allow him or her to understand and make use of the organization's power environment, the positions of the various stakeholders, the times and means to develop and maintain alliances, and how to move around political roadblocks. All of these are skills that require objectivity and sensitivity from project managers in order to be done successfully.

### 3. Understand and Accept WIIFM

One of the hardest lessons for newcomers to organizations to internalize is the consistently expressed and displayed primacy of departmental loyalties and self-interest over organization-wide concerns. There are many times when novice managers will feel frustrated at the "foot-dragging" of other departments and individuals to accept new ideas or systems that are "good for them." It is vital that these managers understand the beauty of a new project is truly in the eyes of the beholder. One may be absolutely convinced that a project will be beneficial to the organization; however, convincing members of other departments of this truth is a different matter altogether.

We must understand that other departments, including project stakeholders, are not likely to offer their support of the project unless they perceive that it is in their interests to do so. Simply *assuming* that these departments understand the value of a project is simplistic and usually wrong. One of our colleagues, Bob Graham, likes to refer to the principle of WIIFM when describing the reactions of stakeholder groups to new innovations. WIIFM is an acronym that means "what's in it for me?" This is the question most often asked by individuals and departments when presented with requests for their aid. The *worst* response project managers can make is to assume that the stakeholders will automatically appreciate and value the project as much as they themselves do. Graham's point is that time and care must be taken to use politics effectively, cultivate a relationship with power holders, and make the deals that need to be made to bring the system on-line. This is the essence of political sensibility: being level-headed enough to have few illusions about the difficulties one is likely to encounter in attempting to develop and implement a new project.

## 4. Try to Provide Project Managers with Some "Equal Footing"

Functional line managers often view the initiation of a new project with a degree of suspicion and trepidation because of its potential to upset the power balance and reduce the amount of authority a line manager has with his or her staff. To a point, these concerns are understandable. A project team does, in fact, create an artificial hierarchy that could compete with the traditional line managers for resources, support, status, talented personnel, and other scarce commodities. However, it is also clear that organizational realities that mandate the need for project managers and teams also need to set up these individuals with some degree of authority or status to do their job most effectively.

We have previously suggested that authority and status typically do not accrue to project managers in most organizations. One approach to giving project managers a measure of status vis à vis the formal functional hierarchy is to give them the ability to conduct performance appraisals on their project team subordinates. On the surface, this suggestion seems to be simple common sense and yet, it is often resisted in organizations. Line managers want to maintain their control over subordinates through keeping sole right to this evaluation process and, hence, may resist allowing project managers this measure of equal footing. Nevertheless, it is a powerful tool because it sends the clear message throughout the company that projects *are* valuable, and project contributions by team members will be remembered and rewarded (Payne, 1993).

## CONCLUSIONS

Implementation politics is a process that few managers, even those who are adept at it, enjoy. Interviews and conversations with a variety of managers across a diverse collection of public and private organizations make it clear that using politics, even in the "sensible" manner suggested in this chapter, is often a distasteful process. We do not enjoy having to cut deals, negotiate for resources needed to develop our projects, and constantly mollify departmental heads who are suspicious of the motives behind a developing project, or any other system that threatens their base of power. Nevertheless, the realities of modern organizations are such that successful managers must learn to use the political process for their own purposes; it is simply wishful thinking to assume otherwise. This chapter has presented some of the major issues in organizational politics: its definitions and causes, as well as suggesting some guidelines for effectively managing project implementation within the political context of organizations. Our goal has been to offer some practical views on the nature and importance of political behavior in modern organizations. If one additional reader of this chapter is made better attuned to the political realities of corporate life as a result of our efforts, they were well expended.

# 4

## *Project Critical Success Factors*

*Failures are with heroic minds the stepping stones to success.*

—HALIBURTON

IN MODERN ORGANIZATIONS today, most project managers are firefighters; they spend their days going from one problem area to another, putting out a succession of small and large "fires" that can threaten the successful development of their projects. They often attend to these critical success factors in an intuitive and ad hoc fashion as they attempt to manage and allocate their time and resources across a number of conflicting demands. What would be helpful is a more refined and specific model of these critical success factors and their interrelationships. It would also be extremely helpful if we possessed an approach to the measurement of these factors to assist project managers in allocating resources and detecting problem areas early enough to enable them to respond in an effective manner. This chapter describes the development of a framework of critical success factors (CSFs) for project implementation. Further, we will argue, as noted above, that research has shown clearly that in the majority of situations, it is the behavioral and organizational factors rather than technical issues that can have the most impact on successfully introducing new projects.

## BACKGROUND

There is an increasing interest in project critical success factors in the field of organizational research. Several authors, writing on the implementation process, have developed sets of CSFs, or those factors that, if addressed, will significantly improve the chances for successful implementation. In this chapter, we will focus on three of the more well-known streams of CSF research and their implications for project implementation. Two of the studies, by Baker, Murphy, and Fisher (1983) and Pinto and Slevin (1987) based on Pinto (1986), examined the CSFs for implementation success using databases of projects from U.S. companies. The third study by Morris (1983), using a sample of British firms, looked at major drivers and inhibitors of project success. The important point to note while examining these findings is the high level of agreement, regardless of the different implementation efforts being studied and the potential cultural differences that exist.

### Morris' Study

The first study, conducted by Peter Morris, was based on a large sample of British firms and their efforts at implementing new technologies. The key factor of this study was its breakdown of the implementation process into a life cycle comprising four stages: team formation, buildup, main phase, and close-out. Among the behavioral factors examined were issues such as personal motivation, top management support, team motivation, clear objectives, client support, technical issues, financial concerns, and so on.

**TABLE 4.1. Principal Success Drivers from British Study on Critical Success Factors**

| *Stage* | *Critical Success Factors (in order of importance)* |
| --- | --- |
| Formation | Personal ambition |
| | Top management support |
| | Team motivation |
| | Clear objectives |
| | Technological advantage |
| Buildup | Team motivation |
| | Personal motivation |
| | Top management support |
| | Technical expertise |
| Main phase | Team motivation |
| | Personal motivation |
| | Client support |
| | Top management support |
| Close-out | Personal motivation |
| | Team motivation |
| | Top management support |
| | Financial support |

*Source: Morris (1983).*

The results of the study, as shown in Table 4.1, demonstrated three important points. First, the relative importance of the various CSFs changes as the implementation effort proceeds through its life cycle. For example, at stage one, team formation, the most important factors are personal motivation and top management support. However, by the time the implementation process is in its close-out, personal and team motivation are most important to the success of the project.

The second point to note is that behavioral and organizational factors far outweigh technical issues in terms of their importance for implementation success. Rather than focusing undue concern on technical issues (adequate budgets and financial support, scheduling, and so forth), this study argues that it is far more important to pay attention to the human side of the implementation process: to remember that "management" does not simply imply oversight, but attendance to the needs and concerns of members of the implementation team as well as the clients. The final point, although closely related to the above two issues, is that these human and organizational issues that are the primary drivers of implementation success can also have tremendous impact on system failure if not addressed. Table 4.2 demonstrates that the inhibitors of successful implementation, once again, are clearly shown

**TABLE 4.2. Principal Inhibitors to Success from British Study on Critical Success Factors**

| *Stage* | *Problems with Critical Success Factors (in order of importance)* |
|---------|------------------------------------------------------------------|
| Formation | Unmotivated team<br>Poor leadership<br>Technical limitations<br>Money |
| Buildup | Unmotivated team<br>Conflict in objectives<br>Leadership problems<br>Poor top management support<br>Technical problems |
| Main phase | Unmotivated team<br>Poor top management support<br>Deficient procedures |
| Close-out | Poor control<br>Poor financial support<br>Objectives<br>Leadership |

*Source: Morris (1983).*

to be primarily behavioral and organizational in nature, rather than technical.

## Baker, Murphy, and Fisher's Study

Morris' study cited above sparked interest in the analysis of CSFs within the project implementation context partially because it pointed so clearly to the tremendous role that behavioral and organizational factors can play in the successful implementation of innovations. A separate study by Baker, Murphy, and Fisher (1983) addressed a comprehensive list of those factors thought to contribute to perceived project implementation success. Their list also included a number of behavioral dimensions (project team spirit, project team and leader goal commitment, project manager's human skills, job security of implementation team, and so forth), as well as organizational issues (parent organization enthusiasm, satisfaction with project team structure, adequacy of change procedures, and so forth), and technical factors (development of a realistic budget and schedule to completion, technical details of the system to be implemented, and so forth). They examined over 650 projects across a wide range of project types, durations, budgeted costs, and goals.

As Table 4.3 shows, the similarity of these findings to those of the earlier British study is striking. Again, the behavioral and organizational factors are clearly most important. In particular, the single factor of coordination and relations, encompassing a variety of items such as capability of the project team, sense of mission, team spirit, goal commitment, and supportive informal relations of team members, accounted by itself for 77% of the causes of implementation success.

These two studies illustrate the important truth that we have sought to emphasize—namely, that any discussion of the factors critical for system implementation success *must* look beyond concerns over the basic technical merits of the system. Too often, particularly among technical personnel, there is a tendency to see

**TABLE 4.3. Factors Contributing to Perceived Implementation Success**

| Determining Factors | Standardized Regression Coefficient | Sig. | Cum. $R^2$ |
|---|---|---|---|
| Coordination and team-client relations | +.35 | p<.001 | .773 |
| Adequacy of team structure and control | +.19 | p<.001 | .830 |
| System uniqueness, importance, and public exposure | +.15 | p<.001 | .887 |
| Success criteria salience and consensus | +.25 | p<.001 | .886 |
| Competitive and budgetary pressure | −.15 | p<.001 | .897 |
| Initial over-optimism, conceptual difficulty | −.22 | p<.001 | .905 |
| Internal capabilities buildup | +.08 | p<.001 | .911 |

*Source: Baker, Murphy, and Fisher (1983).*

problems and possibilities from a very narrow focus. In implementing a project, managers placed in charge of that process must acknowledge that technical mastery of the system provides, in itself, no guarantee of adoption success. In fact, such mastery may actually hurt the prospects for successful introduction if it causes managers to reveal and be influenced by professional biases in their management of the team and implementation process.

## *Pinto and Slevin's Study*

A more recent study of CSFs in the project implementation process (Pinto and Slevin, 1988) looked at over 400 projects varying greatly in terms of the basic characteristics. A wide range of representative samples of project type included R&D projects, construction projects, information system projects, and so forth. The study validated a 10-factor model of critical success factors for project implementation that will be discussed below. Further, Pinto and Slevin were also able to confirm the extreme importance of managerial, behavioral, and organizational issues in successful system implementation. In fact, one of the stated benefits of their research was the determination that, to a large degree, these CSFs remain within the control of the project manager responsible for implementing the project. Rather than being held captive by a chain of events beyond their control, project managers have a strong capacity to influence and improve their teams' chances of implementation success by attending to these CSFs.

## CRITICAL SUCCESS FACTORS: A 10-FACTOR MODEL

There is a growing body of project management literature that focuses on implementation critical success factors. However, in many cases, project management prescriptions and process frameworks are theoretically based, rather than empirically proven. That is, the evidence supporting these sets of factors is often anecdotal, a single-case study, or theory-derived, rather than empirical. Although there sometimes exists strong intuitive evidence supporting the conceptual frameworks of the project management process, there is relatively little empirical basis for the resulting models and theories of project management and implementation. From Pinto and Slevin's research, however, we can begin to explore how these factors offer new insights into the "managerial" nature of project CSFs. Table 4.4 shows the 10-factor model, listing factors and short definitions.

### *Factor Definitions*

- *Project mission.* Several authors have discussed the importance of clearly defining goals, as well as the ultimate benefits at the outset of a project. For example, Morris (1983) classified the initial project management stage as a feasibility

## TABLE 4.4. Factor Definitions

1. *Project mission.* Initial clearly defined goals and general directions.

2. *Top management support.* Willingness of top management to provide the necessary resources and authority/power for implementation success.

3. *Schedule plans.* A detailed specification of the individual action steps for system implementation.

4. *Client consultation.* Communication, consultation, and active listening to all parties impacted by the proposed project.

5. *Personnel.* Recruitment, selection, and training of the necessary personnel for the implementation project team.

6. *Technical tasks.* Availability of the required technology and expertise to accomplish the specific technical action steps to bring the project on-line.

7. *Client acceptance.* The act of "selling" final product to its ultimate intended users.

8. *Monitoring and feedback.* Timely provision of comprehensive control information at each stage in the implementation process.

9. *Communication.* The provision of an appropriate network and necessary data to all key actors in the project implementation process.

10. *Troubleshooting.* Ability to handle unexpected crises and deviations from plan.

study. Are the goals clear and can they succeed? Project mission refers to the condition in which the goals of the project are clear and understood, by not only the project team, but also the clients, other departments in the organization, and any other significant stakeholders.

- *Top management support.* Management support for projects, or indeed for any implementation effort, has long been considered of great importance in distinguishing between their ultimate success or failure. Beck (1983) observed that project management is not only dependent on top management for authority, direction, and support, but ultimately, projects serve as the conduit for implementing top management's plans, or goals, for the organization. Further, the degree of management support for a project will lead to significant variations in the degree of acceptance or resistance to that project or product. Top management's support of the project may involve aspects such as allocation of sufficient resources (including financial, manpower, time, etc.), as well as project management's confidence in its support in the event of crisis.

- *Project schedule/plans.* Project schedule refers to the importance of creating a detailed plan of the required stages in the implementation process. As developed in our model, project schedule/plan refers to the degree to which time schedules, milestones, manpower, and equipment requirements are specified. Further, the schedule should include a satisfactory measurement system as a way of judging actual performance against budget and time allowances. Obviously, we should note that schedules and plans are not intrinsically the same. Planning is a more broad-range process, encompassing resource assessments, work breakdown structures, and other forms of project-monitoring mechanisms. Scheduling, on the other hand, is generally understood to refer to the tasks of creating specific time- and task-interdependent structures, such as critical path and Gantt charts.

- *Client consultation.* We have have identified the "client" as anyone who will ultimately be making use of the result of the project, as either a customer outside the company or department within the organization. The need for client consultation has been found to be increasingly important in attempting a successful system implementation. Indeed, Manley (1975) determined that the degree to which clients are personally involved in the implementation process will cause great variation in their support for that project. It is, therefore, important to determine whether clients for the project have been identified. Once the project manager is aware of the major clients, he or she is better able to accurately determine if their needs are being met.

- *Personnel.* These issues include recruitment, selection, and training. An important, but often overlooked, aspect of the implementation process concerns the nature of the personnel involved. In many situations, personnel for the project team are chosen with less than full regard for the skills necessary to actively contribute to implementation success. Most current writers on implementation are acknowledging the role of effective project team personnel in successful implementation efforts and including the personnel variable in their equation for project team success. For example, one researcher has developed a contingency model of the implementation process that includes "people" as a situational variable, their knowledge, skills, goals, and personalities consequently considered in assessing the environment of the organization (Hammond, 1979). For our framework, personnel, as a factor, is concerned with developing an implementation team with the requisite skills and commitment to perform its function.

- *Technical tasks.* It is important that the implementation be well managed by people who understand it. In addition, adequate technology must exist to support the system. Technical tasks refers to the necessity of not only having the necessary personnel of the implementation team, but also ensuring that they possess the required technical skills and have adequate technology to perform their tasks. Obviously, the decision to initiate a new project must be predicated on the organization's ability to both staff the team with competent individuals and provide the technical means for the project to succeed. A recent example of a technical task failure involved a company that contracted with the U.S. government to create a software system using "C" programming language. The firm belatedly discovered that it did not have enough programmers conversant in C language to perform the contract and lost valuable time and incurred schedule slippages while it sent several of its programmers off-site to take training classes in the language.

- *Client acceptance.* Refers to the final stage in the implementation process, at which time the overall efficacy of the project is to be determined. Too often, project managers make the mistake of believing that if they handle the other stages of the implementation process well, the client (either internal or external to the organization) will accept the resulting system. In fact, several writers have shown that client acceptance is a stage in project implementation that must be managed like any other. Some researchers have even proposed the use of "intermediaries" to act as a liaison between the designer, or implementation team, and the project's potential users to aid in client acceptance (Bean and Radnor, 1979).

- *Monitoring and feedback.* Refer to the project control process by which, at each stage of the project implementation, key personnel receive feedback on how the project is comparing to initial projections. Making allowances for adequate monitoring and feedback mechanisms gives the project manager the ability to anticipate problems, oversee corrective measures, and ensure that no deficiencies are overlooked. Project managers need to emphasize the importance of constant monitoring and "finetuning" the process of implementation. For our model, monitoring and feedback refer to not only project schedule and budget, but also monitoring the performance of members of the project team.

- *Communication.* The need for adequate communication channels is extremely important in creating an atmosphere for successful system implementation. Communication is not only essential within the project team itself, but also between the team and rest of the organization as well as with the clients. Figure 4.1 demonstrates the tripartite nature of communication and necessity of keeping open channels among all active stakeholders in the project's development. As the communication factor has been developed within our framework, it refers to not only feedback mechanisms, but also the necessity of exchanging information with both clients and the rest of the organization concerning the project's capabilities, the goals of the implementation process, changes in policies and procedures, status reports, etc.

- *Troubleshooting.* As several project managers have pointed out, problem areas exist in almost every implementation. *The measure of a successful project implementation effort is not the avoidance of problems, but knowing the correct steps to take once problems develop.* Regardless of how carefully the implementation effort was initially planned, it is impossible to foresee every trouble area or problem that could possibly arise. As a

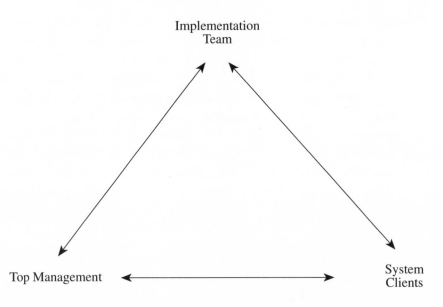

FIGURE 4.1. The three-way path of communication.

result, it is important that the project manager make adequate initial arrangements for troubleshooting mechanisms to be included in the implementation plan. Such mechanisms would make it easier to not only react to problems as they arise, but also foresee and possibly forestall potential problem areas in the implementation process.

## RESEARCH IMPLICATIONS

The framework initially developed by the above discussion can be viewed from both a conceptual and practical standpoint. Conceptually, the model argues for both the sequential and interdependent aspects of factors found to be critical to system implementation success. That is, these factors are seen as arising for consideration separately, but as often having strong influence on each other. For example, the theoretical literature and practical experiences of many project managers demonstrate that initial client consultation will create a strong likelihood of subsequent client acceptance.

Beyond the development of a conceptual framework of 10 critical success factors, recent research has verified the importance of each of the 10 factors to implementation success. Table 4.5 shows the results of a study of over 400 project implementation efforts that assessed the importance of these 10 factors.

## WHAT DOES THE RESEARCH SHOW?

Rather than devote a tremendous amount of space to an in-depth discussion of the results of research on the 10-factor model, we have chosen to condense these findings into a summary based on a series of conclusions from this research:

1. *Keep the mission in the forefront.* On the surface, it seems obvious to state that it is important to keep the mission in mind when implementing a project. However, the point bears repeating

**TABLE 4.5. Critical Success Factors and Their Importance for System Implementation**

| Factor | Beta | T-Value | Sig. T |
|---|---|---|---|
| Mission | .72 | 19.99 | *p*<.001 |
| Top management support | .32 | 10.60 | *p*<.001 |
| Schedule | .32 | 10.92 | *p*<.001 |
| Client consultation | .39 | 11.86 | *p*<.001 |
| Personnel | .31 | 10.54 | *p*<.001 |
| Technical tasks | .43 | 11.25 | *p*<.001 |
| Client acceptance | .39 | 11.46 | *p*<.001 |
| Monitoring and feedback | .29 | 10.89 | *p*<.001 |
| Communication | .32 | 10.38 | *p*<.001 |
| Troubleshooting | .35 | 11.15 | *p*<.001 |

*Source: Pinto (1986).*
*Cumulative $R^2 = .615$.*

and continual emphasis. The research on the 10-factor model demonstrated clearly that adherence to mission was the *number one* cause of implementation success. Remember that what "mission" refers to is not simply *having* a mission to implement a project, but conveying exactly what the goals of the implementation effort are to all concerned parties, particularly the other project team members and prospective users of the system. What will the new project do for us and the rest of the organization? How long do we expect it will take to develop and complete the project? Does every member of the project team understand and buy into these goals? These are just some of the important questions that need to be asked about the project's mission. Nothing will derail a project faster than not having clearly communicated its goals to all groups impacted by the project. When goals change or require updating, that information also needs to be made public.

One well-known problem with getting a project out the door is the potential for the mission to change or metamorphosize as the project progresses. There are many examples of projects that, for whatever reason, underwent major specification, technological, or user changes or got off on such tangents that the originally agreed on goals and purposes became meaningless. Obviously, some modifications are bound to occur as a project is customized for a particular client's uses. The point that must be stressed, however, is that the project's underlying purpose must remain clear and important for all members of the implementation team.

**2. Consult with your clients early.** Remember that "clients" refers to any projected or potential user of the project. Regardless of who the client is for a particular project, it should be apparent that consultation and communication with clients during its development are very important for its successful implementation. Put another way, one of the worst things that a project manager can do is initiate and develop a product or service without engaging in any meaningful dialogue with the external customers or internal departmental clients who could potentially make use of the technology. There is an old saying that *people don't mind "change," they just don't like being changed.* We tend to be leery of anything that can cause disruption in our thought patterns, approaches to decision making, or work habits. The output of a completed project is bound to cause disruptions in all three of these areas. Therefore, knowing in advance that strong potential exists for this project to change forever (it is hoped, in a positive manner) customer attitudes or internal client operations, we suggest that it makes excellent sense to spend a considerable amount of time establishing the groundwork for the successful introduction of the project.

**3. Stay "well connected" to clients.** Client acceptance, a "selling" activity, is necessary during both the initial planning processes as well as the termination phase of the implementation. Often, the sequence of operations concerned with the client follows the pattern of 1) consult to determine specific needs; 2) sell our ideas (including the benefits of the project), budgets, and time frame to completion; and 3) perform a final verification of client acceptance once the project has been completed. This verification may occur in the form of a series of formal interviews or followup conversations with clients who are intending to use it.

In developing and implementing a project, do not underestimate the importance of "selling" the output to the clients, even after having initially consulted with them about the system. An important truth of project implementation suggests that one can never talk to clients enough. A corollary to that rule argues that just because the project manager and team members once spent time consulting with clients about the system, it is absolutely incorrect to now assume that clients will embrace the finished product with open arms. In the time between initial consultation and project development and transfer, too much can change that will alter their perceptions of the product. For example, the technology may be altered significantly or a great deal of time may have elapsed, changing their basic reasons for even needing the system. Or perhaps, one of the department's chief proponents of the project has since left to take another job. The common denominator of all these issues is that time does not stand still between initial client consultation and final project completion. Do not automatically assume that you fully understand the client's concerns. Further, once the completed project is transferred, do not simply expect it will be used. In fact, this topic is so crucial to successful project implementation that we have devoted a chapter to it later in this book.

**4.** *Make sure you have the technology to succeed.* The successful development and acceptance and use of a project assume that the organization has the technology or technically proficient staff to support the system and ensure that it succeeds. Organizations, like many small children, often suffer from the "eyes bigger than the stomach" syndrome. A new technology is introduced nationally and someone within the organization develops great enthusiasm for the concept. The question that needs to be asked at this point is whether or not the organization can support the successful development and introduction of this project with its current personnel and facilities. If the answer is "no," the organization needs to take immediate remedial steps: either hiring additional support personnel who have the necessary technical backgrounds, instituting a department-wide training program to bring potential users up to technical standards or, if necessary, putting the brakes on the project's development until another time when it can be more fully supported.

**5.** *Set up and maintain a scheduling system.* Planning is an activity that many project managers would rather avoid. The process can sometimes be rather tedious and involves an activity that does not have immediate visible results. This is particularly true early in the project's life cycle, when top management begins to issue a string of pointed communiqués demanding to know when project development will begin, somehow assuming that time spent "planning" takes away from time spent "doing." In spite of these external pressures for action, it is impossible to underestimate the importance of comprehensive and detailed planning for successful project implementation. There is great validity to the old saying that "Those who fail to plan are planning to fail." Initiating the action steps in a project without having developed a comprehensive planning and control process may please upper management in the short term, but such is a real recipe for disaster down the road.

An interesting side note based on our research is to offer some ideas of when planning can be most effective. Obviously, during the early startup of the implementation effort, planning is paramount. This type of planning involves setting milestones, breaking down the specific work activities into meaningful segments, and assigning the necessary personnel to tackle each of these duties. However, planning is also very useful during the final, termination, phase of the project. We have found that planning here serves two purposes. First, schedules provide feedback on how well the project team accomplished its goals: They serve as a learning device when projected schedules are compared with actual results. Second, schedules are needed for the transfer of the project to its intended users. Transferring the project, establishing training sessions and maintenance cycles, and getting it on-line usually require an additional series of target dates and schedules.

**6. *Put the right people on the project team.*** Research results demonstrate the importance of recruiting, selecting, and training people who possess the necessary technical and administrative skills to positively influence the ultimate success of the project. Does the organization currently employ people capable of understanding the technology and dealing with the headaches, deadlines, and conflict that a project implementation can bring? Of equal importance is the question, "How are project team members assigned to the group?"

In many organizations with which we have worked, members are assigned to project teams purely on an availability basis; that is, if managers have subordinates who are currently free, those people are put on the team, regardless of whether or not they possess the technical qualifications, people skills, or administrative abilities to perform effectively. In some organizations, the picture is even worse. There, members are assigned to projects as a method of removing them from their departments and making them someone else's problem. In such cases, managers burdened with problem subordinates simply use the project as an excuse to ship these troublemakers to other duties. It is easy to imagine the prospects for projects continually staffed with cast-offs and incompetents. "Personnel" as a factor implies having and assigning the most qualified individuals to the implementation team, not the most available. We owe our projects more than to simply make an implementation team the dumping ground for malcontents.

**7. *Make sure top management gets behind the project.*** It is well accepted that top management can either help or seriously hinder a project. Top management grants the necessary authority to the project manager, controls needed resources, arbitrates cross-departmental disputes, and rewards the final results. Its role in the successful implementation of a new project should not be overlooked. However, top management support must go further than simply "approving" the new system. Its statements of support have to be backed up by concrete actions and demonstrations of loyalty. Actions speak far louder than words and have a way of truly demonstrating how top management feels about the project and by extension the project manager. Is management putting its money where its mouth is or is its support simply pro forma? This is an important question that needs to be resolved early in the implementation process, before significant time and resources have been spent.

Further, top management's support can be most important during the time when the actual "work" of the implementation is being done rather than early on or after the project is being terminated prior to transfer to clients. Top management is most able at this point to make its presence felt, through providing the necessary money, personnel, and support for the system as they are needed. Finally, both project managers and their teams need to know that top management will support them in the event of unforeseen difficulties or crises. All implementation efforts encounter difficulties and "fair weather" supporters are likely to be terribly demoralizing.

**8. *Continually ask the "what if?" questions.*** It is axiomatic that problems will occur with the implementation. All projects run into trouble and the mark of a successful project manager is not one who can foresee and forestall problems; rather, the successful project manager is the individual who has taken the time to puzzle out appropriate responses to likely trouble spots. This idea of troubleshooting is particularly appropriate in the implementation of projects with new or not well understood technology because there are so many human and technical variables that can cause a project to go awry. So the successful project manager has to be cognizant of technical issues and difficulties that can arise, but furthermore, we have made the case in this book that behavioral and organizational issues are often more common, pressing, and potentially damaging to implementation success. Therefore, the act of simply troubleshooting the project's technical features will only be of limited usefulness.

One final point about troubleshooting needs to be made. We

have already discussed the importance of a clear project mission for successful implementation. In fact, it was noted as the number one cause of project success. A followup study was conducted by one of the authors and a colleague to investigate, again using the 10-factor model, the principal causes of implementation *failure.* We discovered that the number one cause of failure in project implementation was a lack of adequate troubleshooting mechanisms (Pinto and Mantel, 1990). The projects that were viewed as unsuccessful due to poor adherence to budget, schedule, specification performance, and user acceptance were almost always associated with an inadequate or nonexistent attempt by the project team at troubleshooting.

## CONCLUSIONS

This chapter has focused on the results of recent research and its implications for successful project implementation using critical success factors (CSFs). The interest in CSFs as a methodology for gaining better control of the project implementation process is still relatively new, but has already yielded some important implications for project managers and those charged with successfully introducing a project. The information offered here suggests some guidelines for project managers to employ in more efficiently assigning their personnel and resources. It is particularly encouraging to note that the critical factors in the three studies cited are all within the control of the project manager; that is, these issues are addressable in that remedial action can be taken in the event problems do occur. Consequently, this chapter has not only listed the important CSFs, it has also offered possible advice on their most effective use. It is through creating an "actionable" set of CSFs that project managers are most likely to employ them in their work and, consequently, their projects are most likely to benefit.

*Part* 2

## *Leader par Excellence*

*T*he central thesis behind this book is the dominant role that the project team leader can play in the success or failure of projects. In this part, we begin to explore in some detail the range of duties and characteristics that effective project managers must possess. The first chapter, "Lead by Following," takes an in-depth look at some of the basic contradictions and confusions in our understanding of exactly what constitutes leadership behavior. We will suggest that the first step toward gaining the ability to understand and lead a project team is to develop a level of self-awareness in that the leader understands and is comfortable with his or her preferred leadership style. Finally, we will demonstrate that the "key" to successful leadership behavior is flexibility.

The second chapter, "A Generalist, Not a Specialist," demonstrates that the most effective project team leaders are usually those who can shed their mantel of technical specialization, adopting a more generalist outlook that recognizes the contributions of all team members, no matter what their functional orientation may be. As part of our discussion, we will present some of the relevant research that encapsulates the generalist nature of successful project managers.

The third chapter, "Project Manager's Duties: A to Z," refers to our attempt to put into a simple, easily understood framework the wide-ranging nature of the diverse expectations and roles placed on project managers. This chapter should give the reader a sense of the often intimidating nature of the project management role, by listing the variety of duties they must perform.

Understanding the process of project team motivation is central to the project leader's duties and we have devoted a chapter to this often confusing and contradictory topic. In this chapter, we will examine some of the more useful and important theories of motivation, arguing that the essential point for project managers to remember is that motivation is the project manager's attempt at finding value for subordinates. Team members motivate themselves to the degree that they perceive value in the process and the absence of risk to themselves. When project managers understand these issues, they can begin to approach this topic with more confidence in their ability to influence project team members positively.

The final chapter in this part, "Total Manager = Total Management," offers a summary and capstone of our discussion by making clear the unique and important nature of project managers in the project development process. As we suggest, there are few functions in business today that are as "leader-intensive" as project management. Bad projects are often saved by good leaders and good projects can easily be ruined by poor leaders. It is usually the project leader who sets the tone for the project and determines its chances of success.

# 5

## *Lead by Following**

*It is not good when he who carries the torch must at the same time seek the way.*

—Colvos

THIS CHAPTER IS about project leadership. There are few topics that are as widely discussed and at the same time lend themselves to such controversy and disagreement as a discussion of leadership behavior. Book after book has been written attempting to show how all managers can become better leaders, how leadership is the key to organizational and even national renewal, and how leadership, particularly when exercised throughout the organization in the form of empowerment, can

---

* Portions of this chapter were adapted from D. P. Slevin and J. K. Pinto (1991), Project leadership: Understanding and consciously choosing your style, *Project Management Journal* XXII, 39–47.

lead to enhanced competitiveness and quality. Trying to help project managers become better leaders will always be a difficult task, but a desirable one. As we have noted often throughout this book, project managers charged with implementing their projects must rely on a variety of skills. Because the implementation process is intensely "people-oriented," some of the most important skills that must be developed are the abilities to motivate, inspire, and lead the implementation team. True leadership from the project manager has been shown time and again to be one of the most important characteristics in successful implementation, not least because its impact is felt not simply within the implementation team, but by other managers and important project stakeholders (Slevin and Pinto, 1988; Posner, 1987). As a result, the more we are able to understand about the dynamics of this concept, the better able we will be to effectively manage our project's development and implementation and train a future generation of project managers in the tasks and skills required for them to perform their jobs.

Leadership is a complex process that is crucial to successful project implementation (Gaddis, 1959; Hodgetts, 1968). The principal difficulty with studying leadership is that we know at once so much and yet so little about the concept. Behavioral scientists have been studying the leadership problem for over half a century in an attempt to better understand the process and arrive at some prescriptive recommendations concerning effective leadership behaviors. Years of careful research have generated a variety of findings that are, at best, sometimes confusing to the practicing manager and, at worst, often internally inconsistent. For example, the following eleven propositions have been suggested to guide leader behavior:

- Leaders will be most effective when they show a high level of concern for both the task and employees (their subordinates) (Blake and Mouton, 1964).

- Leaders should be task-oriented under conditions where they have either high or low control over the group. When leaders have only moderate control over the group, they should be people-oriented (Fiedler, 1978).

- To be effective, leaders must base their decision-making style on how important employee acceptance of the decision will be. They should seek participation by subordinates in decision making accordingly (Vroom and Yetton, 1973).

- Leaders will be accepted and will motivate employees to the extent that their behavior helps employees progress toward valued goals and provides guidance or clarification not already present in the work situation (House, 1971).

- A participative approach to leadership will lead to improved employee morale and increase their commitment to the organization (Fleishman, 1973).

- Under stressful conditions (e.g., time pressure), an autocratic leadership style will lead to greater productivity (Fodor, 1976). A minimum level of friendliness or warmth will enhance this effect (Tjosvold, 1984).

- Even when the leader has all the needed information to make a decision and the problem is clearly structured, employees prefer a participative approach to decision making (Heilman et al., 1984).

- Effective leaders tend to exhibit high levels of intelligence, initiative, personal needs for occupational achievement, and self-confidence (Stogdill, 1984).

- Effective leadership behavior can depend on the organizational setting, so that similar behaviors may have different consequences in different settings (Ghiselli, 1971).

- Leadership behavior may not be important if subordinates are skilled, if tasks are structured or routine, technology dictates the required actions, or the administrative climate is supportive and fair (Dansereau, Graen, and Haga, 1975).

- Leadership behavior can be divided into task behavior (one-way communication) and relationship behavior (two-way communication). An effective leadership style using these behaviors can be selected according to the maturity level of subordinates relative to accomplishing the task (Salancik et al., 1975).

This list of principles of leadership and leader behavior presents a bewildering set of premises for project managers. In some cases, these points seem to actively disagree with each other. For example, some researchers say that a participatory leadership style is best for all situations, whereas other work suggests that a participatory style is more effective in some situations and with some types of subordinates than others. Some of the conclusions argue that specific character traits of the leader determine effectiveness, whereas other work states that it is, in fact, the dynamics of the interaction of the leader with subordinates that determines effectiveness. Finally, other authors have concluded that, under some conditions, leadership style is not important at all (Kerr and Jermier, 1978).

So where does this leave us and the project manager? These research results certainly reinforce the perception that the process of project team leadership is confusing, complex, and often contradictory. What would help project managers is an understanding of the current state of project management theory regarding leadership. What do we know about this elusive topic as it pertains to the project management process? Finally, we will offer a day-to-day working model that clarifies some aspects of the concept of leadership, suggests alternative leadership styles that may be used, and provides some practical recommendations on conditions under which alternative leadership styles might be used. The purpose of this chapter is to describe the project leadership process as fully as we are able, suggesting a *cognitive* approach to leadership that will help the implementation team leader consciously select the leadership style correct for alternative situations.

## LEADERSHIP BEHAVIOR AND PROJECT MANAGEMENT: WHAT WE KNOW

Besides the collection of prescriptive studies listed above that argue for specific "leader-related" actions, we can investigate the results of large-scale leadership research that was aimed at uncovering those traits that are specific to leaders. Because a leader is not the same thing as a manager per se, we find "leaders" in all walks of life and occupying all levels within organizational hierarchies. A recent study that sought to uncover the traits most managers felt were important for leaders to possess is particularly illuminating in the characteristics it suggests we all seek in those who lead us. The study, conducted by Kouzes and Posner (1991), used a large sample survey and asked a total of 2615 managers within U.S. corporations what they considered to be the most important characteristics of effective leaders.

Table 5.1 presents the results of Kouzes and Posner's survey. A significant majority of managers felt that the most important characteristic of superior leaders was basic honesty: Leaders say what they mean and live up to their promises. In addition, we seek competence and intelligence, vision, inspiration, fairness, imagination, and dependability, to list a few of the most important characteristics. These traits offer an important starting point for better understanding how leaders operate and, more important, how the other members of the project team or organization expect them to operate. Clearly, the most important factors that the majority of us seek in people we are willing to view as leaders are the dimensions of trust and strength of character and the intelligence and competence to succeed. The expectation of success is important: The majority of followers do not tag along after failures for very long.

Another study on the leadership roles of senior executives has revealed five broad categories of leadership roles, as perceived by their subordinates (Javidan and Dastmachian, 1993). These roles include ambassador, avatar, driver, mobilizer, and servant. The results of the large-scale study (1687 senior to upper-middle managers in three large Canadian firms were polled) led to the follow-

**TABLE 5.1. Characteristics of Effective Leaders**
**(U.S. Managers, $N = 2615$)**

| Characteristic | Ranking | Percentage of Managers Selecting |
|---|---|---|
| Honest | 1 | 83 |
| Competent | 2 | 67 |
| Forward-looking | 3 | 62 |
| Inspiring | 4 | 58 |
| Intelligent | 5 | 43 |
| Fair-minded | 6 | 40 |
| Broad-minded | 7 | 37 |
| Straightforward | 8 | 34 |
| Imaginative | 9 | 34 |
| Dependable | 10 | 33 |
| Supportive | 11 | 32 |
| Courageous | 12 | 27 |
| Caring | 13 | 26 |
| Cooperative | 14 | 25 |
| Mature | 15 | 23 |
| Ambitious | 16 | 21 |
| Determined | 17 | 20 |
| Self-controlled | 18 | 13 |
| Loyal | 19 | 11 |
| Independent | 20 | 10 |

*Source: Kouzes and Posner (1991).*

ing conclusion: Both the hierarchical level of the superior and the nature of the organization itself influence the effective "mix" of leadership roles. That is, within some firms and at certain management levels, effective leaders use certain roles (e.g., driver versus servant) to a greater degree.

We also can refer to research specifically related to project managers and the leadership traits necessary to be successful in this more specialized arena. Three studies in particular, those by Pettersen (1991), Einsiedel (1987), and Thamhain and Gemmill (1974), shed some valuable light in the nature of the special demands that project managers face and the concomitant nature of the leadership characteristics they must manifest. Pettersen (1991) analyzed data from a number of sources and synthesized a set of factors that most effective project leaders shared in common. Specifically, he pointed to five important characteristics for proficient project management: oral communication skills, influencing skills, intellectual capabilities, the ability to handle stress, and diverse management skills, including planning, delegation, and decision making. Pettersen's study reinforced the points we made in Chapter 3 on the nature of project management power. In effect, as Pettersen found, most project managers do not have the capacity to exercise power that derives from formal positional authority. Consequently, they are forced to develop effective influencing skills.

The second study, by Einsiedel (1987), showed close parallels to Pettersen's (1991) more comprehensive research. Einsiedel also identified five characteristics that he argued are closely associated with effective project team leaders. His five factors were 1) credibility—is the project manager trustworthy and taken seriously by both the project team and parent organization? 2) creative problem-solver—is the project manager skilled at problem analysis and identification? 3) tolerance for ambiguity—is the project manager adversely affected by complex or ambiguous (uncertain) situations? 4) flexible management style—project management situations change rapidly: Does the project team leader possess the flexibility to adapt his or her leadership style to match the situational requirements? and 5) effective communication skills—the project manager operates as the focal point for communication from a variety of stakeholders. Does he or she possess the skills to effectively manage this process?

The final study of project management and leadership behavior, that of Thamhain and Gemmill (1974), addressed some of the effective influence styles that project managers can profitably use in dealing with their team. The three most important influence behaviors of project managers that contributed to project success were 1) emphasis on work challenge and expertise, 2) openness of upward communication, and 3) project involvement and support.

Specifically, project managers who were perceived by their team as emphasizing work challenge and expertise as influence methods achieved better project performance and also tended to foster a greater willingness among team members to openly disagree with each other, voice dissenting opinions, and become personally involved in the project implementation. Interestingly, their other major finding showed that, as an influence tactic, project managers' use of expertise had a positive impact on project success, whereas relying on simple authority over the project team had a negative effect on project outcomes.

It is important to note the commonalties across these studies. In so doing, it is possible to draw some general conclusions about the nature of project leadership. First, effective project managers must be good communicators. Much of their time is spent in one form of communication or another. Whether they chair meetings, brainstorm solutions to problems, or maintain information flows with the client and upper management, effective project leaders are adept at all forms of communication. Second, project leaders must possess the flexibility to respond to uncertain or ambiguous situations with a minimum of stress. The nature of project management work is that it does not follow easily defined or recurring patterns. Each project is, to some degree, unique and each problem that the team will face has to be viewed as a "new" problem requiring flexibility of response and creativity.

The third conclusion is that strong project leaders work well with and through their project team. They are adept at getting the most out of their subordinates by providing an atmosphere of challenge and creativity. They have the ability to build and reinforce a cohesive team atmosphere based on trust and enthusiasm for success. They understand their role in creating an environment in which their team members are able to motivate themselves to perform at levels of excellence. They are encouragers and supportive of their teams and utilize the various "people skills" necessary to help the team perform to its maximum.

The final conclusion from this research is that good project leaders are skilled at various influence tactics. As we had noted in Chapter 3, formal power relationships and chain-of-command

**TABLE 5.2. Five Keys to Establishing Sustained Influence**

---

- Develop a reputation as an expert.

- Prioritize social relationships on the basis of work needs rather than habit or social preference.

- Develop a network of other experts or resource persons who can be called on for assistance.

- Choose the correct combination of influence tactics for the objective and target to be influenced.

- Influence with sensitivity, flexibility, and solid communication.

---

*Source: B. Keys and T. Case (1990).*

authority do not work well in the project environment. Hence, effective project leaders must become well-schooled in the art of persuasion and influence. As in the case of the leadership trait research we have just explored, there is also some important literature that examines the various forms and uses of influence (Keys and Case, 1990), particularly within the context of project management (Thamhain and Gemmill, 1974).

How does a project manager succeed in establishing the sort of sustained influence throughout the organization that is useful in the pursuit of project-related goals? A recent article by Keys and Case (1990) highlights five methods managers can use for enhancing their level of influence with superiors, clients, team members, and other stakeholders (see Table 5.2):

1. *Establish a reputation as an expert.* A project manager who is widely perceived as lacking any sort of technical skill or compentency cannot command the same degree of influence to secure the support of other important stakeholders or be perceived as a true "leader" of the project team (Thamhain and Gemmill, 1974). Remember, however, that the label of "expert" is a perceptual one. That is, it may or may not be based on actual fact. Many of us are aware of project managers who cultivate the reputation of techni-

cal expert, whether the title is deserved or not. A reputation as an expert is very useful for gaining influence: Truly *being* an expert helps to improve immeasurably a project manager's credibility.

**2. Distinguish between the types of relationships that we encounter on the job.** Managers need to make conscious decisions to prioritize their relationships in terms of establishing close ties with those around the company who can help them accomplish their goals, rather than on the basis of social preference. All of us have personality types and influence groups toward whom we naturally gravitate. However, in seeking to broaden their influence, project managers need to break ties of habit and expand their social networks, particularly with regard to those who can be of future material aid to the project.

**3. Network.** Canny project managers seek to establish ties to acknowledged experts or those with the ability to provide scarce resources the project may need during times of crisis. We never know when we may need to call on them, especially when resources are lean.

**4. Do it well.** For influence to succeed, project managers seeking to influence others must carefully select their intended tactics. For example, many people who consider themselves adept at influencing others prefer face-to-face settings, rather than using the telephone or leaving messages to request support. They know intuitively that it is far harder for others to refuse to offer help when the request is made in person rather than through an impersonal medium. If the tactics selected are not appropriate to the individual or situation, influence will not work.

**5. Be socially sensitive, articulate, and flexible.** A clever influencer knows how to best balance the alternative methods for attaining the other manager's cooperation and help. These people can read body language and reactions from the "target" and may instinctively shift approaches in order to find the argument or influence style that appears to have the best chance of succeeding.

Whether the approach is pure flattery or cajolery, persuasion, or use of guilt, successful influencers are often people who can articulate their arguments well, read the nonverbal signals given off by the other person, and tailor their arguments and influence style appropriately to take best advantage of the situation.

It appears, ultimately, that the "bottom line" for understanding leadership behavior is to focus to a greater degree on what leaders *do* rather than who they are. It is dangerous and often imprecise to draw overly large generalizations from the personal psychology of acknowledged leaders in an effort to try to better understand what psychological forces make them operate in the manners in which they do. As Peter Gronn (1993) has noted, the uncritical use of currently popular psychoanalytical theories to investigate leaders ignores the influence of their organizations and ingrained cultural expectations that can heavily influence leadership behavior. In other words, we spend far too much time analyzing leaders *after* they become acknowledged leaders rather than investigating the forces that originally shaped them. If, then, it is more appropriate to examine leadership in terms of its behavior, let us consider some of the more common demands made on project managers and their approaches to responding to these demands.

## THE DIMENSIONS OF INFORMATION AND DECISION AUTHORITY

Beyond attempting methods to best exploit their influence skills, how are project managers to make the best use of their position and personalities in fostering leadership behavior? In order to practically answer this question, let us consider the following scenario. Let us imagine the manager of a five-person project development team. This manager is faced with a problem that is complex, yet a decision must be made. From the standpoint of leadership, the project manager must answer two "predecisional" questions:

1. *Where do I get the information input?* (Whom do I ask for relevant information?)

2. *Where should I place the decision authority for this problem?* (Who makes the decision?)

The first question asks which members of the group the project manager heads will furnish information about a particular decision. The second asks to what extent the manager retains all decision authority and makes the decision him- or herself or to what extent that manager is willing to "share" decision authority with

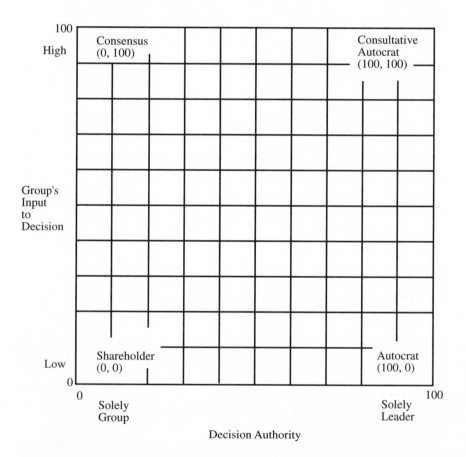

FIGURE 5.1. The Bonoma/Slevin leadership model.

members of the implementation team and have them make the decision with the manager in a more or less democratic fashion.

The first dimension is one of information; the second, one of decision authority. These two critical dimensions are essential for effective leadership and they have been plotted on the graph in Figure 5.1, the Bonoma/Slevin leadership model. As leaders, managers may either request large amounts of subordinate information input into a decision or very small amounts. This is the vertical axis: information input. Second, leaders' decision-making styles may range all the way from making the decision entirely by themselves to sharing their power with the group and having the final decision made entirely as a group decision. This is the horizontal axis: decision authority.

## FOUR LEADERSHIP STYLES

Slevin and Pinto (1988) argue (refer to Figure 5.1) that it is possible to describe almost every leadership style. The four extremes of leaders can be depicted in the four corners of the grid and are characterized as follows:

- *Autocrat (100, 0).* Such managers solicit little or no information from their implementation team and make the managerial decisions solely by themselves.

- *Consultative autocrat (100, 100).* In this managerial style, intensive information input is elicited from the team members, but such formal leaders keep all substantive decision-making authority to themselves.

- *Consensus manager (0, 100).* Purely consensual managers throw open the problem to the group for discussion (information input) and simultaneously allow or encourage the entire group to make the relevant decision.

- *Shareholder manager (0, 0).* This position represents literally poor management. Little or no information input and exchange take place within the group context, although the group itself is provided with ultimate authority for the final decision.

The advantages of the leadership model, apart from its practical simplicity, become more apparent when we consider three traditional aspects of leadership and managerial decision style:

- Participatory management

- Delegation

- Personal and organizational pressures affecting leadership

## Participative Management

The concept of participation in management is a complex and somewhat controversial one with different meanings for different individuals. Most managers will acknowledge that, in keeping with the general industrial move toward greater empowerment for subordinates, participation is a positive step. The problems usually occur when these same managers are asked to act on these views and encourage participation. Frequently, we discover that different managers envision different approaches to participation because they interpret the process in distinct ways. One of the common threads running through many of the managers' views is that participation should *not* be confused with decision making, which they regard as their unique right. For example, when we have discussed the notion of participation with managers in other settings, the following response is typical:

> "Oh, I participated with my subordinates on that decision—I asked each of them what they thought before I made the decision."

To many practicing managers, participation is often an *informational* concept, that is, permitting sufficient subordinate input to be made before the hierarchical decision is handed down. On the other hand, when academics consider the concept of participation, the following directive is more often typically made:

> "Managers should use participation management more often—they should allow their subordinates to make the final decision with them in a consensual manner."

To the academic, the concept of participation is usually an issue of *power*, that is, moving to the left on the Bonoma/Slevin model such that decision authority is shared with the group.

In reality, participation is a two-dimensional construct. It involves both the solicitation of information and sharing of power or decision authority. Neither dimension, in and of itself, is a sufficient indicator of a participative leadership style. Participative management requires equal emphasis on the project manager requesting information and allowing a more democratic decision-making dynamic to be adopted. See Figure 5.2.

## Delegation

Good managers delegate effectively. In doing so, they negotiate some sort of compromise between the extreme of "abdication," letting subordinates decide everything, and "autocratic management," doing everything themselves. Although the advantages of delegation are legion (see Table 5.3), there are also a number of reasons why many project managers have difficulty in delegating work and responsibility to subordinates. Table 5.4 lists some of the most common causes for managers to refuse to delegate. In general, these inhibitors of delegation can be broken down into three major categories: attitudes about subordinates, personal insecurities, and personal preference. Perhaps the most common reasons for project managers' refusal to delegate have to do with their underlying attitudes about their subordinates. In talking with project managers, most of whom freely admit that they have trouble delegating, we hear continually the same basic concerns: "My subordinates are not smart enough to handle this assignment." "My

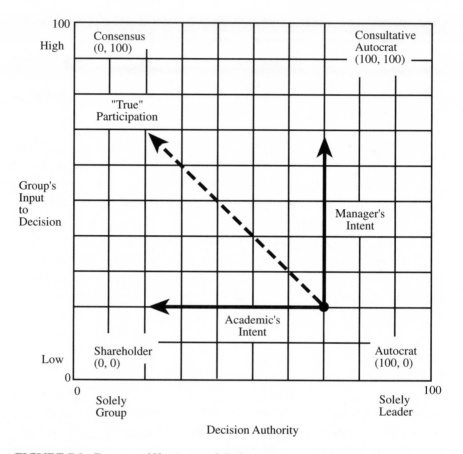

FIGURE 5.2. Bonoma/Slevin model showing participative
decision making.

people only do enough to get by. None of them will take on additional work, no matter how challenging." "None of my people
want the responsibility." These and other comments typify an attitude that pervades many managers' psyches: Subordinates are
subordinates for a reason. They are lower on the corporate ladder
because they do not have the same level of motivation or competence that the project manager possesses.

The second inhibitor of delegation stems from the project manager's personal insecurities (Leana, 1986). Many managers are concerned that in delegating work, they will lose the recognition or

**TABLE 5.3. Advantages of Delegation**

---

- Increases the personal discretionary time of managers: Leads to more effective time management.

- Develops the capabilities and knowledge of subordinates: When they look good, you look good.

- Demonstrates trust and confidence in subordinates: Leads to better interpersonal relationships.

- Enhances the commitment of subordinates to the task and organization: Improves morale, understanding of task, and motivation.

- Improves decision making by bringing to light more relevant information.

- Increases manager's efficiency by getting more done with less effort.

---

status that comes from performing the task by themselves. Further, they may fear the real or imagined consequences of failure if the task is given to a subordinate who cannot satisfactorily complete it. Finally, some managers refuse to delegate purely from personal preference: They simply prefer to do the work themselves, regardless of how tedious or mundane the task is.

Although all the above excuses are commonly voiced in defense of a refusal to delegate assignments to subordinates, we argue that, like it or not, project managers need to become comfortable with this process. The nature of task breakdown in projects is so fundamental to successful project development and the demands are often so diverse that project managers must learn to "bite the bullet" when it comes to developing the trust and commitment necessary to delegate effectively (see Table 5.5). Project-based work requires such a fragmented task structure and wide range of skills that it is simply impossible for project managers to hoard all discretionary power and decision authority to themselves and still perform competently. Given this fundamental requirement for delegation within project management, it is important to

**TABLE 5.4. Inhibitors of Effective Delegation**

ATTITUDES ABOUT SUBORDINATES

1. Subordinates are not competent enough to accomplish the work.

2. Subordinates should possess the skill required by their positions: It is not the manager's job to train them.

3. Subordinates are unwilling to accept additional responsibility.

4. Subordinates are unable to accept additional responsibility.

5. Subordinates should not be involved in certain kinds of tasks or decisions.

PERSONAL INSECURITIES

1. Managers may lose the recognition and rewards associated with accomplishing the task.

2. Managers may lose power if they share their expertise or trade secrets with subordinates.

3. Managers must know the details of all the work for which they are responsible so all uncertainty is eliminated.

4. Managers have to endure too high a cost as a result of mistakes made by subordinates.

PERSONAL PREFERENCE

1. Managers prefer to do some mundane and routine tasks.

2. Managers prefer to do the task quickly themselves, rather than take the time to explain it to subordinates.

3. Managers prefer to put in the longest hours and do the most work of anyone in the organization.

understand what constitutes effective delegation from poor delegation.

We have found the leadership model useful as a learning device for managers as they delegate work to their subordinates. After exposure to the model, managers are often likely to be more

**TABLE 5.5. Principles of Delegation**

---

- Parity of authority and responsibility
- Clarity and completeness of delegation
- Levels of delegation
- Support for delegated tasks
- Participation in delegation
- Upward delegation
- Accountability for results
- Consistent delegation

---

explicit about the informational and decision authority requirements of the delegated task. For example, the project manager might say to his or her subordinate:

> "Get the information that you need from my files and also check with Administration (information). You make the decision yourself (decision authority), but notify me in writing as soon as you have made it so that I am kept informed."

Thus, the subordinate understands both the information and decision authority aspects of the delegated tasks. Delegation often fails when the communication is unclear on either or both of these dimensions. To illustrate, there is a strong likelihood of difficulties occurring when managers phrase their instructions in such a way that subordinates are not clear about 1) what information they are expected to provide and when it is needed, and 2) how much power or discretion they possess to make their best judgment on the action to be taken.

## *Pressures Affecting Leadership*

Project managers must learn that they may be required to act differently as a leader under different conditions, depending on three kinds of pressure:

1. Problem attributes

2. Leader personality

3. Organizational/group

Please refer back to the grid map of the Bonoma/Slevin model. Think of the leadership model in terms of a map of the United States. Table 5.6 summarizes these pressures on leadership style in terms of geographical direction (e.g., a movement "north" is a movement upward on the vertical axis of the leadership model, and so on).

### Problem Attributes

Problem attribute pressures generate eastward forces on the leader. In other words, they often cause leaders to take the majority of or sole decision-making authority on themselves. This is especially true when problems are characterized as:

- Time-bound (a quick decision is required)

- Important

- Personal

- Structured and routine

In such cases, it is very tempting to take control over the decisional process personally and "get the job done." This phenomenon is particularly apparent with managers who are new to the job or insecure about their status as team member vis à vis their subordinates. They may not be inclined to trust subordinates to make either an accurate or timely decision, believing instead that

**TABLE 5.6. Pressures on Leadership Style**

| *Type of Pressure* | *Direction of Pressure on Leadership Grid* |
| --- | --- |
| **PROBLEM ATTRIBUTES PRESSURES** | |
| Leader lacks relevant information; problem is ambiguous. | North: More information needed. |
| Leader lacks enough time to make decision adequately. | South and east: Consensus and information collection take time. |
| Decision is important or critical to leader. | North and east: Personal control and information maximized. |
| Problem is structured or routine. | South and east: Little time as possible spent on decision. |
| Decision implemented by subordinates is critical to success. | West and north: Input and consensus required. |
| **LEADER PERSONALITY PRESSURES** | |
| Leader has high need for power. | East: Personal control maximized. |
| Leader is high in need for affiliation, is "people-oriented." | North and west: Contact with people maximized. |
| Leader is highly intelligent. | East: Personal competence demonstrated. |
| Leader has high need for achievement. | East: Personal contribution maximized. |
| **ORGANIZATIONAL AND GROUP PRESSURES** | |
| Conflict is likely to result from decision. | North and west: Participative aspects of decision making maximized. |
| Good leader-group relations exist. | North and west: Group contact maximized. |
| Centrality: Formalization of organization is high. | South and east: Organization style matched. |

one of the leader's prerogatives is to retain decision-making authority. However, northward pressures (involving the quest for additional information) can occur as well, given:

- Important decisions

- Decisions in which leaders lack the resources to make the decision themselves

- Problems in which subordinate implementation is critical to success

In these cases, information input and exchange will be maximized. Time pressures tend to push one toward the east, into an "autocratic mode." Implementation concerns push one to the northwest, in search of both more information and the active participation in and support of the decision by subordinates. It is a well-known behavioral finding that people cooperate more in implementing decisions they have helped make.

**Leader Personality**

Some managers tend to be inflexible in their leadership style because of who they are and how they like to manage. For example, both past research and personal experience have led us to conclude that, in many cases, such managers:

- Have a high need for power

- Are task-oriented

- Are highly intelligent

Managers of this type will make many decisions themselves that might otherwise be left to subordinates, and they also may make decisions without acquiring information from the group. People-oriented leaders, on the other hand, will act to maximize information inputs from their subordinates and share their decision authority as well. Both these activities are "people processes."

**Organizational/Group**

If conflict is likely to result from any decision made, effective managers are most likely to want their subordinates as involved as possible in both the input (northward) and authority (westward) dimensions, so as to help manage the potential conflict. Should good leader/group relations exist, pressure northward (but *not* necessarily westward) will be felt. The leader will feel great pressure to fit into the "culture" of the organization. The R&D lab expects a consensual approach; most business groups expect a consultative autocrat approach; the factory floor may expect an autocratic approach. It is important to match your style to the norms, needs, and expectations of your subordinates.

## FLEXIBILITY

Our basic argument is for a contingency model of leadership. No one style is best for all situations. Rather, the successful manager is flexible and adapts the model as appropriate to a given situation. If time pressures are overwhelming, autocratic decision making may be appropriate. For a majority of management decision making, the consultative autocratic approach may be the best alternative. And in dealing with high-tech professionals, engineers, and other specialists, the project manager may choose a more consensual style. The key to success is for project managers to *match their leadership styles to the situation.*

## FINDINGS FROM PERSONAL EXPERIENCE

Based on the presentation and discussion of this leadership model with literally hundreds of practicing managers, we would like to share some conclusions with the reader concerning project management and leadership style (Slevin, 1991):

**1. *You are more autocratic than you think.*** In the eyes of subordinates, it is clear that most managers are probably closer to the autocrat on the graph than they themselves perceive their leadership style. Why? Because the manager is the boss and they are the subordinates. Many managers have an idealized vision of their leadership style. Please note that, in most cases, these leaders are not trying to fraudulently claim a style not theirs. They may truly believe that they are consensus managers who actively solicit information from subordinates and involve them in the decision process. Unfortunately, subordinates rarely see it that way. No matter how easy-going, friendly, participative, and supportive managers are, they are still the boss. There is almost always a difference in leadership style as perceived by supervisor and subordinates.

**2. *But it may be O.K.*** Often, when we have asked subordinates where they would like their boss to move, they respond, "Things are O.K. as they are." Even though there are perceptual discrepancies concerning leadership style, there may not necessarily be a felt need or pressure for change. The status quo may be acceptable. In effect, this is the case of leaders calling their subordinates' bluff. In some situations, subordinates truly desire more freedom and autonomy in decision making. However, in other cases, although the rhetoric of decision-making freedom is employed, when directly offered autonomy, subordinates prove to be more comfortable with allowing the boss to shoulder the responsibility for decision making. As we have stated, there is no hard and fast rule here. Leaders need to address the personalities of their own subordinates and develop and encourage those who are willing to take on decision-making responsibilities. Often, those individuals are the future leaders in that organization.

**3. *It is easy to move north and south.*** It tends to be much easier to move vertically on the graph. The reason is that management is a job of communication. It is easy to collect more or less information from subordinates before making a decision. Even if the intent of the manager is not to make use of the information that is collected, it is easy to ask for or not ask for input from subordinates. The information dimension is the least resistant to change.

**4. *It is hard to move west.*** Most managers, in our experience, find it quite threatening to move westward too quickly. "West" implies the willingness to give up some decision authority to the group. The primary reason for most managers' hesitation is that a westward movement upsets the basic power realities in the organization. If the manager is under severe time pressure, the decision is of major importance, or problems are continually plaguing the implementation effort, it is very difficult to turn the decision-making process over to subordinates.

**5. *If subordinates' expectations are not met, morale will suffer.*** Team members often have expectations about the decision-making and leadership style of the project manager. Based on past experiences and beliefs about how a leader "should" act, they become comfortable with certain styles from their leaders. If the project manager does not employ the expected style, it can have a detrimental effect on morale. For example, if subordinates are expecting their leader to use a consensual style and the leader prefers an autocratic decision-making style, subordinate morale is likely to decline. Interestingly, the reverse case is also often true. When subordinates are used to and expecting their manager to make all decisions in an autocratic style, they can become very uncomfortable when confronted with a manager who prefers group decision making. They are simply not used to being asked their opinion and hence, once again, morale may decline. The essential point here is that the decision *process* can be as important as the decision *outcome,* especially from the standpoint of motivating subordinates.

**6. *Be flexible.*** Successful managers are autocratic when they need to be, consultative when necessary, and consensual when the situation calls for it. It is possible and, indeed, desirable to adjust leadership style to fit the needs of the situation. Unsuccessful managers are inflexible and resort to the same style in all situations. In our consulting experiences, when we have asked these managers why they do not adopt more flexible leadership styles, they tend to be very resistant to the idea that they do have options—that is, they can develop flexibility in their approach to practices such as delegation and participatory decision making.

## IMPLICATIONS FOR LEADERSHIP STYLES

The leadership framework presented in the Bonoma/Slevin model requires the manager to ask two key questions concerning decision making:

- Whom do I ask?

- Who makes the decision?

The manager's ability to obtain accurate information input from subordinates is crucial to effective project implementation. Similarly, decision-making authority must be located in the right place vis à vis the leader's group. Successful projects are implemented through sufficient access to and judicious use of both information and power. At the start of any implementation effort, the project team leader might be well advised to review the status of project information and power. Among the key questions that must be considered are issues such as who or what will serve as the primary source(s) of information for this implementation? Does the team have access to accurate and plentiful information from all relevant stakeholders? Who has the power to make decisions and get those decisions implemented?

These and other questions form the basis for determining the viability of the leader's various options for decision making. Unless the members of the team have access to and are able to collect necessary information, a consensual leadership style will be wasted; it does no good to ask uninformed sources their opinions. Likewise, do team leaders in this company have the authority (given the organization's culture and norms) to give up some of

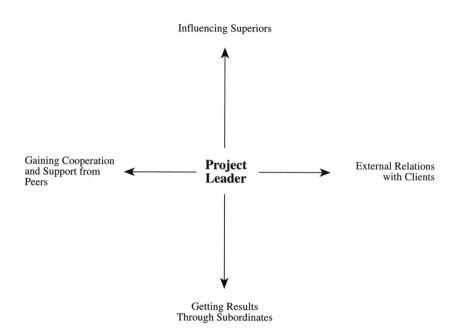

FIGURE 5.3.  Four roles of the leader.

their decision-making authority or are they expected to make all decisions by themselves? Although these questions are appropriate, they point to the fundamental basis of decision making: the leaders' flexibility and self-confidence that allow them to be flexible and make appropriate choices in decision-making situations. Making use of the Bonoma/Slevin model and understanding the nature of leadership (see Figure 5.3) can help project managers more effectively manage their programs, while at the same time encouraging subordinates' professional development and maintaining high levels of team morale.

# 6

# *A Generalist,*
# *Not a Specialist*

PROJECT MANAGERS REMAIN the focal point of all activities relating to their project. However large the project, that one individual must have an appreciation for the project as a whole. That presents a tremendous challenge, and it is a major objective in this present work to see the way in which that task is accomplished. In effect, the project manager is the head (the chief executive, as it were) of a new company with a specific life span, extending from concept to completion of the particular project on which he or she is engaged. The manager's team is drawn from elsewhere: from within the parent company, if they are not "hired in" for the project. These individuals are selected for their specific functional skills and operate as simplified functional departments.

Project managers are responsible for every aspect of the job from conception to completion—in effect, for every service required to carry out the work: planning, scheduling, costing, designing, engineering, purchasing, inspection, shipping, construction, and commissioning. And, of course, they bear a special relationship of responsibility to the client. Their position calls for wide experience, broad knowledge of every group within the organization, the ability to decide and control progress. Logically, this position calls for a generalist rather than a specialist. We define a "specialist" as an individual who possesses a *depth* of skills within a narrowly defined area of expertise. In other words, what they do, they do well. A generalist, on the other hand, is one who has a *breadth* of skills, albeit not to the same degree of mastery as a specialist. However, the range of knowledge this individual possesses gives him or her the ability to converse intelligently across a variety of project management issues, both technical and managerial in nature.

One of the true challenges facing project managers is the need to acknowledge that they are not necessarily chosen to run a team based solely on their technical qualifications and expertise. Typically, the project core team is composed of the technical specialists that help project managers make those decisions. Rather, project managers must learn to adopt a more generalist attitude, one that allows them to monitor and supervise all aspects of the project. Further, this generalist attitude puts them in the position to operate in both the short and long term: dealing with the day-to-day demands of their position while still maintaining a sense of strategic vision for the project.

Project managers usually evolve from technical disciplines, typically engineering. They may be expert in their general area or a subspecialty, but can be totally ignorant of the management aspects of their work. We think of engineers as working with things and managers with people. However, due to the nature of their assignment, project managers are managers first, engineers later or last! These "people skills" can be extremely difficult for engineers to acquire and cultivate; this illustrates, quite eloquently, why effective project managers are hard to come by. After all, project managers have to get people with diverse backgrounds and functional loyalties to work together as a team—an extremely difficult task.

The business magazine *Harvard Business Review* has come to be recognized in the management field as a "torchbearer" and is

People are by far the most valuable resource in modern corporations and it is they more than other physical resources, including money, that determine the success of a project. Naturally, therefore, selection of the project personnel must have top priority. Before actual selection, specific qualifications of the project manager and team members must be spelled out. The necessary tools for this purpose have been provided by Mikkelsen and Folmann (1982). Unfortunately, as we have noted, in many organizations the project directors and senior management feel that candidates' potential can only be developed and tested on an actual job. Trainees are selected, and it is hoped that they will graduate to suitable positions on a project team and eventually take over as project managers. Though this is a commonly held view, it seems a difficult and expensive way of acquiring the right people. It is much like teaching infants and children to swim, except that the real-life "swimming pool" is an actual project where time is of the essence and it may prove far too expensive to let trainees learn, especially when the "taxi meter" is running. We find it extremely useful to liken a project to a taxi; in both cases, the "meter" starts running right from time "zero," even though there may be no progress on either for some time.

extensively quoted in management literature. Reporting cutting-edge issues on practically everything under the management umbrella ranging A to Z, this journal was prescient enough to recognize at an early date the importance of project management for business success. As early as 1959, an article entitled "The Project Manager" (Gaddis, 1959) appeared and it may be considered a classic in this area. The article lists some of the main characteristics and functions of project managers, briefly thus:

*Unique Characteristics*

- Different approach
- "Blind flying"
- Taking risks

*Authority and Responsibility*

- Keeping things moving
- Dealing with perfectionists
- Organization planning
- Heading off
- Selling and reselling

*Man in Between*

- Reasonable "projectitis"
- Free communications
- The next project

*Friendly Differences*

- Tactics versus strategy
- Reporting progress

*Thinker and Doer*

- Using lab output
- Two streams of knowledge

## ROLE IN THE FUTURE

The above is quite a formidable list! Though compiled over 35 years ago, these characteristics seem to be equally valid even now. Some of the desirable qualifications of a competent and effective project manager follow logically from the foregoing. Briefly, these are:

- A career molded in technology environment

- Should have working knowledge of many fields of science

- Must have a good understanding of general management problems

- Must have a strong, continuous, active interest in teaching, training, and developing their supervisors

Notice particularly the integrative function of joining many parts into a systematic whole. Though somewhat indefinable, an integrative mind must deal with intangible factors apart from the tangible ones, and there is also need at times for an intuitive process in the formulation of judgment and decision analysis. In this respect, the outlook of a project manager differs greatly from that of a normal functional manager. It is the project manager's analytical mind that produces the concepts by which the project advances toward its goal. But without the integrative function, the concepts cannot be translated into actual practice.

## CAPTAIN, COMMANDER, AND CONDUCTOR: ALL IN ONE!

One method for assessing the role of the project manager is through metaphor. We can liken the project manager, in the first instance, to the captain of a ship or commander of an aircraft. While at sea or in the air, the immediate need is for quick decisions. Those decisions will often have to be made on the basis of incomplete information or data, but they must be made quickly. What is more, the crew have to implement those decisions without question and delay, or else a disaster is certain. Another analogy likens the project manager to a conductor, who with the right movement of the baton, can get musicians to play in unison. When orchestra members are unmindful of the manager or their own roles, they cannot create the synergistic product that comes from a well-trained group of professionals.

The information that comes to a project manager concerning the project needs a firm decision response and prompt action, and only courageous and competent project managers, with a wealth of experience or training, are really able to fulfill this role. Their major contribution, as we shall see, is not technical, but more in the area of "human relations." Project managers can and do have a variety of technical backgrounds, usually engineering in one of its many forms: chemical, civil, electrical, mechanical, or structural. However, the key to their success will lie in not technical qualifications and capability, but their ability to handle people.

Let us be clear that though the project manager controls the project, the real center for action lies with the team members. This relationship is essentially reciprocal; however, for the team to be truly effective, a competent leader (project manager) is a must. Effective teamwork makes a major contribution to the success of the project and thus the company.

When considering the role of the leader, we should distinguish between a leader and a manager: They are not necessarily the same. Although some say that leaders are born, rather than made, we are convinced that leadership can be learned through practical experience and training. Consequently, we have established some guidelines in this context. One key to successful leadership is to put people (the employees) first and foremost. We further demonstrate the essential difference between management groups and management teams, using the sports arena by way of analogy. The team has a leader, is creative, and has well-defined goals. But its success depends on the quality of coordination and leadership.

Involving the project manager right from the start ensures his or her early attention to direct the project. A project manager will then have a more complete understanding of the project and can thus present forcefully the company's qualifications to a prospective client. The broad qualifications of a project manager include (Langley and Meyer, 1986):

- Ability to organize, plan, build, and motivate a team
- Ability to resolve personality differences and foster an environment of cooperation, productivity, and progress

- Excellent oral and technical writing skills

- Strong leadership and good judgment in selecting team members

- Sound technical understanding and experience in similar work

- Ability to develop concise scope of work and schedules

- Ability to negotiate a fair contract with the client

- Sensitivity to environmental issues and experience with federal, state, and local permit requirements

## ACCOUNTABILITY AND PLANNING

For effective project execution, it is essential to have a combination of skills and experience in a diverse set of backgrounds: technical training, basic accounting and cost control, operations and production, and basic management skills. This point was brought home eloquently at a recent meeting when Prudential's chief executive told an audience of organizational members, "Technical proficiency alone is now unlikely to be sufficient for effective performance. . . . " For successfully managing new projects and other innovations, he identified the following key attributes:

- Communication skills

- High personal motivation

- Personal qualities

- Interpersonal skills

- Decision making

- Management and organizational abilities

The message is clear: The day of the technically competent project manager who can painlessly ignore the human side of the task is past. Future project managers must acquire and use a variety of skills, both technical and administrative/behavioral, if they are to succeed (*AACE Transactions*, 1988).

## TEN PRINCIPLES AND NINE CHARACTERISTICS

Two academicians (Randolph and Posner, 1988) in a down-to-earth article offer ten common sense principles that every project manager needs to know and follow for achieving project success:

- Set a clear goal.

- Determine the project objectives.

- Establish checkpoints, activities, relationships, and time estimates.

- Draw a picture of the project schedule.

- Direct people individually and as a project team.

- Reinforce the commitment and excitement of the project team.

- Keep everyone connected with the project informed.

- Build agreements that vitalize team members.

- Empower yourself and others on the project team.

- Encourage risk taking and creativity.

These ten principles can help a project manager integrate the technical and human aspects of project management. The first four help develop a sound plan and the final six manage the plan effectively by anticipating problems before they become severe. Together, these principles keep team members committed to project success—namely, its completion on time, within budget, and according to the quality standards expected by the clients.

As a simple proof of the last principle, we would point out

that few novels and even fewer scientific articles are published anonymously. To encourage creativity in projects, the project manager must not only recognize it, but also praise and even reward it at all opportunities. At the same time, really effective project managers plan time for thinking, experimenting, and creative behavior. Creativity takes time, and to encourage it, companies like 3M have established a system by which their engineers and scientists are not only allowed, but even encouraged, to spend some 15% of their time working on unscheduled and unprogrammed activities.

In fact, at 3M an 11th commandment exists: Thou shalt not kill a new idea. It has been discovered that the most stimulating and rewarding projects are often much like a rollercoaster ride—you never really know when and where the dips, twists, and turns will come. 3M likes to tell its project managers that this feature is the real challenge of their work and they might as well learn to enjoy it, as they are committed to completing such a journey until its bitter end. Somewhat like a turtle, project managers make significant progress only when they stick out their necks.

A distinguished project manager (Toft, 1988), one who came up through the ranks having "done time" on every rung of the engineering ladder beginning as a laborer, has given us the benefit of his wisdom by virtue of his long experience with a variety of capital projects in the chemical plant field. The essential qualities of an effective and successful project manager are diverse, but broadly they can be summed up by four characteristics:

- Engineering ability, including design background

- Leadership and team motivation

- An ability to generate trust

- Literacy, foresight, and forward-thinking

It is clear that up to a certain level in engineering, one has to concentrate on the way things are done, but in the management function, particularly on projects, one has to be able to recognize when things are going wrong through the so-called early warning signals. Such knowledge of largely unwritten "tricks of the trade" is an invaluable asset for a project manager. Summarizing a lifetime of rich experience, Toft (1988) tells us:

- Lead your team and maintain their morale.

- Project managers must make team members aware of the *whole* picture.

- Work closely and build up mutual respect with contractors' team.

- Beware of an unreasonably low price, a sure recipe for trouble.

- Attempt to foresee difficulties.

- Hold frequent informal chats with your staff to keep them informed.

- Make letters to clients clear in intent and reasonable in tone.

- Maintain good technical and financial records for monitoring.

- Act with integrity and honesty, maintain absolute goodwill.

## ENGINEER TO MANAGER: EASIER SAID THAN DONE!

Because project management is one of the most challenging disciplines in industry, with requisite skills and abilities that differ from those required in traditional management work, there is very little training support for those assuming project management functions. How to turn technical types into top-notch managers is the subject of an excellent paper (Thornberry, 1987) with a no-nonsense, down-to-earth approach. Unfortunately, as Thornberry notes, due to sheer ignorance and carelessness, far too much time and money are wasted in the development of project managers through the use of ineffective programs. This area has remained relatively uncharted. The entire area of project management training is an extremely important one for not only the individual, but also the project organization. Proper selection, conscientious skill-directed training, and objective assessment for project managers can provide measurable, bottom-line results for companies operating in the project management arena.

To further solidify this point, consider the following study in which one of the authors and his colleague interviewed 110 project managers and their direct supervisors, as well as some of their training managers from 20 high-technology firms. Their purpose was to learn about the kind of company-sponsored training programs specifically aimed at engineers moving into project management positions. Perhaps not surprisingly, only one-fourth of the companies had any formalized training, and of these, only a few employed a well thought out, comprehensive project management training program. Most of the programs were confined to the more technical side of project management. Further, most of the training was the "swim or sink" type of on-the-job learning. It is clear that with projects costing millions and now even billions of dollars (mega-projects), this kind of "hit or miss" on-the-job training can prove to be an expensive and high-risk strategy, which no company can afford (Kharbanda and Stallworthy, 1990).

The potential candidates for project manager positions should be given a realistic job preview, including an understanding of the likelihood of long working hours, relocation to construction or development sites—often far away from so-called "civilization"— moving to another site at the end of a job, and last but not least, postings away from headquarters with the possibility of being ignored at the time of promotions on the basis of the adage, "out of sight, out of mind." The selected candidates should be exposed to realistic expectations (Thornberry, 1987):

- Functioning as an understudy to a successful project manager (PM)

- Serving as a PM apprentice or an assistant PM

- PM simulation training

Thornberry helped design a project management "in-basket" exercise that simulated many of the responsibilities, duties, and activities of a project manager. The prospective candidates are asked to assume the role of a project manager and make decisions about the items in the in-box. Though some of the training for project managers is, necessarily, conceptual, much if not most of it is skill-based, with a particular emphasis on people skills. Possible modules in preappointment training could include (Thornberry, 1987):

- Written and, most important, oral communications

- Influencing (persuasive) skills

- Conflict-resolution skills

- Group decision making

- Project-planning and -tracking skills,
  and last but by far the most important skill

- Organizational politics

We have demonstrated clearly in Chapter 3 that to be successful, project managers must possess political savvy to be able to survive and thrive amidst their sometimes onerous cross-departmental and cross-functional responsibilities. However, prior to any training program teaching the skills of successful project management is the very crucial step of selecting the most appropriate candidates/engineers. An assessment center can help in this process and will pay enormous dividends in selecting the right candidates, as well as upgrading the project management skills of existing project managers. Choosing a training program from those offered in-house or through outside vendors can be counterproductive, since the choice may well be based on interest rather than need. Assessment centers facilitate the selection of project managers on the basis of assessed skills and needs rather than their personal interest.

Let us be candid; not every engineer can or should become a

project manager. Often, engineers see faster career development on the management side and are therefore tempted to move across the "fence" and climb up the "right ladder." As one engineer put it quite bluntly to the interviewers in the course of an exhaustive research study (Thornberry, 1987):

> "Our company has dual career ladders. Unfortunately only one ladder has rungs."

Experience in this area has shown that, unfortunately, some of the best engineers may be ill-suited for a project manager's job. For example, many engineers relish the technical challenges of their work, the creative problem solving, and freedom to work at their own pace and with their own schedule of priorities. Fortunately, or perhaps unfortunately, the promotion to project manager changes the dynamics of their work situation markedly. It places the former engineer, who valued his or her independence, in a managerial position with responsibilities for which they were never formally trained. One has only to examine the curricula of major engineering programs in our universities to discover that exposure to even minimal management training is usually sadly lacking.

## PROJECT MANAGER VERSUS FUNCTIONAL BOSS

In the course of selecting a project manager, we must know how this person differs from a functional manager. Both are bosses but with a difference that, although subtle, can make all the difference! In a previous section, we likened the project manager to a conductor of a symphony orchestra, which with a perfect blend of individual sounds can produce a musical masterpiece. A functional manager is, however, in the business of conducting a "business symphony." In sharp contrast to a project manager, a functional boss is concerned with the ongoing activities of a functional department. The work is more often repetitive, less unique, and does not have time and budget constraints. Further, functional manag-

ers, because of their position within the formal organizational hierarchy, can make use of a prescribed and well-defined chain of
command, one that gives them the formal authority to exercise
command and control over subordinates. On the other hand, the
characteristics of a good project manager have been listed (Deeprose, 1992) as:

- Does very little telling, instead asks the team members about
  their opinions and suggestions. This not only satisfies them,
  but also produces some good advice and suggestions. The
  leader then lays down the guidelines and lets the team work
  out the details and complete the implementation.

- Is a helper to other team members. The leader first of all
  defines reality, and at the end of a project thanks everyone.
  In between, the leader acts more as a "facilitator" than doer.
  A good leader guides the team members along by constantly
  asking the right and relevant questions and encouraging
  them to solve their problems—with the right kind of help as
  and when required.

- Shows people that they matter. Lets team members write
  their own job descriptions and share them with their colleagues who would then be more than willing to help in
  every possible way. The project leader must, however, look
  for any omissions, overlaps, and discrepancies. An excellent
  team works together toward the true final goal with contributions from everyone.

- In case of any problem, the leader must get the team to
  pinpoint the source and acquire their input on how best to
  solve the difficulty. For this to work, team members must be
  certain that the leader will not "shoot" the messenger or bash
  the person who owns the problem. In the case of a time
  constraint and/or the need for confidentiality, the leader
  may have to act unilaterally to solve the problem.

- Is there a better way?" must be a constant and repeated
  question, so also "Does it meet our needs?" This attitude

will not only ensure continuous improvement, but also help involve everyone in achieving the desired goal. Complacency is avoided.

In sharp contrast to the above, a unit boss, for example, an operations engineering manager, must excel in technical leadership/judgment, and in general, pure technical engineering skills are far more important than pure leadership and organizational skills. A project manager's success or failure directly affects the work within the project and its outcome. A strong project manager is likely to select strong lead engineers for the project team. Further, for project work, a matrix organizational structure has generally proved to be superior to line organization to enable coordination and exchange on a daily basis within the operating team (Larson and Gobelli, 1989). This helps eliminate problems before they can seriously impede a project.

## SELECTION OF PROJECT MANAGER/TEAM

As we suggested in previous sections of this book, a critical skill for project managers is the ability to wield influence and persuasion, since usually, team members are "on loan" to the project from their respective functional departments. Team members have, therefore, a dual reporting role that can cause many problems, unless the project manager is diplomatic and tactful, and able to command respect without any real authority. One method for easing possible friction is to adopt a more proactive policy toward selecting a project team. Within most organizations, it is common to find project team members assigned on an availability basis; that is, rather than the best person from a particular functional department being sought, most team members are picked because their current duties (or lack of them) free them up to serve on a project team. This ad hoc approach to member selection has the obvious disadvantage of assembling a group of people with varying levels of interest in the project, motivation, and ability to perform effectively.

The best (and, admittedly, rarest) method for team member selection is to work in close consultation with department managers from the various functional areas, making clear what the project entails and the skills that will be needed from each potential team member. In a cooperative organizational environment, the departmental managers are able to understand the importance of the project and, more important, the importance of their willingness to facilitate the effective staffing of the project team. Unfortunately, in many instances, these same managers are more likely to jealously guard their best people to perform their functional duties. It behooves intelligent project managers to network with influential departmental managers in order to develop the personal contacts and relationships that enable them to gain the best individuals for upcoming projects, rather than the person who is currently available or simply unwanted.

The selection of project managers is even more challenging in cases of overseas projects. A great deal has been written about this process (e.g., Mikkelsen and Folmann, 1982; Kharbanda and Stallworthy, 1986). Clearly, it is an expensive undertaking and something of a gamble that may or may not pay off. Even for normal managerial appointments (other than the project manager), the cost of placing expatriates is prohibitive, as has been evidenced by the myth of the "Euromanager" in the context of the European Common Market. Equally, there is a risk for the person as well. It appears that the top 5% of a multinational firm's managers are likely to feel frustrated being in one place for too long and may well choose to leave a company unless they receive frequent new postings. The good news is that the rapid advances in communications technology are beginning to change this picture as the growth of electronic mail and video conferencing enables most departmental managers to handle international duties from their home office.

For a project to succeed, the human relations among team members must be healthy and supportive. The one person who can set the standard for the team is, to the rest of the core team, the most visible symbol of the project, the project manager. In setting the example, his or her preaching must be accompanied or preferably preceded by practicing. Good human relations are a must, but this does not necessarily imply or demand warm feelings and pleasant words, though these can help "lubricate the friction."

A healthy relationship to achieve the desired goals will survive an occasional but at times necessary unpleasant word. The basics for good human relations are:

- Teamwork

- Development, of self and others

- Communications

Yes, we have come full circle in mentioning yet again the word "communications," which we consider most important. We stress this term advisedly in that it is so obviously essential to the creation and continual improvement of relationships among team members and between the team and project manager. In selecting a project manager, this book can serve as a guide in providing many of the features that characterize the project manager role. That is, a careful reading of this book will show clearly that there are myriad demands placed on project managers, who require a number of technical, administrative, and leadership qualities. Certainly, these features should be the basis for an organization's selection of project managers.

An experienced Danish executive researcher, Jorgen Lisberg (1982), tells us of three main reasons for the wrong choice of project manager:

- Lack of precise description of the job requirements

- Too much reliance on candidate's previous experience

- Inaccurate and insufficient evaluation of elements determining teamwork and its results, for example, leadership skills, attitudes, and managerial knowledge

Mikkelsen and Folmann (1982) provide a tool for project manager selection, which according to the authors is "no guarantee," but certainly of some help to both prospective project managers and their parent organizations. The basis for this tool:

- A master for description of the project job

- A list of factors in which the job characteristics form a job profile, showing requirements to the candidates

- The same list to match candidates' skills and qualifications

In particular for the job of a project manager, personal contacts are of extreme importance. Effective project managers are often individuals with large coworker circles or contacts with other functional areas in the company. The social, working, business, and cultural relationships and norms are particularly crucial, as is, of course, the project manager's ability to cultivate political influence and assimilate practical methods of contact and cooperation. The project manager selection "tool" provided by Mikkelsen and Folmann (1982) contains a user's guide to the personal interview. It is desirable that an optimum number of persons participate in the evaluation of candidates and preparation of their profiles. This profiling process will guide the search for more information about the candidate and thus ensure qualified evaluation.

The search for a project team must start as soon as a project is identified. In effect, the availability of qualified team members constitutes one of the important capacity assessments an organization needs to perform to determine its ability to conclude the project. Ideally, project managers should be involved in the project at stage "zero" and even earlier. While the project is being developed, a project manager should be forming the team to execute the project. Apart from this function at the inception stage, a project manager must be involved with budgets, schedules, and technical matters.

We cannot help asking the age-old question in the present context: Is an ideal project manager born or made? Perhaps a "bit" of both, but far more, we believe, the latter. Project managers must have certain skills, some listed above and more in the rest of the book, that *can* and *must* be acquired through experience or learning. Project managers need not be trained at Harvard, MIT, or Sandhurst, or at the scores of seminars/workshops proliferating worldwide. Many are trained "on the job," a hard but still effective way, and unfortunately often expensive, time-consuming, and based largely on trial and error. And having learned the job on the job, we have found, as no doubt many readers have as well, that experienced project managers can be the best teachers. What is the stuff that good project managers are made of? Hundreds of books and thousands of articles delve deep into this vital aspect, but in trying to encapsulate the commitment and single-minded determination to succeed that characterizes successful project managers, the following is hard to beat in driving home our point (Lucas, 1981):

> I remember a project manager, working in a very remote and hostile location who received a very attractive offer of a new job, in a very civilised location and with many "perks." To his pleading wife and son, his first thoughts expressed were, "But I can't leave—the reservoir has not been filled, and the penstock hasn't been tested. The turbine check is not due for six months."

This, it is hoped, conveys some measure of the stuff of which project managers are made. Project managers truly represent the essence of the specialized professional, the generalist who can (and often does) do it all. One senior manager, in referring to the project management group within his company, liked to think of them as his "special forces" team, named in honor of the special forces branches of the armed forces. He considered the special skills and mental "can do" attitude of his project managers, like those of actual special forces, features that set them apart from the typical manager. Also, as is the case with the more famous special forces groups, such as the British SAS or American Green Beret or Delta Force, this executive used his project management team for the most difficult assignments, knowing that they were capable of operating without formal power or hierarchy, dedicated to completing the task, and having the wide-ranging knowledge and contacts within the company to complete the project with a minimum of fuss and bother. We submit that all organizations using project management techniques are capable of building their own team of "special forces" if they are willing to understand the characteristics of effective project managers and are committed to providing the supportive atmosphere and resources needed to develop these people. It is our hope that this chapter has offered a glimpse into the sort of professionals that any organization can aspire to develop, provided the basic understanding and commitment are in place.

## SOME PROFILES

Throughout the book, we have identified some major projects and their respective project managers and revealed some of their dynamic managerial qualities as an illustration of what makes them stand out as exceptional members of their profession. To further solidify these points, we want to share with you the stories of two project managers who typify this "new breed":

1. *The San Diego Unified Port District* had invited bids for the construction of a 1.75 million square foot convention center that would be leased back to the city. The first set of bids were not considered satisfactory and Billy G. Crockett, project manager for Fluor Corporation, was called in to help prepare a revised bid. Through the use of value engineering, Crockett revised the bidding process and the initial time frames, established good communication links with all potential bidders, and streamlined the bureaucracy of the actual bidding. The architect, Alberto Bertoli, saw Crockett as the epitome of the exceptional project manager and commented: "I don't know how many people . . . could be qualified to do his job!" His efforts helped save the city of San Diego as much as $13 million dollars, winning him Mayor Maureen O'Connor's appreciation. As a token gesture, three days after the revised bids came out (February 14, 1987), the mayor sent

Crockett a bouquet of roses with a card that she had signed, saying:

Thirteen million reasons why you're my valentine!

Crockett's background, a combination of technical and administrative duties, illustrates the importance of project managers developing the vision of a generalist. After graduating from the University of Arizona, Crockett joined the Civil Engineering Corps of the U.S. Navy, working on projects worldwide. After retiring from the Navy, he worked for several companies on a variety of projects from casino construction to gas pipeline development and even for the Los Angeles Olympic committee in 1984. Crockett's success is attributed to his broad-based technical background, willingness to apply his talents to diverse projects, and ability to "abandon" a purely technical allegiance in order to attain the general management skills necessary to succeed in leading projects (*Engineering News Record*, 1989).

**2. *Our second personality sketch*** demonstrates that although project management was, like much of business in general, a male-dominated field, it is changing dramatically. It also demonstrates that not all project management demands are job-related. Kathi Littmann, project manager for Lehere McGovern Bovis (LMB), is one of a number of highly-paid female project managers. LMB's chairman is clear: "It doesn't matter to me whether someone is male or female. I care about ability." Kathi's immediate superior, Peter Marchetto, is more direct in his assessment of her abilities: "She is tough . . . she has the ability to command a meeting . . . and make contractors toe the line . . . [she is] innovative in making up bid packages."

While experiencing several moves related to her husband's financial management career, Kathi has held a series of jobs, including assistant project manager for developer Gerald Hines on Houston's Texas Commerce Towers, field superindent for U.S. Homes, and project executive for Morse Diesel. In the midst of her career rise, she took time off to have two children. She and her husband have recently moved to New York City where she has taken a job working for LMB on the $95 million Security Industry Automation Corporation building, part of the $1 billion Metrotech development project. Her present position, while demanding, gives her the flexibility to juggle her schedule between business and family. Her motto for kindergarten programs is (*Engineering News Record*, 1989):

> "Just be there. My colleagues schedule meetings around golf games. I schedule around school activities. What matters is that the job is on time and on budget."

# 7

# *Project Managers'*
# *Duties: A to Z*

THE DUTIES AND responsibilities of project managers are so incredibly diverse and wide-ranging that it is sometimes difficult to accurately encapsulate the true nature of their unique challenge. In this chapter, we attempt to synthesize some of the salient issues in the previous chapters with the extensive literature on the duties and expectations of project managers. They are presented here in an easily comprehended framework. We will address each of the major duties, characteristics, and responsibilities that project managers are expected to acquire or undertake as part of their job. This chapter serves as a capstone for the previous chapters in this part and will reiterate many of these duties within our A to Z format. We would refer the reader wishing to examine any of these duties in more detail to the specific chapter or chapters where we discuss them at length.

## PROJECT MANAGERS: A TO Z

**A:** *Arbiter of conflicts.* Project managers are constantly enmeshed in a variety of conflicts emanating from a number of sources, both within the project team and due to pressures brought by external stakeholders. The test of an effective project manager is that manner in which he or she is able to recognize impending conflict and manage the conflict process to minimize the potential loss in terms of time, goal commitment, and personal energy from the project team members. As part of this process, project managers often serve as "referees" for intragroup conflicts in which team members from different functional departments or with disparate personalities discover the tension that comes from working closely with team members possessing significantly different traits, goals, time frames, and backgrounds. Successful project managers recognize that conflict, if handled effectively, is not necessarily bad. In fact, it can lead to more informed decisions based on project team synthesis. However, project managers must learn to deal with conflict, distinguishing damaging, personalized conflict from that which can serve the team and project, by focusing attention on ambiguities and misunderstandings so they can be addressed and corrected.

**B:** *Believability.* Project managers must cultivate a reputation for authenticity in order to inspire trust and confidence from team members and stakeholders. Being authentic with subordinates means being completely up-front with them in delivering news and status reports, both good and bad. Some novice managers imagine that they can withhold important information from their people, either because they prefer to exert complete control over the group or they have information that they believe could be potentially demoralizing to team members. This attitude is almost always counterproductive; bad news eventually surfaces no matter how hard we try to suppress it, and this process can have disastrous results. Project team members are much more inclined to commit to project goals when they perceive that the project manager is someone they can trust. If the news about the project or potential rewards is good, tell the team. If the news is bad, tell the team. A reputation for believability, once discredited, is almost impossible to regain. On the other hand, a reputation for deviousness, once acquired, is almost impossible to shake.

**C: *Communicator.*** The essence of management is communicating. Managers spend the vast majority of their days involved in some form of communication, either telephone calls, face-to-face get-togethers, or team status meetings. Developing communication skills, particularly those of good listening and persuasion, is key to facilitating the project development process. In dealing with a wide range of project stakeholders, the project manager serves as the central conduit for filtering and transferring information. The ability to speak and write well (clearly and concisely) is a quality that is important to develop. Sound communication has saved many projects from oblivion, just as poor communication has consigned many to the limbo of cost and schedule overruns.

**D: *Delegator.*** Project managers cannot perform every task, both technical and administrative, in their projects. The purpose of devoting time and energy to developing a cohesive and capable project team is to make use of their energy, commitment, and skills in furthering project team goals. Hence, project managers must become good delegators. "Good" delegation does not mean that the project manager hands off every job, exciting or boring, to team members while remaining impervious and above the fray. Many times, it is necessary for project managers to get involved in day-to-day operations and perform their share of the drudge work. Likewise, good delegation means neither retaining full control nor absenting oneself from the project decision-making process. Effective delegators understand that the key to using delegation well is to give subordinates adequate information and authority to make the necessary decisions while ensuring that accountability stays where it ultimately belongs: with the project manager.

**E:** *Expert.* Research suggests that project managers can function more effectively in leading their teams if they are perceived by team members and other stakeholders as possessing sufficient technical knowledge of the project (Kouzes and Posner, 1991). Expertise is an important quality to possess and maintain. In dealing with subordinates or outside stakeholders such as clients or top management, sometimes the best ally a project manager has is his or her reputation as a technically qualified manager. Not only is this quality important in offering team members a secure backstop for their operations (i.e., someone who can evaluate properly the work that has been performed), but the project manager's expertise gives subordinates an immediate and convenient source of information for the questions that will inevitably arise.

**F:** *Finisher.* The mark of successful project managers is those who complete what they start. Persistence and a strong will are very important traits for those charged with implementing projects in a high-stress environment. As Posner (1987) has demonstrated, effective project managers seem to understand intuitively the importance of developing personal coping skills to deal with the rigors and demands of project-based work. Important to their ability to cope with the demands they face is a single-minded determination to see the project through to completion. An important additional characteristic that "finishers" need is the ability to be creative, think on their feet, and react to events as they occur. Obviously, despite our best attempts to be proactive and predict future events, everything is not foreseeable. In untangling the occasional snags and roadblocks that threaten to halt a project, the project manager's own unflagging optimism and commitment to seeing the project through to completion represent vital character traits that can play a tremendous role in project facilitation.

**G:** *Goal setter.* One of the best methods that project managers can use to help their team members develop higher motivation to perform is to engage in mutually developing performance goals with subordinates. Goal setting does more than create an atmosphere for enhancing team member motivation. Goal setting also takes much of the ambiguity out of project planning, for not just team members but the project manager as well. Setting clear, challenging, but attainable goals allows subordinates to operate at their own peak levels. They also paint a vivid picture of the attributes the finished project is expected to possess. When goals are made and communicated to all team members, they have the effect of serving as a rallying point around which all members can gather. Further, in the case of disagreements or difficulties in blending diverse personalities and attitudes, goal setting serves as a unifying theme for team members. If everyone knows what they are seeking, it is easier to engender cooperation among subordinates.

**H:** *Highly energetic.* It should come as no surprise to the reader that the portrait we paint of successful project managers includes an extremely high level of personal energy. Earlier in this book, we suggested that few activities in organizations today are as "leader-intensive" as the project management process. Projects are often made or broken by their leaders, and one of the best resources that project managers can employ lies in maintaining a high level of energy. When readers examine various leaders from a variety of public and private organizations, across cultures and the political spectrum, one of the commonalties embedded in the characteristics of these individuals is the energy to create a vision, but also to see it through to fruition. Subordinates take their cues from team leaders. When they have direct, clear evidence of a project manager who practices what he or she preaches, demands much of himself and others, and operates at a personally energetic pace, it offers the best possible object lesson for the team.

**I:** *Influencer.* Project managers have to understand the nature of organizational politics. Distasteful as that message may be for some readers, it nevertheless is true. In gaining the resources so necessary for successful project development, satisfying and enlisting the support of important stakeholders, and managing the delicate relationships between the project team and the organization's functional departments, political savvy and effective influence tactics can be a project manager's best tools. To simply dismiss politics as the province of the unsavory or amoral is naive and most likely damaging to the chances of the project team successfully implementing the project. Project managers must learn to recognize and develop the necessary connections and channels of influence that can be so important for project success.

**J:** *Joiner.* A true challenge for even the most seasoned project manager comes from trying to develop a functioning, cohesive team from a group of people from different functional backgrounds. "Joining" refers to the process of team building, in which the project manager must act with a deft touch in gaining cooperation and commitment from people who are often suspicious of each other's backgrounds and motives. Teams can work wonders and perform at much higher levels than the sum of individual contributions; however, in order to develop the degree of synergy that elevates all members to higher performance, project managers must set the tone. They need to be aware of the stages through which teams progress. Further, they need to recognize that the conflict of the storming phase is a natural by-product of cross-functional teams. Project teams can operate in a number of ways of which individual members would not think themselves capable, but the challenge of molding and creating a team ultimately lies with the project manager.

**K:** *Keeper of the flame.* No one has a better vision of the project than the project manager. Somewhere around the middle of the project development process, when team members have settled into routines and sometimes become very tunnel-visioned about their own specific tasks, it is very common for team members to start forgetting the overall purpose of the project. It becomes difficult, many times, to distinguish the forest for all the trees that we continually confront. During these project doldrums, project managers can play an important facilitating role in keeping the project team oriented toward the project's ultimate goals. It is this "eyes on the prize" mentality that refers to our notion of the project manager as the keeper of the flame. Project managers, because of the position they occupy, have the capability to think both strategically and tactically, projecting a vision for the project in the long term while also dealing with the day-to-day minutia that they must confront. It is in projecting this vision for the project, in keeping the flame lit, that project managers offer a visible and powerful symbol to the team.

**L:** *Leader.* Leadership is key to the project management role. Although the idea of leadership means many things to many people, no one can deny its impact on project performance. The leader must set the tone for the project, establish the schedules and work pace, and deal with both strategic and minute issues on a daily basis. Further, leaders implicitly understand that the project is only as effective as is the project team in working together. Consequently, much of the project manager's time is spent working with the team. Canny project team leaders involve subordinates in decisions as much as possible. Further, they understand the essence of effective delegation. Most important, they present themselves to the project team as an immediate, living embodiment of what the project represents. It is through their personal enthusiasm and energy that the project team can draw the inspiration necessary to carry them through the rough periods and occasional trials to success.

**M:** *Motivator.* In a sense, the label of "motivator" is a misnomer. We will argue in a future chapter that no individual is capable of motivating another person; rather, each of us has our own internal generator that we consciously decide whether or not to turn on. Project managers are motivators to the degree that they understand that the way to get their subordinates to "turn on" that generator is to create a project atmosphere that taps into those elements that each of us seeks in our work experience. People are motivated by a wide range of issues, including challenging work, opportunities for new learning, chance for advancement or praise, and money. To motivate a project team member, the project manager has to become familiar enough with that individual to understand what "buttons to push" in order to get positive responses. Treating subordinates as unique individuals and creating an atmosphere in which they can grow as employees and human beings are the underlying challenges of motivation.

**N:** *Need for achievement.* Successful project managers often foster an almost relentless personal dynamism. They have a passion for their work, performing at high standards, and doing whatever is necessary to succeed. An early theory of human needs (McClelland, 1961) argued that each of us has a mix of three basic needs: the need for affiliation (friends), need for power (control), and need for achievement (success). Although the relative strength of the three needs may vary from individual to individual, in successful project managers the most important need is to achieve: to bring the project to a successful conclusion. While careful to foster good interpersonal relationships with team members and stakeholders, all parties involved in the project must be aware that for the project manager, the overarching concern is to get the job done.

**O:** *Organizer.* Organizing refers to the planned composition of the project team. In many organizations, project team members are assigned to projects on an "as available" basis; that is, when a project manager requests the use of an individual from a functional manager, the person most often assigned to the project is whoever is available. In organizing an effective project team, project managers should not be passive about member selection. Strong people are often the key to strong projects. To illustrate this point, consider the situation that had been allowed to evolve in a large manufacturing organization headquartered in the midwest. Over a period of time, functional managers discovered that their input or lack of input in support of project teams had no impact on their personal evaluations. Consequently, they began to use project teams as a dumping ground for their poor performers. In effect, every time project managers requested that someone be assigned to their teams, functional department heads used the requests as an opportunity to transfer malcontents and poor performers to someone else's jurisdiction. Needless to say, the word quickly got out that assignment to a project was akin to a notice of incompetence, with the expected drop in project team member motivation. As you might imagine, this situation deteriorated to the point where few of the company's projects were being successfully implemented. Although this problem has since been corrected, it points to the potential problems that can arise from paying inadequate attention to the fundamentals of project team organizing. Effective organizing means conscientious staffing and task selection.

**P: *Planner*.** A fundamental feature of project-based work is the concept of working under the pressure of tightly defined time schedules. Either in relation to core team members or by themselves, project managers are expected to develop comprehensive (and often tremendously complex) plans for the project's development and implementation. These plans include work breakdown, cost sheets, PERT and Gantt charting, and so forth. Even with the aid of computer-generated scheduling, much of the work of planning still resides with the project manager. Planning is particularly difficult in that it can consume tremendous amounts of time, while providing top management and other interested stakeholders with no visible evidence of progress. There is a strong temptation for many novice project managers to shorten the planning cycle, assuming that time spent planning is time taken away from "doing," as if planning and acting are contradictory forces. This is a temptation that absolutely must be resisted. In reality, project managers must understand the importance of the planning process, even in the face of demands for progress updates from top management or the client. Conscientious planning early in the project life cycle can go a long way toward eliminating potential problems down the road. Likewise, sketchy or incomplete planning has a way of boomeranging on the project, usually at the worst possible times.

**Q: *Qualifications*.** By this point, we suspect that we have managed to successfully convey the impression that effective project managers need to master a wide range of skills, both in the technical and behavioral areas. Most research that has examined the characteristics of successful project managers bears out this point; project managers must have or develop a number of diverse qualifications and skills in order to perform their jobs. To illustrate, consider Table 7.1 that lists the findings of a recent study by Barry Posner (1987). His list of the tools necessary for successful project managers is far-ranging and again demonstrates that in order to be an effective project manager, it is necessary to be technically

**TABLE 7.1. Project Management Skills**

1. *Communication skills*
   - Listening
   - Persuading

2. *Organizational skills*
   - Planning
   - Goal setting
   - Analyzing

3. *Team-building skills*
   - Empathy
   - Motivation
   - *Esprit de corps*

4. *Leadership skills*
   - Sets example
   - Energetic
   - Vision (big picture)
   - Delegates
   - Positive

5. *Coping skills*
   - Flexibility
   - Creativity
   - Patience
   - Persistence

6. *Technological skills*
   - Experience
   - Project knowledge

*Source: Posner (1987).*

qualified, a dynamic leader of the project team, sensitive to issues of subordinate diversity and motivation, and so forth. It is precisely because the demands made on project managers force them to become highly qualified that there is such a shortage of capable project managers in most corporations. The individuals who can measure up to these characteristics are rare and, once located and trained, jealously guarded.

**R:** *Resource provider.* In addition to maintaining a high level of personal energy, project managers also act as facilitators for their project team members. Among the facilitative duties they perform are finding ways to keep team morale high, smoothing the political waters, devoting time to enhancing cohesion, and ensuring that project team members have the necessary resources to perform their tasks. In operating as a resource provider, project managers work to insulate, or "protect," the project team as much as possible in allowing it to perform its tasks with a minimum of external interference. In this sense, the project manager is the conduit or filter for external stakeholder communications to the project team. Likewise, while acting as this filter, the project manager constantly works to maintain budget levels in the face of threats of spending cuts and protect schedules from the impatience of top management and clients. One of the truly unheralded acts project managers perform is that of resource provider, because only when problems arise, are the team members aware of missing resources. It is when team members can continue to work without excessive outside interference that the project manager shows direct evidence of being a good resource provider.

**S:** *Salesperson.* The project manager is the best marketer the project will ever have. If the manager and his or her team have taken the time to keep clients abreast of project developments, solicit their opinions, and seriously work to fulfill their requests, the project transfer process can be relatively smooth. On the other hand, it is a serious mistake to assume that, having once talked to the clients, the project team is now free to develop the project in comparative isolation, creating a project that is sure to be accepted and used. In reality, unless care is taken to prepare a detailed presentation of the project, plan for the transfer, and try to anticipate problems or resistance, project transfer can be haphazard and problem-filled. While staying in contact with clients throughout the development process, as the project nears completion, project managers must readjust their focus and begin operating in a "sell" mode. Remember: A project is only as useful as the clients deem it and their judgments are often emphatic and final.

**T:** *Theatrics.* A trait of successful project managers that does not receive nearly enough attention is that of showmanship. The ability and willingness to do the outrageous or unexpected often convey a more profound and lasting message to team members than all the more traditional communication approaches put together. One recent example illustrates our point.

A medium-sized manufacturing plant made glass tubing that is used in the construction of lighting equipment. Specifications for the width of the glass have to be rather precise: Too thin and the tubing will shatter, too thick and light will defuse inefficiently. A new plant manager discovered that the specification standards had been allowed to slip over a period of time to the point where the tubing was of increasingly poor quality. Some major clients were threatening to cancel their future orders unless changes were made. Following the afternoon shift in his second week at the plant, the new plant manager called a meeting of all workers and supervisors at the factory. Standing on a platform piled with bundles of the last shift's output of glass tubing, the plant manager proceeded to smash over $10,000 of tubing before the stunned crowd of workers. When he was finished, he delivered a simple message: The days of poor quality were over. If the glass did not meet specifications, it was not acceptable. In that five minutes of destruction, the plant manager sent a more eloquent message and ultimately accomplished more toward upgrading quality than the previous manager had done in four years on the job.

**U:** *Up-to-date.* Project management is a steadily evolving profession. Some of us retain images of project managers as they have been caricatured through the years: hard-hatted and hard-headed. In fact, the science of project management has seen many significant changes in recent years. The explosive growth of membership in professional bodies such as the Project Management Institute and the International Society of Project Management, the development of a unifying body of knowledge and carefully monitored accrediting program, all demonstrate that project management continues to grow in size and sophistication as new and better techniques are applied to the problems of project management. Today's project managers need to remain in the forefront of the movement, staying current in terms of new technologies and techniques, constantly seeking to expand their range of skills and depth of knowledge of both computers and people processes. Much has been written and continues to be written in an effort to help project managers improve their skills. Successful project managers are those who acknowledge the dynamic nature of their field and seek to remain up-to-date with regard to the latest trends.

**V:** *Voice of the project team.* It is important that project managers become comfortable in the role of ambassador. They often function as the sole representative of the project to external stakeholders. Further, they filter a large quantity of information for their project teams. As the spokesperson for the project, team leaders negotiate for additional resources and extra time when possible. This role is demanding in that stakeholders have such differing agendas and criteria that are important to them: Clients want the flexibility to change the specifications, accountants want costs kept down, top management wants the project completed expeditiously, and project teams want as much time and as large a budget as they can get. The person directly in the middle of these disparate viewpoints is the project manager. Acting as an ambassador, he or she must find ways to manage relations among these various stakeholder groups.

**W:** *Walks the talk.* The expression "walks the talk" suggests that the project manager sets a personal example for the rest of the project team. It is easy to offer pronouncements and exhortations to team members, particularly when the project manager refuses to engage in direct, project-related tasks. Unfortunately, as W. Edwards Demming (1986) and others have pointed out, these types of exhortations, without the support of a visible managerial presence, do little to aid in motivation or productivity. As leaders, we have to eschew gimmickry in favor of authenticity, whether our goal is leading a functional group or within the confines of a project team. In walking the talk, the project manager sends a clear message to the project team as well as the rest of the organization: The project *is* important, individual and team contributions *do* matter, and working together, the team and project manager can create a product of which they and the organization can be proud. When the project manager sets a personal example, this offers the best possible evidence to the rest of the team that the project is important and worth devoting their time and energies in its successful pursuit.

To take this walking function literally, we know of no better way of feeling the "pulse" of the project than just walking around the project site. A walk-through with all or part of the project team not only gives the project manager a first-hand picture of the work's status, but also helps explain why certain activities are running behind schedule. Further, the team members begin to develop the image of the project manager as someone who is interested in them personally and the specific role each subordinate plays in the development process. No amount of reports, let alone computer printouts, can effectively substitute for this walking the talk.

**X. "X-citement."** Potency is the term for the team's belief that it can successfully complete the project. The project manager is the natural epicenter for conveying and maintaining a sense of excitement about the project. Whereas some members of the team are naturally enthusiastic, others need the personal example of the project manager's interest and excitement. In our experience, nothing can sidetrack team member interest in the likelihood of a project's potential for success faster than the perception that the project manager is just "going through the motions" with the project or is attempting to generate noticeably false enthusiasm.

It is important to note that, in truth, not all projects are exciting. There is no doubt that every project manager and team member has served or will serve on projects that simply are not exciting. We have been asked by project managers facing these situations how to create a sense of excitement. Generally, our response is to reinforce the importance of authenticity in dealing with subordinates. Authenticity means telling team members the good news as well as the bad news. If a particular project is not likely to generate a great deal of enthusiasm, we feel that it is important to tell the team the truth. At the same time, canny project managers will often create psychological bargains with their subordinates. For example, a project manager may say the following to a team member:

> "I'll be honest with you—this project is not all that interesting. Still, it is important and has to get done. However, I have another one slated to come on-line two weeks after we finish this job and it's exactly what you like to do. I'll make a deal with you: Work hard for me on this project and I'll remember your contributions when I have to staff the next project."

In our experience, we have found that honesty (authenticity) on the part of the project manager goes a long way toward creating a sense of interest and enthusiasm in team members. Not every project is exciting, but if the team members feel that the project manager is being authentic and working to give them the kinds of challenging work they seek, they often will reward that honesty with diligence.

**Y: *Young at heart.*** Exuberance, creativity, and expressed joy are just some of the traits and characteristics we associate with the young. It seems that as we get older and "mature," many of us lose our sense of wonder, our attitude of "can do." In suggesting that successful project managers are "young at heart," we argue that they never get over their sense of excitement for challenges or lose their dogged determination to master a new skill. The young at heart are not depressed by failure, but regard past failure as a challenge for future success. Someone once cogently observed that it is good that we learn to walk when we are young, before the disillusionment of older age sets in. Think of how many times, in learning to stand and walk, we fell. Our response to those failures was not dismay, but the desire to come out on top. How many of us, as adults, would apply the same single-minded determination to a task in the face of repeated failures as we did routinely as children? As project managers, we must remain young at heart.

*Z: Zeros in on problem areas.* Project managers are problem solvers. They have to be. If there is one constant for projects, it is that they are activities in which problems are the rule, not the exception. Consequently, effective project managers are individuals who are comfortable with a certain level of ambiguity and stress. They have to be able to adapt to and deal with the variety of problems they face as part of their daily activities. In developing a problem-solving style, it is important that project managers understand the difference between solving problems and assigning blame. One clear sign of a new or insecure project manager is someone who, when confronted with problems, reacts by first searching for culprits. There is an important message that project managers need to internalize: *Fix the problem, not the blame.* Rather than devoting time to finding a convenient "fall guy," let us accept as a natural side-effect of project management the fact that problems of all types arise as a result of normal operations. Project managers need to create a team atmosphere in which worry and fear are replaced by a willingness to get to the root of the trouble and solve it.

## CONCLUSIONS

It is clear that project management appears to offer a thousand challenges to those who wish to master it. Likewise, in order to become competent at the process, it is necessary that project managers acquire a wide variety of skills for their personal arsenal. The good news is that although some of the characteristics and traits we have examined appear to be difficult for the average manager to attain, many, if not all, of these necessary elements can be learned if individuals are willing to apply themselves to the challenge. The demands placed on project managers are varied and great and the rewards, both in terms of personal satisfaction and professional advancement, can be tremendous. In order to achieve a level of competence in managing projects in today's organizations, more than a basic technical understanding is required. Likewise, having a fundamental knowledge of human processes such as motivation and leadership, although helpful, is also insufficient by itself.

This chapter has offered a simplified framework based on an alphabetized listing of some of the important features of the project tasks and necessary personal characteristics of project managers in an attempt to illustrate just how difficult the challenge is that awaits project managers. Readers need to realistically and above all, honestly, assess their own skills in terms of strengths and weaknesses to discover those aspects of the project management process they are currently suited for and those that need to be developed further. If such an honest assessment is undertaken and corrective action initiated, this chapter will have offered a starting point for future project managers intent on better developing the skills necessary to excel.

# 8

# *Motivation and the Project Manager*

MOTIVATION PRESENTS A challenge for every project manager intent on obtaining the most effective performance from his or her team. The "challenge" in applying the concept of motivation to a group of subordinates lies first in understanding exactly what motivation is and how far project managers can go in attempting to exploit or improve on the motivation of their teams. If, then, the first challenge in motivation is simply understanding what the concept implies, the second and by far most important task has to do with learning how best to make use of motivation techniques and theory to gain maximum performance from project team members.

The rewards that can be derived from a highly motivated project team are impressive. We usually characterize these highly motivated individuals with traits such as creativity, independence of decision making, quick and energetic response to challenges, tolerance for ambiguous or uncertain task situations, and more.

Most project managers have known the pleasure of working with a group of motivated team members. On the other hand, many of us have also known the frustration that comes from being put in charge of a group of dissatisfied or unmotivated subordinates. Those past experiences have solidified in our minds the value of motivation as a technique for deriving the maximum potential from those with whom we work.

## WHAT IS MOTIVATION?

Motivation is defined as "the set of processes that arouse, direct, and maintain human behavior toward attaining a goal" (Greenberg and Baron, 1993). There are two important aspects of this definition. First, the process of motivation is concerned with arousing behavior—that is, finding a method to stir individuals or energize them. For example, when people are hungry, they are aroused to search for food. The second part of the definition refers to the idea that motivation is directed toward the attainment of some goal. It is not enough to energize or arouse someone without providing an acceptable outlet for that drive. As a result, in using the motivation process, managers seek to appeal to a need or drive within each subordinate that will impel the subordinate to seek a socially or organizationally sanctioned goal.

An important element in the motivational process that is usually not explained clearly has to do with the nature of the originating force behind a subordinate's arousal. We frequently hear athletic coaches and managers referred to as "good motivators." The obvious implication is that these people are adept at finding ways to motivate their subordinates. In reality, this characterization is something of a misnomer. True motivation is due to each individual turning on his or her own internal generator. As someone external to that person (whether as a coach or superior), the project manager cannot *motivate* someone to do something. Motivation comes from the decision by that subordinate to arouse or energize him- or herself. However, although the project manager cannot motivate this person, as if able to manually turn on that individual's "generator switch," it is possible to create an atmosphere in which this person wants to motivate him or herself. For example, if an important motivational drive is the need to eliminate sources of tension, such as hunger, one can seek to influence other individuals by offering to provide the food that they seek. Likewise, if project managers have subordinates who are motivated by the potential for advancement, they can make it clear to their subordinates that successful performance on the project will lead to recognition and, possibly, a promotion. Notice that in neither case did the manager actually "motivate" the subordinate. Rather, the manager discerned what that subordinate valued and created an atmosphere in which such a person would be able to satisfy that need or drive.

This point is important in that much has been made of certain managers as being "good motivators." We suggest that in reality, these managers are sensitive to the various needs and motives of their subordinates and have been highly effective in offering the challenging work environment, support, and facilitative atmosphere that will allow their subordinates to excel. Good motivators are actually good managers who have taken the time to learn what it is their subordinates seek from their work experience. Consequently, the more we can learn about the processes that underlie motivation (the attitudes and psychological constructs that anticipate our ability to lead our subordinates), the better project managers will be able to help their project team members ignite the internal generator that can lead to enhanced project performance.

## McGregor's Theory X/Theory Y

McGregor's (1960) theory regarding the assumptions that we make about other people offers important background for our discussion of motivation. McGregor suggested that each of us holds a set of assumptions about other people, both peers and subordinates, in the workplace. Further, his theory holds that these assumptions have important implications for the way in which we behave toward others—how we manage them and reward them. The specific theory argues that collected managers' assumptions regarding their workers form a continuum from hard-core theory X beliefs to hard-core theory Y attitudes. Each of us, as managers, has attitudes about our subordinates that place us somewhere along the continuum.

At one extreme, McGregor suggested that there were managers who held similar, theory X assumptions about subordinates. These assumptions are as follows:

- People are lazy and will avoid work whenever possible.

- People dislike responsibility. They seek only safety and security and will willingly forego leadership roles, preferring to be directed.

- Because of their general attitudes regarding work, most people respond only to threats and punishment. They need coercion in order to put forth any effort.

At the opposite end of the continuum are managers who hold an entirely different set of assumptions about their subordinates. McGregor termed this set of beliefs theory Y and suggested that theory Y managers assume:

- Given the right circumstances, people want to work. They want to feel productive.

- People will seek out responsibility and they like to make decisions.

- Once committed to organizational or project-team goals, people are capable of self-direction and self-control.

- The capacity for leadership is widely distributed throughout the organization and exists at all levels in the firm.

The reason these basic beliefs are so important for understanding motivation is that in most of us, initial beliefs quickly become self-fulfilling prophecies. If we believe a priori that our subordinates cannot be trusted and, further, we give evidence of that belief every time we talk to our people, they will quickly perceive our attitudes and begin to respond in accordance with that belief. Consider a real project example in which a manager is notorious for his belief that the best way to "motivate" his workers is to impose harsh time pressures on them every step of the process. To illustrate, he firmly believes that, if given the chance, all his project team subordinates will attempt to "pad" their time estimates for specific tasks. Consequently, he has adopted a rule of thumb that no matter what time estimate a subordinate gives him, he will immediately trim it by 20%. As you can imagine, the subordinates immediately catch onto this game and begin to retaliate in the only logical way: by expanding their initial time estimates for various tasks by 20%! As a result, conversations between the project manager and his subordinates often proceed along the following path:

> Manager asks, "Do you have the estimate for how long it will take to program those lines of code for the subroutine?"
>
> Manager thinks, *"Whatever this lazy so-and-so tells me, I'll just shave it by 20% to keep him honest!"*
>
> Subordinate says, "Yes, it should take 100 hours to complete the coding."
>
> Subordinate thinks, *"Actually, this should take me about 80 hours, but I'm not stupid. I know the game he likes to play."*
>
> Manager says, "Sorry. I can only give you 80 hours."
>
> Manager thinks: *"That should keep his feet to the fire!"*
>
> Subordinate shakes his head and says sorrowfully, "I don't know. I guess I'll just have to do my best."
>
> Subordinate thinks, *"Got you, boss!"*

As this scenario illustrates, rather than engage in an honest exchange of information, the theory X boss has simply created a theory X subordinate who understandably is looking out for his or her own best interests. The subordinates are responding to an obvious message and sending back a clear one of their own (Graham, 1992): *If you do not take my estimates seriously, I will not give you serious estimates.* On the other hand, theory Y assumptions argue that an atmosphere of trust and self-direction will bring out the desire in subordinates to respond in a similar fashion to the manager, proving that they are, in fact, capable of the self-control the manager has offered to them.

Obviously, not everyone will respond to one single style of management from the project manager. Just as the theory X/theory Y model represents a continuum, so too do the subordinates with whom project managers must work. Effective project managers learn to know their subordinates, to understand which respond to theory Y challenges and freedoms and which seem to react only when a theory X approach is employed. The essence of McGregor's theory is that managers need to maintain the flexibility necessary to deal with each subordinate on an individual basis, offering a theory Y atmosphere to those subordinates who are motivated by the challenge of the project and maintaining a theory X attitude toward those subordinates who, for whatever reason, refuse to operate under any motivational technique, except that of coercion and threat of punishment.

## MASLOW'S NEED HIERARCHY

McGregor's theory X/theory Y model offered an important first step to understanding motivation by focusing on a manager's preconceived notions of his or her subordinates. Another useful starting point to understanding motivation in subordinates is to focus on their general psychological needs as precursors and drivers of an individual's motivational requirements. Maslow's (1943) hierarchy, while criticized by some as simplistic and others as overly complex, places human needs in an ordered sequence that is arranged in the following five categories:

*Most Basic*

   1. *Physiological needs.* Basic survival needs such as food, water, etc.

2. *Safety needs.* The need for security and freedom from threat

3. *Social needs.* The need for affiliation and social acceptance

4. *Ego/esteem needs.* The need for self-respect and peer recognition and appreciation

*Highest level*

5. *Self-actualization needs.* The need to perceive in oneself a sense of personal growth and self-fulfillment.

Maslow suggests that any individual's needs are arranged on a similar hierarchy of "prepotency," in which the lower-order needs must be fulfilled before one feels secure enough to attempt to satisfy the next level of need. For example, were one to be freezing to death in the middle of a snow storm, obviously that person would have little interest in satisfying ego-esteem needs. Recent research has suggested that Maslow's five levels are too rigid and, in reality, we rarely follow them in such a lock-step fashion. It is not at all uncommon for some individuals to violate the order or seek to satisfy higher-order needs while ignoring the most basic (e.g., the "starving artist" willing to sacrifice all for his muse). Nevertheless, from a managerial perspective, Maslow's hierarchy offers project managers an important starting point when attempting to formulate a plan for seeking to gain the maximum involvement and commitment from project team members.

Project managers need to examine their subordinates individually to get a realistic sense of where that person is in terms of needs' satisfaction. For example, it is not at all uncommon for those who are young and new to an organization to be more concerned with satisfying monetary needs or seeking challenging work assignments. Older employees, on the other hand, may be more concerned with maintaining satisfying working relationships with those around them or seeking an acceptable work environment. Some subordinates will crave status and public recognition. Others will be content to be accepted as part of a team and are perfectly happy to blend into the background. Still others demand the opportunity to perform in creative or nontraditional roles. Chances are, a project team will contain an assortment of members who encompass all the above types of needs. From a management perspective, a starting point for seeking to uncover the motivational concerns of subordinates is to ask oneself three questions:

1. Based on my best reading of this subordinate, where is he or she on Maslow's need hierarchy (i.e., what sorts of concerns does this person continually voice)?

2. What needs will motivate this person?

3. As the project manager, what can I do to help this subordinate satisfy these needs?

Maslow's appeal lies in his recognition that motivation is a process requiring project managers to abandon preconceived notions that there is "one best" method for motivating employees. Rather, members of the project team carry their well-developed attitudes, opinions, needs, prejudices, past experiences, and learning with them from one project to the next. The effective project manager will seek to uncover each team member's set of needs in order to best determine how to create an atmosphere in which these subordinates can satisfy those needs. The key lies in learning to "read" your subordinates; get to know them as complex and complete human beings rather than simply in terms of the functional expertise they bring to the project team. Once this step is taken, the project manager is in the position to try and find ways to appeal to the "internal generator" that exists with each individual member of the project team.

## HERZBERG'S MOTIVATION HYGIENE THEORY

Herzberg (1968) has suggested that there are two types of motivational factors: hygiene factors and motivators. He argues that the hygiene factors are necessary conditions for a satisfied worker, but do not guarantee satisfaction. That is, if they are absent, you will have an unhappy worker, but their presence does not assure contentment. These hygiene factors include company policy and administration, supervision, relationship with superiors, working conditions, salary, relationship with peers and subordinates, personal life, status, and security. The impact of these factors lies mainly in what they prevent, rather than in what they encourage. Should workers believe that any of these factors are deficient to a significant degree, it can have the effect of demotivating the subordinate.

On the other hand, Herzberg posited a second class of factors that, he argued, account for worker satisfaction and enhanced job performance. These factors he labeled motivators and stressed that, unlike hygiene factors, motivators are the blocks on which top management can build a contented and motivated workforce. Some of these factors include sense of achievement, recognition, challenge, responsibility, advancement, and feelings of personal growth. According to Herzberg, these motivators offer workers the opportunity to pursue important personal needs within the context of performing their work as part of the project team. For example, Herzberg argues that job challenge and the opportunity of new learning are important motivators for most subordinates. A strategy that project managers could usefully employ might be to allow, when possible, subordinates to self-select themselves into the various subtasks for the project. Certainly, this strategy is constrained to some degree by the nature of the work and the fact that on many project teams, there may be only one obvious choice to perform some of the tasks. Nevertheless, if subordinates believe that they have some discretion over the nature of the work they will perform or a chance to enhance their technical or managerial skills as part of the project, they are likely to become more motivated to perform well as part of the project team.

Herzberg posits a two-stage process for creating an atmosphere of motivation within the project team. First, he suggests, project managers must critically evaluate the nature of their team and task responsibilities to determine if as many potential dissatisfiers (hygiene factors) as possible can be removed. For example, a step in this direction would be to ensure that working conditions are pleasant and supervision and pay are perceived as equitable and fair. Once project managers have explored methods to remove these negative hygiene factors, they need to "load" the project-related tasks with additional motivators. Some strategies for performing this step might be to push responsibility downward rather than retaining all decision authority at the management level, increase job freedom and the learning that can accompany it, introduce new, novel, or difficult tasks that offer a challenge and encourage creativity and nontraditional thinking, and perhaps most important, involve subordinates in planning and other operational decisions so that they feel they have a voice at all stages of the project's development and implementation.

It is a well-known truth that individuals tend to do what is satisfying to them. They are more likely to repeat behaviors for which they are rewarded and not repeat those for which they receive no positive encouragement or reinforcement. Consequently, when project managers spend the extra time to attempt to redesign a work environment in which individuals are reinforced by the work itself, they are likely to experience much greater effectiveness as the project leader and manager.

## LOCKE'S AND LATHAM'S GOAL SETTING THEORY

One of the most important theories of motivation to emerge in recent years has been the goal setting theory of Ed Locke and Gary Latham (1990). Locke and Latham agree that individuals are motivated to satisfy needs on the job. However, they argue that in addition to seeking to satisfy these needs, human beings are also motivated to strive for and achieve goals. Their central argument is that a goal serves as a motivator because it permits the subordinate to compare his or her present abilities with those necessary to perform the job. Further, having a goal helps subordinates learn on the job. If they succeed in fulfilling the goal, they are able to process information to determine how to improve their performance. On the other hand, if the subordinate does not fulfill the goal, he or she can assess the areas of shortcoming to pinpoint training deficiencies or flaws in goal development. If workers believe that, with hard work, they have the capacity to achieve the goal they seek, they will become motivated to perform to the higher level necessary to attain the goal. On the other hand, if a subordinate evaluates a goal a priori and determines that it is either 1) too difficult, or 2) not something the individual values, that subordinate will not be motivated to perform in such a way to meet the goal.

This discussion highlights some of the practical aspects of goal setting theory. Locke and Latham suggest that in order for goals and goal setting to be effective as a motivational tool, it is important the goals have certain attributes. Specifically, Locke and Latham suggest that there are three characteristics goals must have if they are to be a valuable motivational source:

- They must be specific.

- They must be meaningful.

- They must be perceived by the subordinate as difficult but attainable.

Let us examine each of these characteristics in turn. First, Locke and Latham note that in order for goals to have meaning and, therefore, motivational force for subordinates, they need to be specific—that is, well-defined. Goals that are ambiguous or too general are not much help to project managers or team members. For example, if a project manager is given a goal to "improve relations among the various functional departments," he or she is likely to perceive that goal as far too nebulous or ill-defined to be meaningful. Further, uncertain or vague goals usually create conflict and animosity at some point in the future, since it is likely that the subordinate and manager will disagree on whether and to what degree the goal has been realized. On the other hand, if the above goal were to be restated, "Hold informational meetings at least once a week in which the various functional departments are involved," the project manager would have a specific, concrete goal to attempt to complete.

The second necessary feature of motivational goals is that they be meaningful. Another way of stating this is to suggest that they must be viewed as personally important by the subordinate. The underlying premise of this point is that goals can only motivate so long as the subordinate perceives that they represent a challenge or accomplishment he or she seeks. In this light, when presented with a goal, subordinates will usually ask themselves a salient question: Is either the goal itself or the reward offered for attaining the goal something that I value? If the answer to this question is "no," it is unlikely that the goals, as stated, will compel a subordinate to become motivated. Project managers need to carefully consider the personality of each subordinate when formulating motivational goals, as it is a mistake to assume that all team members will be motivated by challenge, creativity, freedom of action, or any one of the other potential goals or rewards that the project manager can offer.

The final defining criterion for meaningful goals is that they must be perceived by subordinates as difficult but attainable. In assigning goals for subordinates, there are two equally serious mistakes that managers can make. On the one hand, they can assign targets that the subordinate believes are easily attainable. Consequently, the subordinate is not motivated to exert any energy or effort on their behalf. The second mistake lies in erring in the opposite direction: creating goals that are perceived as being beyond the subordinate's reach. Goals that the subordinates feel are too far out of line with their capabilities do not motivate, but will actually demotivate the worker. For example, a regional sales manager who arbitrarily increases a sales representative's quota by 100% for the coming year, in the hopes that this will "motivate" the sales representative to perform, will, in fact, discover that all he or she has done is demotivate the subordinate. The sales representative's thinking would probably be, "There is no way I can make those numbers, so why bother trying?"

A recent article by experienced project managers pondered the difficulties in creating an atmosphere of motivation within project teams (Tampoe and Thurloway, 1993). Lamenting the difficulties in gaining any sustainable level of motivation and goal commitment from temporary subordinates such as those found on project teams, the authors pointed to five important keys for establishing an environment in which subordinates feel willing to work to their highest potential. Specifically, they list five key motivators, including:

- *Mutuality.* The belief that project leader and subordinate share a common ground and set of objectives.

- *Recognition of personal achievement.* The willingness of the project leader to give credit and public accolades where they are due.

- *A sense of belonging.* The belief that each member of the team is a valued and valuable commodity performing an important task.

- *Bounded power.* The pragmatic and measured use of authority by the project manager over the members of the team.

- *Creative autonomy.* Giving team members free rein to perform creatively while taking care not to oversupervise.

## IMPLICATIONS FOR PROJECT MANAGERS: UNDERSTANDING VALUE AND RISK

Taken together, these various models of motivation offer project managers a valuable resource for creating the kind of environment in which project team members may be inclined to motivate themselves to higher performance levels. The key, as we have said, is to treat each subordinate as a separate motivational challenge. Project managers need to realize that they, by themselves, cannot motivate anyone. Rather, their task is to establish and encourage an atmosphere that allows team members the opportunities to be the best they can be. There are two concepts that project managers must

FIGURE 8.1.  Understanding motivation: risks and rewards.

Value of Reward                     _____
        ×
Probability of Value                _____

   = Expected Value                 _____

Minus:

    Cost                            _____

    Risk                            _____

   = Decision Outcome               _____

understand thoroughly if they are to use them to their advantage in creating such an atmosphere of self-motivation: value and risk.

Figure 8.1 offers an example of a simplified decision model of subordinate motivation. It suggests the sort of thought process a subordinate might go through in evaluating the rewards offered by a manager in an effort to create a sense of motivation. To illustrate, consider a situation in which you, as the project manager, sought to help your subordinate enhance his or her motivation for a project. Using the model, you would most likely seek the team member's active participation in the project and offer some type of reward of value to the subordinate in an effort to get his or her commitment and enhance motivation. What typically happens next is that the subordinate will consider this offered reward in light of his or her past project experiences, knowledge of you as a truthful individual, and general belief that what you offer, you are able to deliver. That evaluation process is illustrated in the model by the line denoted as "Probability of Value." In the case where the subordinate has complete confidence in your ability and willingness to follow through on the offered reward, that probability will be close to 100%. On the other hand, if unpleasant past project experiences or basic distrust of the organization factor into the subordinate's decision, they may evaluate your offer as a more chancy proposition and lower their probability figure accordingly.

The result of this internal calculation that every subordinate performs is the *probability of value.* In other words, the reward offered multiplied by the perceived likelihood that the subordinate will ever receive it. In the case of complete trust, the expected probability will be essentially no different than the initial value figure. On the other hand, if the subordinate is cynical or distrustful of your intentions, you could find the expected value to be considerably lower.

The probability of value figure is just the starting point, however, for additional thought processes that subordinates will engage in while considering whether or not to commit themselves to the project's goals. Notice that the next two lines of Figure 8.1 refer to subtracting *cost* and *risk* from the probability of value figure. Cost refers to the perceived or actual cost to the project team member of committing to the task. Such a cost could be in terms of out-of-pocket expenses of some sort or perhaps the cost to be incurred in the eyes of colleagues for agreeing to take part in an unpopular project. Generally, the cost figure for most project-based work is low because few subordinates make personal economic investments in their projects. Risk, on the other hand, is a more fundamental concern for project managers. Risk refers to the potential risk to a subordinate's career or standing in the organization if he or she begins working on the project team. Further, risk could refer to concern for status, the potential risk of foregoing future raises and promotions if the project fails, or any other form of perceived personal risk from agreeing to take part in the project. In many instances, a team member who could make valuable contributions to the project will view serving on either a "low visibility" or highly risky project as presenting too much potential for downside risk. These people will do everything they can to physically and psychologically distance themselves from the project, perceiving that the costs of participation do not equal the potential gain from performing well.

Figure 8.1 illustrates these two fundamental concerns that all project team members have in considering whether or not to wholeheartedly commit themselves to a project: the concern over probability of value and the potential risk involved. It is important that project managers, reading about these concerns, do not minimize them or assume that they will not occur on any of "their projects." Team members carry their perception of the probability of value with them from one project to another. In effect, project managers are fighting past history. In spite of their own best efforts to be authentic with subordinates, it is important to remember that these team members have had other project team experiences prior to ever joining their current team. If those past experiences on other projects were bad, the project manager seeking to gain their motivation and commitment for a new project is facing an uphill battle. The best tool that they have to use in their fight to gain team member commitment is the recognition that their subordinates' suspicions are not personal, but understandable residue from past experience. The more open, honest, and authentic project managers are with subordinates, the better the managers' chances of realizing a higher degree of commitment from them.

One question that we are often asked by project managers is how to get someone motivated when there are simply no monetary rewards that can be offered. Our response does not change: When a project manager's rewards are limited, subordinates need to be made aware of this fact and understand the reasons behind it. It is vital not to make a set of promises when chances of delivery are dicey at best. Put another way, a good rule of thumb for subordinate motivation is to *never promise something you cannot deliver and always deliver on your promises.* We do not suggest that by being honest, all the subordinate's fears and qualms about working on the team will vanish: They may not. However, in being authentic with subordinates, the project manager is sending a clear message that he or she can be trusted and is looking out for the best interests of team members.

We have one additional point to make about rewards. When faced with a situation in which monetary rewards are limited, project managers need to exercise some creativity in finding other rewards that their subordinates value. For example, we have said earlier in this chapter that money is only one of many things that employees seek as a reward. In fact, Herzberg, in his two-factor model, argues that money serves only as a hygiene factor, not a motivator. Consequently, there are any number of nonmonetary rewards and incentives that project managers can offer to their team in order to induce their commitment and enhance their motivation. Challenging work, the opportunity for new learning, high visibility, and recognition are only a few of the many nonmonetary rewards over which project managers do have discretion. The key is getting to know your subordinates: what each of them seeks and values. As a result, when you offer a reward, you are tailoring it to that subordinate.

## CONCLUSIONS

Motivation is one of the most complex and challenging concepts that most managers will ever face. The problem is often compounded within the project management context due to the limitations of most project managers in making rewards available to team members. As a result, they are often faced with a job in which they must find ways to gain the maximum commitment from a motivated project team while not possessing the resources necessary to induce that commitment. This chapter has explored the nature of the motivation problem, arguing that many of the challenges involved in getting subordinates motivated to perform well on the project team lie in our basic lack of understanding about 1) the motivation process itself, and 2) the nature and use of rewards to encourage motivation. Just as there is no such thing as a "universal subordinate," so too, there is no such thing as a universal standard or guide for motivation. Each subordinate is different and responds to a different set of needs. The key to effective motivation lies first in acknowledging these differences and tailoring attempts at enhancing motivation to each individual. Once that lesson has been truly internalized, project managers are much further down the road to creating the sort of well-motivated team that can greatly enhance the prospects for project success.

# 9

## Total Manager = Total Management

*The two great movers of the human mind are the desire to do good and the fear of people.*

—SAMUEL JOHNSON

FOR A PROJECT manager to be effective and successful, the quality of leadership is most essential. People want to be led, rather than managed, for to be managed implies manipulation, and no one likes to be manipulated. When we come to assess what we expect of project leaders, and what their qualifications ought to be, it begins to look as if we are calling for a superman or superwoman. He or she has to bring together qualities, some of which appear to be self-contradictory, as we demonstrate in the previous chapter and here as well.

Project managers are the focal point with any and every project. It seems that their abilities are the one factor that can make or break a project. Although many project managers will have a specialized background, most probably, in a certain area of engineering, they must try and forget all that. As part of their core project team, they will have specialists in the concerned disciplines to advise them; they must rely completely and absolutely on these specialists. That is, they must not consistently allow their own specialist knowledge or commitment to a certain functional area to influence their judgment. Indeed, project managers may well be out-of-date in their own engineering discipline. But what is far more important, as we have said, than their technical qualifications are their qualifications as people.

Project managers usually enter a profession, such as civil engineering or chemical engineering, that first brings them into contact with projects. Then they develop an interest in that aspect and find themselves first on project teams and finally leading such a team. The obvious implication is that the training and development of project managers occur largely—indeed almost exclusively—via experience. The most fruitful training ground is obviously within the organizations of the major construction contractors or entrepreneurial companies, some of whom have as many as 300 to 500 project managers on their payroll.

The roles of project managers vary considerably from one who is strictly a project monitor or expediter, through one who oversees or exercises broad supervision over a project, to one who exercises total authority and accepts full responsibility for the execution of the project. It is within this *total* context that this chapter and indeed the entire book are focused. The responsibilities of a project manager include planning, organizing, coordinating, staffing, leading, decision making, motivating personnel, and monitoring and controlling operations on the project.

## A TO Z FUNCTIONS, CONTINUED

A previous chapter, "Project Managers' Duties: A to Z," catalogued, alphabetically, the characteristics and roles of project managers. Quite independently, another study set out to do the same and came up with the following list (Stallworthy and Kharbanda,

1983). Interestingly, although generally distinct from our set (only four entries seem common), its similarity derives from the wide range of roles and tasks that project managers are expected to perform:

- Adaptable

- Benefactor

- Communicator

- Delegates

- Enthusiast

- Flexible

- Go-getter

- Handler of people

- Initiative taker

- Jovial

- Keen

- Listener

- Motivator

- No-nonsense approach

- Organizer

- Persuasive

- Quietly in command

- Reliable

- Sensitive

- Team builder

- Understanding

- Versatile

- Winsome

- X-ray view

- Yearns for the best

- Zestful

You will see that although we have managed to represent every letter of the alphabet, this list is in no way complete. We have no doubt that successful project managers must have these attributes and many more. They really have to excel in every area. Some of the qualities may appear to be contradictory (e.g., zestful versus quietly in command), but that aspect mirrors the complexity of the life of project managers: needing to adapt, sometimes with the versatility of a chameleon. One must be kind but firm, to give another example—and although neither of those two attributes are even included in our lists, they offer additional demands on the project manager. It is in this sense that we have used the word "total" to describe this person.

The role and management style of project managers in turnkey contracts have been discussed by Merna and Smith (1990). Such a contract has the advantage of entrusting the entire responsibility to a contractor right from the beginning of design, through engineering, construction, and maintenance. The fully operational plant is finally handed over to the client—hence, the term "turnkey." The client deals with only one contractor who takes on complete responsibility for entire execution of the project, including all the "headaches" associated with it. Obviously, an experienced project team is essential to carry out all the phases of a turnkey contract, and the project manager of such a team must have the requisite managerial skills and technical ability to coordinate and manage the corresponding multidisciplinary contract. The total number of persons involved in a turnkey contract is less than those involved in a nonturnkey contract, since in the former much of the work is subcontracted. Essential for success is the free flow of information between the site and head office. And, the project manager has a pivotal role in this activity.

On a major contract, the project manager has to deal with a host of technical professionals, a subject important enough to warrant a special issue (August 1992) of the *IEEE Transactions on Engineering Management*. In an editorial to this issue, the guest editors (Katz and Lee, 1992) point out that the real problems here are people-related rather than technical. Breathtaking developments have occurred in various fields, and it is left entirely to the respective professionals to keep abreast of them. The project managers' responsibility covers a broad spectrum of such specialists' concerns in respect to security of employment, technical challenge, professional recognition, competent and supportive collegiality, freedom of exploration, preparation for an eventual entrepreneurial start-up, or the achievement of a balanced lifestyle between work, family, and leisure time.

It is essential that the project manager be fully competent to meet the needs of the professionals on the team. Good professionals are often rather ambitious and wish to advance fast. They are also frequently more demanding of a desirable work environment, apart from good pay and good benefits. They may even go so far as to assess their organization on the basis of the quality of its mission and goals, the quality of its career support, and the freedom from arbitrary restrictions. And, most important, truly gifted technical professionals are in a position to pick and choose! One has only to read some vignettes in Tracy Kidder's (1981) Pulitzer Prize-winning book, *The Soul of a New Machine*, to get a sense of the challenge of selecting, managing, and placating technical professionals.

## A HOTBED OF PARADOXES

As we have just suggested, some of the qualities called for in a project manager seem to be contradictory, and this presents us with a paradox, perhaps even a series of paradoxes. The present business environment is, in fact, so chaotic and paradoxical that

Peters (1989) is able to list some 18 paradoxes large and small, and he says that these are only "a small sample." To deal with a paradoxical situation, the effective leader has to be unconventional, adaptive, and very flexible.

The leader needs clear vision to see where he or she is going in order to encourage risk-taking. This is all very necessary if change is to be encouraged. On the other hand, the nature of project management is to constantly shift from a proactive, visionary stance to that of a reactive "firefighter," trying to douse the fires of setbacks and unanticipated outcomes. The effective leader has not only to face these paradoxes, but also accept them, learn to live with them, and indeed thrive on them. Although it is the case that project leaders need to be paradox lovers, how can this be facilitated? They need to be visible and aware; they need to listen and provide a listening forum; they need to accept and indeed applaud failures; they need to adapt their preferred decision styles and encourage speedy action-taking by all members of the team. The list seems endless: Not only the leader but also the whole team have to learn to live with paradoxes. Indeed, as such paradoxes are encountered, they should be discussed openly and appropriate solutions found.

Abraham Zaleznick (1977), a Harvard Business School professor, argues that true leadership encompasses three elements: substance, humanity, and morality. He further charges that most of us are painfully short of all three qualities in our collective lives. Our corporations, he states, are governed by caretakers, executives who substitute mediocrity and manipulation for substance and vision. The managers have seized control and left leadership behind. Zaleznik further asserts that modern executives organize operations without improving them. They control their employees with psychological pressure instead of motivating them with good examples. Instead of thinking innovatively, it seems, managers fall back on what has succeeded in the past. They are afraid to deviate from the known and practiced procedures. Zaleznik encourages the development of management courses to teach leadership, but he sees many problems overall. The majority of today's managers are in love with the present situation, their position and status, and are not likely to willingly give up these things. So, the creation of a new class of leaders is required, and this demands a complete revolution. The team concept, with the development of leaders rather than managers, lies at the core of the creation of this new generation of leader.

Many organizations seem enamored of new gadgetry; that is, high technology in general and computers in particular are considered to be the magic solutions to all problems. Certainly, these innovations offer companies and project management excellent and useful tools. As Sweet (1994) notes, project managers need to be constantly aware and updated on:

- Where costs are being incurred

- How good forecasts are

- Whether break-even returns need to be adjusted for the future

However, these tools and techniques do not offer a panacea for project managers through eliminating the need to consider the human element in their operations. Further, they can be dangerous in leading novice project managers to assume that the essence of their profession is to become computer-literate and software-sophisticated. Appropriate software can, of course, be a great help in weighing the numerous variables involved, also in keeping track of costs. Drawing up the project plan on paper is easy enough, but by the end of the first week and steadily thereafter, changes occur and the plan needs to be redrawn. A software package is *no* solution to the project manager's problems, since it has been observed that:

A fool with a tool is still a fool!

With a large number of variables involved in project management, there has to be a lot of juggling and human intervention seems a must.

## THE KEY TO LEADERSHIP

We have repeatedly stressed the importance of the role played by the project manager or project leader. The project leader, more than anybody else, is the one able to develop an effective team, by inculcating the right attitude in team members. Although a company should encourage participative management and see that such is put into practice, it is project leaders who actually achieve results through their people. The project leader needs to be fully aware of the problems of human relations and personal sensitivity. He or she needs to be constantly on the lookout to prevent personal conflict and ensure mutual respect among the team members.

In spite of our images of the leader as the rugged individualist, they do not stand alone. Although the respective functions of the leader and the team are different, they are completely complementary. The one cannot exist without the other. Both are equally essential to successful project execution. Just as a leader helps his or her team members, so team members can help the leader. If the project goals are well-defined, then all will be working toward a common goal. The last thing we wish to do is to create the impression that it all depends on the leader. The leader has indeed a very important role to play, but his or her prepotency does not come at the expense of the rest of the team. Without an effective team, leaders will achieve nothing.

There is no simple recipe for becoming a leader other than to note that it is not simply a trait with which one is either born or not, like red hair or blue eyes. Leadership skills can be acquired, but it is a hard road. They have to be cultivated through hard work and nurtured carefully. It is difficult to define the steps in acquiring leadership skills, but here are a few vital hints:

1. *Show the way.* A leader has to be, in effect, a path finder.

2. *Have a compass.* It is obviously necessary to lead in the right direction.

3. *Give due credit.* People should always be praised for effort, without fail.

4. *Take risks.* A leader must be prepared to take risks.

5. *Keep faith.* It is crucial that a leader keep faith with the team and superiors.

6. *Act the part.* An effective leader sounds and looks like a leader.

7. *Delegate.* It is most important to delegate work.

8. *Be enthusiastic.* Enthusiasm is highly infectious.

9. *Be competent.* The leader should know something about everything.

10. *Thrive on change.* Change is the order of the day, accept or adapt to it.

## LEAD, DON'T MANAGE

The project team members look up to their project manager for almost everything, but above all for providing leadership. A remarkable book on the subject (Brine et al., 1990) from the Ashbridge Management Development School (UK) establishes this point very clearly. The book is mainly about the leader and deals with the subject in three main parts: the project leader, managing the project, and action summary. The main function of project leaders is seen as their ability to manage the visible and invisible teams in order to meet the needs of the stakeholders. In their analysis, the Ashbridge School provides a clear and important link between the "assigned" duties of managers and "assumed" roles of leaders.

The field of management is looking for people like Jack Welsh, Chief Executive Officer of General Electric. The achievements of these men have been acclaimed in the media, but there are many more "unsung heroes" of whom we have never heard. Appointed to the highest office in his company in 1981, Jack Welsh feared that he would be perceived as "abrasive," but in spite of his style, he proved to be a model leader. An intuitive revolutionary, he preached and practiced the concept: "If it ain't broke, fix it." What was he getting at? We have to realize that such a statement is, in fact, a radical departure from the conventional wisdom, expressed in the words: "If it ain't broke, leave it." Welsh loved change and in the process caused GE to shed itself of a number of unprofitable, low-growth enterprises, concentrating on those that were doing well. This was a radical departure from previous policy. In the process, he eliminated more than 100,000 jobs and revitalized General Electric. It is this type of leader that transforms an organization and in the process creates a brighter and better future for the company, its employees, its suppliers, and its customers.

The subject of leadership has assumed great prominence in the management literature over recent years, and there are a host of titles addressing the subject. There is even a chair of leadership (named after Konosuke Mutushita) at the Harvard Business School. We can read of "the leadership factor," "the leadership challenge, the transformational leaders," and simply, "leaders." These are just a few of the titles to be found on the shelves, and they are all of value, highlighting various aspects of the need for leadership in management.

We have suggested that although some leaders may be born, in practice, most are "made." Leaders can be trained to do the job very effectively, but such training has traditionally been best carried out "on the job." It is extremely difficult trying to teach leadership in college. College coursework can teach managers to be more imaginative, communicate better, and be more self-aware. However, it cannot teach them to exercise sound judgment, thrive on chaos, work with energy, and be curious about all that happens. That only comes with practical experience—perhaps a hard way to learn, but by far the most powerful.

Nevertheless, there are a number of courses that seek to teach leadership. The Wharton School, in the United States, initiated its first course on leadership in late 1987. The dean, Russell Palmer, set the course in motion even though his faculty colleagues insisted that this was one subject that cannot be taught. Palmer's course was not the first: The first such course was probably that instituted in 1984 by the Northwestern University Business School. Since then many other business schools have followed suit and such courses are growing ever more popular. The Center for Creative Leadership at Greensboro, North Carolina, reports that the number of its students, sponsored mainly by corporations, has tripled over the last five years. In spite of such courses' popularity, leadership remains a challenging subject to teach effectively.

In order to drive home the lessons relating to leadership, some appropriate management games have been devised. Typical of these is what is called the "boat exercise," which demonstrates that it is very hard to get things right while managers keep meddling. The moral, it seems, is that to be a good leader, you must leave your team alone to get on with its work, ensuring a positive and supportive working environment.

The distinction between a manager and a leader, although rather subtle, is becoming clearer as the significance of leadership in management is more widely recognized. If we see leadership as something different from management, we then recognize that there are a number of leadership styles, which we have sought to enumerate in Table 9.1. Specifically, we can categorize four classes of leadership behavior under this model, recognizing, of course, that some forms of "leadership" here represented are, in fact, *anything but* leadership. The table is undoubtedly an oversimplification. We show the main features of the various styles of leadership, but there is a considerable overlap in both leadership style as well as the various schools of management. Our presentation exists only for illustrative purposes.

## LEADERSHIP IN THEORY AND PRACTICE

We have explored some of the early leadership theories in a previous chapter. At this point, we would like to discuss some of the more contemporary views that are held in the popular literature

**TABLE 9.1. Leadership Styles**

| Function | Scientific | Bureaucratic | Human Relations | Team |
|---|---|---|---|---|
| Production | Line/staff. Close control. Rewards and punishment. People are commodities. | Systems. Regulations. Technology. Traditional values. | Cooperative participation. Happy family is a productive family. | Best results through gaining individual goals. Team management. |
| Decisions | Management. | Informal negotiations. | Employees. | Shared, with management accountable. |
| Role | Boss runs a tight ship. | Technician. Salesman. Compromiser. | Father figure. | Team handler. Coach. Change agent. |
| Motivation | Good working conditions. Loyalty and expectation. | Status. Achievement. Recognition. | Involvement. Acceptance. | Teamwork. Self-managing leads to actualization. |
| Feelings | Keep them out of the workplace. | Controlled but low-key. | People want what they get. | Creative ideas will overcome hangups. |
| Communication | Get instructions. | Openness. Information exchange. | Openness. Accentuate the positive. | Two-way dialogues. |

*Source: Kharbanda and Stallworthy (1990).*

on leadership. Because of the almost "faddish" nature of the concept, our decade has given rise to a proliferation of books on leadership. This is not surprising since, as noted earlier, the word "management" is being increasingly replaced by "leadership" and "manager" by "leader." Here, we bring you just a brief synopsis of some of the most well-known recent additions to the leadership library, particularly noteworthy for their relevance to the project leader.

- Cohen (1993) presents an executive guide to issues such as change, teamwork, and leadership. He considers the interpersonal styles and personal needs of leaders, power and political behavior, and career development. Once having addressed the individual processes that go into leadership behavior, he then addresses the leadership model at the organizational level, focusing on organizational design, human resource management, and diversity. His book offers both practical examples and conceptual models and is an excellent tool for managers intent on learning more about the process of leadership development and behavior.

- Kouzes and Posner (1993) emphasize the importance of trust and credibility as prerequisites of leadership behavior. They argue that unless the manager has achieved a reputation for integrity, that individual can never be viewed as a leader by others. Through interviews and a comprehensive survey of over 15,000 managers, they have identified the six characteristics of credible leaders: self-confidence, appreciation, affirmation, empowerment, purposefulness, and encouragement.

- Mancuso (1993) offers an in-depth look at one of the chief tools in the leader's personal inventory: the power of persuasion. He notes that persuasion is the act of selling, negotiating, and motivating others. Along the way he suggests some practical methods for improving persuasive skills.

- Wheatley (1992) takes as her starting point the relationship of the classical business organization to the biological concept of an evolving organism. Although seemingly esoteric in treatment, the parallels she draws between organizations and natural science has some interesting implications for leadership behavior.

- Chemers and Ayman (1993) have assembled a state-of-the-art anthology of leadership theory, integrating concepts such as legitimacy; power and influence; transformational, charismatic, and visionary theories; and managing cultural diversity.

## Don't Ignore the Company Culture

It is clear that groups and organizations have unique personalities and value systems, somewhat characteristic of their company's culture. The project manager, especially as an outsider, must know and understand the company's culture in order to be effective and in gaining support to guide the project through organizational mazes (Cleland, 1990). Elmes and Wilemon (1988) present various models of culture that should help project managers identify what to look for in terms of cultural values and nuances. This analysis should enable project managers to devise strategies to interact effectively with the identified culture. Of course, some exceptionally strong project leaders can create and shape the cultures of their project teams, sometimes in spite of a contrary organizational culture. However, one should never minimize the potential impact that an organization's culture can have on the effective workings of a project team and the real limitations it can place on the project manager's prestige and influence.

It is mainly due to its conservative corporate culture combined with conservative financial management that one of the oldest and largest companies, Exxon, has managed to survive, amidst the tottering of former American giants such as GM, IBM, and Sears. Exxon's continued solid performance is all the more remarkable in the face of a number of significant challenges, including:

- The Valdez environmental disaster, costing the company over $2 billion

- Prolonged softening of oil prices

- Stagnant home market

- Company's "remoteness"

Exxon continues to look as solid as any big company in America. Its obsession with quantifying everything has been a major factor. For example, the company does not initiate any project unless the return on capital is projected at 12% or greater.

Intragroup conflicts on the project team can also be minimized by understanding the cultural frames of representatives from different groups. As we suggested in the chapter on politics, because of differentiation, team members enter any project team with divided loyalties and commitment to their departmental goals and attitudes. The project leader must make a concerted effort to speak and listen in ways that take such differences into account. A headstrong, reactive approach can be counterproductive and polarize differences, escalate conflict, and make project completion not only difficult but in an extreme case even impossible. Some characteristic cultures of a few major companies may interest our readers:

Intel Corporation: clan culture
Proctor & Gamble: market culture
Meridian Telephone Company: hierarchical culture
3M: adhocracy culture

Managing each of these unique cultures requires a distinct and different type of strategy. Project managers can help their teams achieve high performance in one of three ways: 1) by buffering most of the interference that the team might encounter both from within and without; 2) through the values they transmit to the team members—directly as well as symbolically; and 3) by sharing with team members different task review roles, for example, clarifier, critical evaluator, devil's advocate, etc., on a rotating basis in the course of project meetings.

*Part* 3

*Teams Achieve Wonders*

*A* key component of the project management pro-
cess involves the effective performance of the core project team. Although the
project manager exerts a tremendous impact on the potential for project success,
it would be fatuous to exclude the importance played by the project team as well.
Indeed, the manner in which project managers direct and mold their teams lies
at the heart of project management. In this section, we will examine the importance of teams in the successful completion of projects from a variety of perspectives. In Chapter 10, we will attempt to better define the team-building process,
arguing that unless a solid groundwork is laid at the beginning of a project, it
will be almost impossible for project managers to gain the full measure of support
and performance from their subordinates on the project team.

Chapter 11, "1 + 1 Can Equal 11," refers to the importance of developing and
sustaining synergy within the project team. In this chapter we will take a closer
look at the various stages that project teams go through, the ways in which they
can develop closer working relationships, and the manner in which they begin to
gain benefits from working as a team rather than as a collection of individuals.

Chapter 12 explores the process of team building. We will examine the various
characteristics that typify successful and effective project teams and identify the
steps in creating such teams. In this context, we will also address some of the
more common interpersonal processes that often occur during team building.

In Chapter 13, we will explore an extremely important process in project management: the nature, causes, and various methods for dealing with conflict, both
within the team and between the project team and external stakeholders. Conflict
is a ubiquitous characteristic of project management due to the resource limitations placed on the team, the nature of disparate personnel working in close
proximity with each other, and the various demands placed on the team and the
project manager. We will argue in this chapter that conflict, although serious, is
also a natural side-effect of the project management task and if managed appropriately, is not the disaster it is commonly misperceived to be.

The final chapter in this section, on project team meeting skills, represents an
interesting challenge to most project managers as they discover early in their
careers that most of their time is spent communicating with others. Specifically,
project managers spend a great deal of time in meetings, with team members and
other project stakeholders. Most of us know from our own experiences that
meetings can run the gamut from productive to tedious. This chapter will offer
some important suggestions on how to run more effective meetings, so that the
project manager's time spent will be maximally useful.

# 10

## "Excellence" Says So!

THE NATURE OF project management work is inspiring maximum performance from a disparate group of individuals coming from different functional backgrounds, having dissimilar goals and value systems, and often possessing little appreciation of the roles performed by other functional departments and team members. One of the most difficult roles that project managers undertake is influencing their team members to appreciate the strengths and contributions that other team members can bring to the project.

The title of Part 4 and also that of this chapter happen to be connected. "Excellence" comes from the title of a classic management book, *In Search of Excellence* (Peters and Waterman, 1982). It was a trailblazer in the field of management literature, if we judge by a spate of books (e.g., Peters and Austin, 1985; Waterman, 1987; and Peters, 1989, among many others) on this and related subjects in the 1980s and even now. Many of these titles have been bestsellers. In them, we are told that project teams and task forces have indeed achieved wonders in the corporate world. Before we bring you some examples of this, let us first consider some of the slogans and/or missions that these "excellent" companies established for themselves.

- *Bechtel.* Fine feel for the doable.

- *Fluor.* Taking an idea and making metal out of it.

- *Hewlett Packard.* Communicate, communicate, communicate. . . .

- *3M.* Informal communications.

- *NASA.* Ad hoc team structures.

- *P&G.* Tests, tests, and tests.

- *Texas Instruments.* A fluid, project-oriented environment; swift followup.

- *United Airlines.* Visible management and MBWA (manage by walking around).

Consider some of the innovative "wonders" achieved through teams and task forces in the past 30 years. Each of these examples or corporate attitudes was, in some sense, so groundbreaking that it set a new benchmark for the industry in which it occurred.

*Activision.* Build a game as quickly as possible.
*Canon.* AE-1 project.
*GM.* Downsizing.
*Honda.* CVCC program.
*IBM.* System 360.
*Sony.* Walkman.
*Taylor & Ng.* No. 1 goal: develop a prototype.

As we have said above, this is just a sampling of some "excellent" companies and how they specifically achieved excellence. Of course, it is interesting to note that just a few years after *In Search of Excellence* was published, some of the companies specifically cited in the book ceased to be excellent. For example, Atari Corporation quickly developed a host of product development and administrative problems that sent it into a multiyear tailspin. It just shows the very dynamic nature of the corporate world in that nothing can be taken for granted. In our fiercely competitive world and fast-changing global economies, one has to stay constantly on one's toes to remain excellent—even after achieving excellence (Kharbanda and Stallworthy, 1990).

## THE TEAM'S ROLE IN EXCELLENCE

The real strength of a project manager is the project team. In the previous chapters, we have emphasized the exceptional personal abilities of a project manager, even to the extent of calling this person a "superman" or "superwoman." However, project managers cannot operate just on their own, without full support from the project team. Although the project manager may well make or break a project, the project team is vital and its contributions are crucial to the ultimate success of a project. Consequently, one of the primary duties of a project manager is to build a dedicated group and knit it into a team through his or her leadership skills. This implies that the project manager should have a powerful voice in the choice of the members of the project management team right from the time of a project's conception.

However, let us approach this issue directly. What is the primary role or purpose of a team? Why should people act together as a team at all, rather than work as individuals? Barrett (1987) puts it thus:

> ... Teamwork and cooperation ignite and fuel the engines of the individual and the enterprise, and they make a new level of competence possible.

In other words, we work more effectively when we are part of a team. When the primary role of a team is to execute, or carry out, a project, it is naturally called a project team. A recent advertisement by an American company in the technical press proclaims:

> Bell South is not a bunch of individuals out for themselves . . . we're a team!

Notice the very subtle but important distinction. A group of individuals is not necessarily a team: They have to be welded together by their leader if they are going to be an effective team. To offer yet another example from the other side (literally) of the world and in an entirely different industry, let us consider the phenomenal success of the Vijay Bank in Bangalore, India. In the first four years of his appointment as chairman and managing director, Sadanand Shetty succeeded in tripling the bank's deposits and increasing profits a hundred-fold. The youngest person ever to be chairman of a nationalized bank, he is nevertheless a soft-spoken, modest leader. Shetty credits his bank's phenomenal success not to himself, but his team, saying (Purokayastha, 1989):

> "I feel I have done what I was expected to do as a chief executive. I built up an efficient team, something this bank needed very badly, and that is primarily responsible for its current success."

## MOLECULES ARE MORE POWERFUL THAN ATOMS!

Compared to a single person, teams are far more energetic and resourceful. They are positive and consistent and their members grow in skills and understanding as team building proceeds. Further, they are capable of solving complex problems far more competently than the single individual. In general, it also seems teams have a greater commitment to change than team members on their own. However, it has to be recognized that teamwork should not be confined to the lower echelons of a company: Teams also have a role to play in senior management. In this regard, the importance of a leader in holding together the team is demonstrated and emphasized.

The Nobel laureate, Dr. Polanyi of Toronto, takes the analogy even further. He points out that when atoms join together to form molecules, such a union is accompanied by the emission of energy. So, union produces energy. He suggests it is the same with teams and draws the following comparison:

The atom = the individual
Physics = the discipline of psychology
The molecule = the group (or team)
Chemistry = the discipline of sociology

What Polanyi seems to be saying is that psychology helps us to understand individuals and the way they think, whereas sociology helps us to understand the way people react and relate to one another. This kind of understanding is, of course, very necessary when we must deal with people working together in teams.

We know for certain that when individuals join together to form goal-oriented teams, an intense and powerful human energy develops, which has physical, intellectual, and moral attributes. There are many things that simply cannot be done by one person, working alone. However, it is not a question of mere numbers alone. Teams develop a sort of synergy that enables them to accomplish tasks that one might otherwise have thought impossible. What is the secret of this power that develops within the team? It is the consequence of collaboration, coordination, communication, and integration toward a common purpose. These features lead to unity of action, all effort being directed toward the goal that is to be achieved. There seems to be some magic in integrated effort, which results in the effective concentration of force and energy focused in the desired direction.

At the risk of repetition, we contend that in order to build and maintain a consistent, high-performance team, an effective leader is needed. A leader is required rather than a manager, although of course the leader has to manage as well. Further, the quality of a team's performance is effectively determined by the personality and leadership style of its leader. The leader is at the center of the team's activity, supposedly leading, but for the best results the leader should really lead from behind. Proper cooperation should also exist between teams engaged in the different steps comprising the total operation.

To illustrate this point, let us cite the case of a factory engaged in making shoes. There are four managers whose activities are fundamental to the effective working of the company: the raw materials buyer, production planner, market forecaster, and distribution manager. The efforts of these four should be cooperative: The work of one affects that of the others. If these individuals do not work together as a team, their current, narrow profit margin will disappear. However, when we look at the organization chart for the company in question, we see these four managers listed below the production director, hanging like apples from a tree. There is no indication that their efforts are interdependent, yet that is what is essential to their success. Cooperation may well be happening, but the chart shows the four individually responsible to the production director, as though their partners in the business did not exist. But they should all be one management team—in effect, a team of teams! Therein lies the success for *all* concerned!

## EVEN IN HOSPITALS, TEAMS CAN DO WONDERS!

We see that teams are far more prevalent than one might have first supposed. Not only do teams work individually, but they work in parallel and cooperate with other teams as well. We also observe that when teams are at work, a great deal depends on the team manager or leader and the way he or she succeeds in encouraging the team to work together for its common objective. A hospital is an intriguing example in that it represents, in all probability, one of the most complex knowledge organizations, and for it to provide sound and efficient service, a number of diverse specialists have to work together as a team.

When we think of a hospital, "the doctor" is perhaps the first image that comes to mind. But in addition to doctors, and to some extent under their direction, we have nurses, dieticians, pharmacologists, X-ray technicians, laboratory technicians, physical therapists, and the like, all working on and for the benefit of the patient. They carry out their duties as a matter of routine, with only general direction from doctors. Functionally, they report to their respective department heads, and each professional's work has to be properly synchronized with those of his or her colleagues. If a careful routine is not established, there are liable to be conflicts and problems. Each individual in this team working on and for the patient is a responsible professional, but unless they all recognize that they are indeed part of a team, called on to work and cooperate together, the results can be disastrous. Indeed, so clearly is the fact and benefits of teamwork in this context recognized that it is now being projected in an advertisement of hospital services.

For instance, an advertisement for the Hinduja Clinic, a branch of the Hinduja National Hospital and Medical Research Center in Bombay, states:

> Everyone knows the advantage of teamwork—at the Hinduja Clinic, it's applied to health care.

This is easily explained and understood: For the patient, a proper diagnosis could mean a series of visits to several different doctors and diagnostic clinics, a process that can take weeks to complete. But when, as happens at the Hinduja Clinic, specialists from related fields work together under one roof, as a single team, and meet often to discuss each case, the benefits can be enormous. Cost savings are incurred, wasted time is eliminated, and more efficient communication among professionals, all working for the care of the patient, is realized.

Such a multidisciplinary approach means a quicker and more comprehensive diagnosis. For the patient's family doctor, it means a single, comprehensive report, and a clearcut treatment plan for the patient. Everyone comes out a winner! The advertisement goes on to say, this is "teamwork where it does the most good," and there is no doubt this phrase highlights the fact that teamwork is essential to good hospital practice.

Another example of teamwork in the hospital field exists in the United Kingdom. Vinton (1989) reports that 10 hospitals there formed a consortium to work on both their own and each others' problems. Although the advertisement we have just quoted highlights the application of the team principle to the patient, there are, in effect, a number of separate teams whose efforts are directed toward the patient through the specialist, or consultant, who actually examines the patient. These several teams are all working in parallel and have a common objective.

This system can also be seen working in industry, with teams pulling together like a team of horses "in harness" to achieve success. The most common example occurs when a contractor is appointed to run a project on behalf of the owner of that project. A project manager is then appointed by the contractor and made responsible, within the contractor's organization, for every aspect of the project. Here is what one such contractor says of this individual (Foster Wheeler, 1981):

> He is responsible for every aspect of the job from inception to completion. He is responsible for every service required to carry out the work: planning, scheduling, costing, designing, engineering, purchasing, inspection, shipping, construction and commissioning. And he is responsible to you, our client. He is your direct contact. And you will know him personally. His position calls for wide experience, broad knowledge of every group within the organization, the ability to control progress and make decisions.

Notice the similarity between this organization and that which relates to the hospital. The project managers are similar to doctors, with the project as their patient, and they are able to call on a wide range of specialist groups to perform the various services required, such as design engineering, purchasing, inspection, construction, and so on. Representatives of these various technical groups serve on the project team. However, the owner also has to have a parallel project team, since certain responsibilities exist that cannot be delegated to the contractor. Then we have two project teams working in sequence toward a common goal. There is no doubt that this method of working both alongside and in parallel, just like a team of horses in harness, is highly successful and should therefore be the standard. How does it work? To quote once again from a brochure issued by a contractor (Kharbanda and Stallworthy, 1990):

> The project control team under the direction of the project manager sets the control guidelines for the project. On major projects a project control manager heads the project control team. Each supervisor within the engineering, procurement and construction areas involved in the development of the project controls that which affects his area of work. Thereafter, he is responsible for the execution of the project within the control plans and budget established for his area of work. The project manager, the project control manager, and his project control team constantly monitor performance, making adjustments as may be required to plans as they may affect the interfaces between the specialty groups.

## COOPERATION VERSUS COMPETITION

It is said, and no doubt it is true, that for each winner there must be a loser. Winners and losers are the inevitable result of competition, which has erroneously been stressed in business situations in an endeavor to improve efficiency and performance. Some companies believe that in order to secure the best results, they should pit people one against the other, believing that the competitive spirit thus invoked will bring out the best in them. However, Waterman (1987) points out that research on this issue seems to point in exactly the opposite direction. Studies at both Columbia University and the University of Texas have proved conclusively that the best results are secured not through competition, but through cooperation and teamwork.

The most productive scientists, it was found, were not moved by competitiveness, but looked for proper work orientation and they much preferred challenging tasks. In other words, they looked for their challenge in the work they did, not their coworkers. This research was later extended to include airline pilots, airline reservation agents, business executives, and college undergraduates, and in every case the answer was the same. The conclusion is inescapable: It is a simple canard that injecting competition into the workplace will serve as a spur for enhanced productivity and satisfaction. In fact, the opposite is more often the case: Across a variety of jobs and personality types, increasing competition usually has the effect of downgrading employee satisfaction and productivity, creating suspicion and limiting information flow and teamwork, representing a huge potential loss to the organization in terms of productivity.

No wonder that companies noted for the constant renewal of their organizational systems and consequent success put a high emphasis on trust and teamwork. Competition erodes both: It is a highly negative force. Dana Corporation is an example of one outstanding company that places trust and intergroup relations above all else. Dana has an enlightened management operating with a unionized workforce, and it remains one of the most successful companies in the truck and autoparts business. Trust and teamwork are at the heart of operations at Dana. Employees do not have to earn the trust of their managers and coworkers: It is imputed to them from the very beginning. It is assumed that everyone working for the company does "what's right for Dana." Those who do not live up to this concept just do not last long with the company.

Morgan Guaranty is another company where trust reigns, and this example is interesting because the bank is so different from Dana, operating across international boundaries. It is said that Morgan Guaranty's company culture has trust built into it, and that this is demanded by the very nature of its business. No one's motives are questioned, and trust is built into the company culture right down to the counterclerks and tellers. A bank has to have integrity, and this demands trust. Everyone has to work together as a team. This attitude is demonstrated by the company's approach to the profit center concept. At Morgan Guaranty, this concept has been given the rather ill-sounding title "profit denteritis" on the basis that (Kharbanda and Stallworthy, 1990):

> It's not that we don't have profit centers, but [it] is not the be-all and end-all that you see in other institutions. There's a very strong desire

to get this bank operating together as a team and pulling together for the long term—doing our best to have every decision we make the best decision for the long haul. . . . The way to get on the manure list around here is not to do something because the profit doesn't go to your unit.

At Buckman's Lab plant in Ghent, Belgium, a "perfect" communications system was installed: Walkie-talkies were issued to some 18 employees. This allowed warehouse workers to speak to the shipping department and laboratory supervisors to speak to production department personnel. But it so happened that the walkie-talkies of two workers did not work properly, and they ended up overhearing a lot of chatter that did not really concern them. They became so involved in the problems discussed on the walkie-talkie system that they volunteered a solution to some of them. Management quickly and correctly identified this as an unexpected windfall. As a consequence, it downgraded the system, so that everyone heard what everyone else was saying. Communication improved tremendously, and so did performance.

## CONSENSUS CAN HELP—AT TIMES

It has been found that consensual groups exhibit superior performance on tasks such as selecting R&D proposals for funding, planning innovative projects, and exercising quality control during implementation. Soliciting views from group members and then averaging their input or acting on the judgment of a single group leader or best member have been found to lead to plans of lower quality than those developed through consensus. Research has been undertaken to investigate whether the performance of consensus groups on project planning tasks could be further improved by diagnosis and feedback intervention regarding the nature of a group's rational and interpersonal processes. The best impact was observed with rather limited intervention by an outsider or neutral observer. Some positive interpersonal behaviors include active listening and clarifying by group members, supporting and building on others' opinions, and differing with and confronting other team members.

Groups are usually more receptive to and willing to implement a diagnosis developed by the group itself. A recent study collected data from a total of 114 groups (547 individuals). Feedback on rational processes had a more significant impact on performance than feedback on interpersonal processes, but only for high-ability groups. In other words, more highly productive teams are able to concentrate their evaluation on the task, rather than the social side of their group, perhaps due to greater confidence and trust in each others' abilities (Thamhain and Wilemon, 1987).

In another example, a project planning simulation was used to ensure proper experimental controls and maximize the number of groups participating in the experiment. This exercise for technical training at the Ford Motor Company showed significant overall improvement in the performance of the participants. In the case of training project engineers to become project managers, the simulation exercise for group decision making and project management showed very positive results. Although such results need to be validated in field settings, findings through the use of a simulation are quite relevant and important. According to Kernaghan and Cooke (1990) some of the practical implications for management of project planning groups, drawn from this relatively inexpensive and time-efficient intervention, include:

- Improved planning performance.

- High-ability groups benefited the most from the intervention.

- For low-ability groups, prior training/seminars are recommended to help develop the necessary task skills.

## CONCLUSIONS

One of the true secret weapons in any effective project manager's arsenal is a motivated, cohesive team. Teams that operate in cooperation with each other, rather than through competition, provide project team leaders with a powerful tool for achieving project success. Successful companies have long understood the importance of fostering and maintaining a spirit of teamwork and mutual support for organizational activities. Decision making is typically more accurately done with cooperating teams allowing equal input and open communication among all members. Further, these communication patterns, although frequently informal, can go far toward aiding project implementation success (Pinto and Pinto, 1990). When a team is open to applying its collective mind and will to a mutual problem, it offers a potent and often irresistible force for excellence.

# 11

# 1 + 1 Can Equal 11!

IN SPORTS, GROUPS are usually termed teams, which originally in Anglo-Saxon meant a family, or offspring. Work groups such as orchestras also bear some resemblance to a family. Some employers, including those of family-owned and/or -controlled businesses (e.g., Birlas and Tatas in India, Mars and Walmart in the United States), treat some ("fair-haired" children) of their staff somewhat like children and develop into "father figures." The family is also a potential matrix for learning a variety of skills, including problem solving, interpersonal relations, time management, and conflict resolution.

This concept of group synergy is perhaps best exemplified by a simple Indian proverb, which states that "1 and 1 can be 11." But let us be honest about this. The mere formation of a team is no guarantee of success. It is very difficult to say what makes a team "tick," nor is it easy to establish why one team performs so much better than another. However, as this metaphor was used in a previous chapter, if we venture to liken individuals to atoms, a team is rather like a molecule—an entity by itself. In that earlier example, we brought to you the opinion of a Nobel laureate who claimed that when atoms join together to form molecules, the union is accompanied by the emission of energy. Thus, a molecule of water is far more than a mere combination of oxygen and hydrogen atoms: It is a substance in its own right, with its own very special qualities and attributes. This we venture to describe as the "chemistry" of teams: The team is very different than the sum of the individuals that make up that team.

Based on the phenomenal project success that has been achieved with teams, the concept has now been extended to all fields of endeavor, including manufacturing and services industries, as well as design, production, and marketing. The "project team" approach is equally valid in the case of the mega- or macroproject (over a billion dollars in value) by breaking down the project into a number of subprojects, each of which can then be tackled on its own. But it is advantageous to have centralized coordination, so that a single agency knows what is happening across the board and how it all fits into the whole, much like a jigsaw puzzle.

## THEORY AND PRACTICE—PROJECT TEAMS

In an earlier chapter, we touched briefly on two of the better-known motivation theories, theories X and Y. The main features of these are summarized in Table 11.1. We will now examine some other theories on management, together with research relating specifically to teamwork in somewhat greater detail. We can then apply these theories to organizational management to see how theory and practice relate.

How can individuals perform effectively as a group? How do we bring the arrangement shown in diagram B of Figure 11.1 into being (Kharbanda and Stallworthy, 1990)? In general, with team building there are four stages: forming, storming, norming, and performing. These words in sequence are easy to remember and are also, to some degree, indicative of the stages that should be

**TABLE 11.1.  Motivation Theories**

| Traditional Theory X | McGregor's Theory Y |
|---|---|
| Safety and security | Self-esteem |
| Motivation: extrinsic | Motivation: intrinsic |
| Autocratic | Participative |
| Slavelike | Allies |
| God of fear | Loving, kindness |
| Exploitation | Mutual satisfaction |
| Materialistic | Democratic partners |
| Fear | Courage |

*Source: Kharbanda and Stallworthy (1990).*

followed. These concepts will be discussed in greater detail in the next chapter. The group must perform together and act in a cohesive manner, with all seeking to fulfill its project goal. A leader or project manager can help a great deal in this process of pulling together a team so that it cooperates fully, but a truly good leader will take to heart the saying:

To lead is to serve, nothing more and nothing less.

This discussion serves to highlight the $64 million question: Exactly how and when does a group of people working together become an effective team? This is illustrated diagrammatically in Figure 11.2. When they are first brought together, the several individuals in a team retain their personal identity, with their likes and dislikes, and chances are that they are unable to work together for their common cause. However, with the passage of time the situation often stabilizes, the status of some team members becomes established, and this process continues until all know their

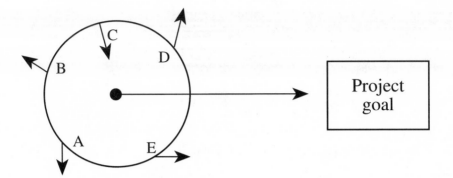

**Diagram A**

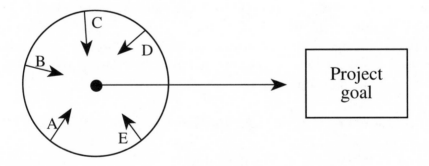

**Diagram B**

FIGURE 11.1. Individuals performing ineffectively and effectively as a group (Kharbanda and Stallworthy, 1990).

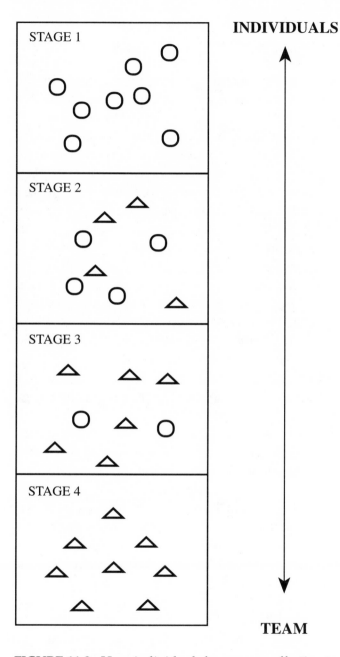

FIGURE 11.2. How individuals become an effective team. ○ = Team member who has not found a place. △ = Team members whose status is established.

place in the team. This process of stabilization seems to start at both ends of the scale at the same time; the senior members and most junior members rapidly establish their status, whereas those in the middle may take some time to sort themselves out. But finally everyone knows their position and role in the team. It is then that we can say the team has been formed. How long this process of team formation takes will vary from case to case and depend to some extent on the ability of the leader or project manager.

If we add 1 and 1, we get 2, but in situations involving people, such a simplistic equation just does not apply. We can get zero, or even a negative result, if the two people are antagonistic to one another. On the other hand, if synergy develops, we may get 3, 4, or even more. As we said at the onset of this chapter, ideally 1 and 1 can equal 11—this is the real payoff in cases of groups and teams. Although we begin by believing that there is strength in numbers, there can also be weaknesses. Unless two individuals are able to work together as a team, they may serve to simply cancel one another out. The example we have just noted is obvious enough, because in a number of real-life situations we have all seen it happen. However, is this concept backed by adequate theory, either basic or applied?

Social scientists have been busy for many years studying the various factors, both positive and negative, that govern human interaction. It has been established, for instance, that there is a need for managers to know and understand the implications of unconscious or covert factors in human interactions, since they have direct relevance to the workplace. Much of a manager's work is largely dependent on interpersonal relations within his or her workforce. This finding means that an understanding of these relationships will help him or her cope with the problems that are most likely going to arise.

Now, we ought to consider a bit of the practical side. We start with Aesop's famous fable of the father and his sons. It seems that from time immemorial, sons have been known to quarrel not only among themselves but more particularly with their parents as well. In the fable, as expected, the father's exhortations to his arguing sons to make peace failed, so he hit on a practical solution. He asked his sons to bring him a bundle of sticks; he then requested that they break the bundle into pieces. No matter how hard they tried, the sons could not break up the bundle. The father finally opened the bundle into individual sticks, and the sons easily broke the sticks one by one. Hence, his lesson (Sparks, 1982):

> My sons, if you are of one mind, and unite to assist one another, you will be as this bundle, uninjured by all attempts of your enemies; but if you are divided among yourselves, you will be broken as easily as the sticks.

Of the three M's, man, materials, and money, we are convinced that the first, man, is by far the most valuable resource in every walk of life. Though just one individual, the leader, can make all the difference, to really achieve anything, he or she has to be supported by an effective team. It is the team, far more than single individuals or techniques, that translates successfully the initial concept into a working reality. Project teams are invariably cross-functional and project managers integrate, liaise, and coordinate the various functions. And irrespective of the team's formal structure, there is intense, frank, and informal communication within the team and also with the various agencies with whom that team must work. More and more progressive companies everywhere have now started to use the project team approach quite extensively. It is interesting to see that this "team" focus has been extended to suppliers and subcontractors as well, for not only project execution but also product development and other functions—and with great benefit. Teams can indeed achieve far more than the sum of their members can ever achieve individually.

Having adopted the principle that the real owners of the company were the people who worked there, the Dana Corporation began to proclaim this with a major institutional advertisement appearing in a number of American business journals, such as *Fortune, Forbes,* and *BusinessWeek.* This advertisement said, *inter alia* (Peters, 1985: quoted in Kharbanda and Stallworthy, 1990):

> Talk back to the boss . . . it's one of Dana's principles of productivity. Bosses don't have all the answers . . . workers know more . . . but all that [knowledge] can't be used unless he's free to talk about it to his boss. . . . At Dana, bosses listen . . . giving people the freedom to work well to grow and share in the rewards. Our productivity [has] more than doubled in the last 7 years. [We] have also improved our earnings year after year—not bad for a bunch of people who talk back to their bosses.

The company did not stop there. Dana eliminated a maze of corporate control procedures, such as excessive reporting, signing on and off and the like, replacing all with trust. Employees were to be treated as responsible, honest adults. Eventually, the majority of employees (more than 80%) became stockholders. The Dana Corporation is by no means the only major corporation to adopt such policies. IBM is another notable example. Its management is reported as saying: "We don't need checks and balances. We need trust." The point is that trust begets trust, and this is the real secret to success.

## STEPS TO A SUCCESSFUL TEAM

There are a series of stages discernible in the development of a team, and Woodstock (1989) has established some of the more common features. In all, there can be said to be four separate stages. Figure 11.2 illustrates how the team through these steps evolves from a set of uncommitted individuals into a group working together.

**Step 1.** *The undeveloped team.* This type of team is the most common. It has been formed, but not much thought has been given to the way in which it should operate. The characteristics of the pyramidal organizational structure still prevail, with the result that unusual ideas are not welcomed, the team members are disheartened, distrust is high, and personal weaknesses covered up. The team members do their allotted work, but senior management is still making all the decisions. This, manifestly, is not real team-work.

**Step 2.** *The experimenting team.* The team has reached the stage where it is willing to experiment or face the unknown. Problems are dealt with openly, and the wider options considered. Arguments proliferate as team members develop a higher comfort level with each other. Hitherto taboo subjects begin to be discussed, personal issues are raised, feelings come out into the open, and the team members begin to understand one another. Although the team is operating in an open and increasingly effective way, it still lacks the capacity to act in an economic, unified, and methodical manner. Some lessons have been learned, but those lessons have yet to be put to profitable use.

**Step 3.** *The consolidating team.* This type of team has much more confidence in itself, and adopts an open approach, and team members are prepared to trust each other. The rules and procedures that prevailed at step 1, but were later rejected, are now being readopted, but as mutually agreed on operating rules rather than managerial edicts. Despite the better relations within the team that developed in stage 2, the team learns that some basic rules are crucially important. Decisions are taken by clarifying the purpose of the team's task, establishing the objectives, collecting the required information, considering the options, making detailed plans as to what should be done, and finally reviewing the outcome and using that knowledge as a basis for improving future operations. The team is learning as it goes.

**Step 4.** *The mature team.* The lessons concerning openness learned during step 2, and the systematic approach to problems developed through step 3, have now resulted in a truly mature team, made wise by experience. Different approaches are adopted to meet different needs and a completely flexible approach to problems exists. No one seeks to defend his or her position or status, and leadership is decided by the situation that emerges, rather than protocol. The typical management hierarchy has been completely abandoned, there is individual commitment, and everyone is striving toward the same objective.

When teams are close together physically, communications are relatively easy, any misunderstandings can be resolved, and clarification of ideas obtained and built on (Pinto, Pinto, and Prescott, 1993). If they are far apart, the team leader and team members must take active steps to ensure that there is free, constant, and quick communication not only between themselves, but between themselves and other teams with which they may be involved. There are both formal and informal methods of communication, and some of the informal methods are very effective. One informal method that we believe to be invaluable is what is called "huddling" (Merrell, 1979). *Huddling—The Informal Way to Management Success* is the unusual title of a book dealing entirely with business communications. The concise Oxford Dictionary defines "huddle" colloquially as a close or secret conference. Merrell demonstrates that results are often produced not by organizations but by people, a special kind of people—the "huddlers," who are able to work intimately and informally in small groups. According to him, huddling is one of the most effective means of communication.

Huddling, of course, is nothing new. It has always existed in the area of interpersonal relations. It is effective and achieves results. A few minutes of informal conversation with subordinates, peers, and superiors, along the corridors of the office, in the washroom, or in the lunchroom, can be most effective. The practice of this technique, therefore, needs to be encouraged. It is an essential element in good management. It is not the only element, of course. Other informal techniques include the notice board with relevant news items, weekly project team lunch where problems can be identified and discussed, and the occasional telephone call to team members whom you have not seen for some time, to ask how they are getting along. Project team leaders have a more particular responsibility in this area. They need to be in close contact with all team members. One way of achieving this is MBWA, short for manage by walking about, or manage by wandering around. So many managers rarely leave their offices to see what is happening about them, but they must do so regularly to remain aware.

## MORE TIPS FOR SUCCESS IN PROJECTS

As we have pointed out, a very substantial volume of literature exists on the subject of teams and team building, and some important research has also occurred to date. There are some interesting findings in relation to a series of research studies on the effect of the restriction of communication channels on productivity and the morale of individuals and teams. Five-man groups were given the problem of finding which symbols were held in common by all members, whereas the communication facilities were varied in a controlled manner. The results of the findings suggest:

- The most effective group had a "wheel" pattern, where the four members communicated with only one central person.

- The least effective group was that which operated in a "circle." However, that type of grouping had the greatest overall morale, since each individual was more involved and hence happiest with the group task.

- The intermediate form of grouping, in terms of results, was what can be called the "chain," or "Y" structure.

The research established that the restriction of communication led to greater efficiency. Although this may be true in relation to simple problems, where information must be collated to establish the correct answer, we do not believe it is true in relation to the far more complex problems dealt with in manufacturing. The wheel structure may save the group time in relation to organization when problem solving, but it is rather inflexible and hence not very efficient when the problems become more complex. In the case of complex problems, a less restricted network, with free communication between all team members, becomes far more efficient. Since that is the more typical situation in industry, a decentralized group structure is preferred.

Informal get-togethers, such as project lunches, outings, and so forth, can be a good long-term investment in the group's psyche, encouraging the exchange of ideas and information and helping build working relationships. Another useful method for building team member commitment to the project is to communicate publicly and frequently with the team members' department heads so that they know about the work of their people assigned to the project (Katzenbach and Smith, 1993). Finally, as Vincent (1988) has pointed out, responsibility is often a good motivator, just as boredom breeds dissatisfaction and challenge creates enthusiasm.

## TIME MANAGEMENT

Time is the most valuable resource, but often one of the most neglected and wasted too. Specific guidelines on how to get more done, quickly and efficiently, suggest (Ballard, 1993):

- It is not how busy you are that is important; it's what you accomplish.

- Saving just one hour per workday through proper work management can provide a full month per year to use more effectively.

- Managing time is harder than you think since most rules of time management contradict laws of human nature (e.g., ego, fear of offending, procrastination, ambition, inability to say no, etc.).

The real trick to accomplishing more is to get organized and manage time effectively. The first step in this process consists of keeping an accurate time log throughout the workday, noting how much time is spent on the telephone, in meetings, in "productive" work, and so forth. Likewise, as part of the time log, consider honestly how much time is spent in "nonproductive" activities: wasting time in nonessential meetings at which a subordinate could represent you, taking every telephone call rather than having a secretary screen them first, allowing others to pile their problems on top of your own, and so forth. We have found that it is best to write down your daily schedule, then alone are you able to track it. Of course, schedules should be flexible; they may need to be revised and finetuned. For this to succeed, managing time effectively is absolutely vital. This may well require a change in the project manager's habits and even values. Table 11.2 lists some

**TABLE 11.2. Time Wasters**

- Attempting too much
- Poor communication
- Confused responsibility or authority
- Poor delegation
- Drop-in visitors
- Inability to say "no"
- Incomplete information
- Leaving tasks unfinished
- Management by crisis
- Ineffective meetings
- Paperwork
- Personal disorganization
- Poor controls and progress reports
- Poor self-discipline
- Socializing
- Inadequate staff
- Telephone interruptions
- Travel

*Source: Ballard (1993).*

of the biggest time wasters (Ballard, 1993). These include attempting too much; poor communication; confused responsibility or authority; and so forth. All sound very familiar!

An excellent book published recently (Covey, Merrill, and Merrill, 1994) is hailed as a real breakthrough in time management. Rather than focusing on techniques of time management per se (calendars, prioritizing, etc.), this book emphasizes relationships as a basis for gaining results. Instead of efficiency, it aims at effectiveness. In sum, the authors argue that the true "villian" in time management is the superficial nature of the relationships we develop with team members, peers, and subordinates. If we focus on enhancing these contacts, we are in the position of being able to make our time on the job more productive.

One of the best practical tips that has been developed on executive time management refers to the difficulty in managing time when other members of the organization or project team are adept at imposing their problems on the project manager. The article by Onken and Wass (1974) refers to these time wasters as "monkeys" and asks the question, "Who's got the monkey?" Their point is that it is sometimes difficult to determine who is working for whom with regard to some subordinates. They are masters at the art of transferring their problems and, hence, the intiative to solve those problems to their managers. For example, suppose that a project manager for a software development project met with a subordinate to discuss a problem with a coding sequence. The subordinate speaks up and says, "Look, we have a problem with this procedure. What should we do about it?" After considering the problem, the project manager decides she does not have enough information to make a decision and says, "Well, let me think about it and get back to you."

What just happened here? The subordinate was the one with the problem and by the end of the conversation, the monkey had ended up on the project manager's back as she promised to "get back" to the team member. This response is just what the subordinate had been hoping to hear. The problem and responsibility for finding its solution are no longer his, but belong to the project manager. Now, in addition to her other problems, the project manager must add the subordinate's monkey to her back and consider how to solve *his* problem. From both a leadership and time management perspective, a far better response would have been to refuse to let the subordinate off the hook, pressing him for alternatives and drawing out his thinking. For example, suppose that the previous conversation had proceeded along the following lines:

> Subordinate: "Look, we have a problem with this procedure. What should we do about it?"
>
> Project Manager: "What are the different alternative approaches?"
>
> Subordinate (after a pause): "Well, I'm not sure. I guess we could . . . I mean, maybe, . . . ."
>
> Project Manager: "Here is what I would like you to do. Go over the sources of the problem with this procedure. Come up with two or three alternatives that we can discuss, along with your recommendation. When we get together in two days, you can give me an update on how you are dealing with the problem."

The result in terms of time saved for the project manager is dramatic. No longer is she allowing subordinates to transfer their problems to her for a solution; she is forcing them to address the difficulties they uncover. Not only will this approach enable the project manager to save a great deal of time, by focusing on her work rather than her subordinate's tasks, but it will also often make subordinates better at their jobs, as they learn to address and solve their own problems without feeling it necessary to bring each one to the manager for a decision.

Time is money and putting a higher value on your time is one effective way to save it. On the average, a working person spends about 500 hours per year in commuting, dressing, showering, shaving, and eating. This time can be used profitably in reading or listening to informative tapes. To jot down ideas that may "pop" up in your mind during the night, keep a pad and pen on your bedside table. An excellent problem-solving tool is to pose a problem to yourself at night just before going to sleep; chances are that you may have a meaningful answer when you wake up.

But when all is said and done, persistence is important: Decide on a workable schedule and stick to it consistently. Lo and behold, things will really get done according to schedule. Make sure to do the more important things during your peak energy and creative periods each day—and also, of course, in the shortest time possible. Work not only hard, but also (and preferably) smart! In the case of projects, of course, time is of the essence and even one day's delay in completion of a mega-project can cost millions of dollars. For the Chunnel project, which made headlines even before it opened in late 1994, the final price tag is likely to be £ 15 billion, and in terms of interest alone, the cost of one day's delay is over $3 million. Some readers may find it useful to consider the taxi meter analogy for projects and have a prominent sign board at the entrance of the project proclaiming that

The cost of one day's delay on this project is $ . . . million.

## FROM DUMPS TO TOPS

In 1984, Julian Pritchard took over as chief executive of Penley's Bank, almost a national institution in Great Britain. Established in 1762 by the Penley family, the bank had suffered from declining profitability, especially in the years following the 1973 oil crisis. In speaking with his board of directors, Pritchard said (Adair, 1986):

> Look, we are in the middle of a revolution in the City of London, not to mention new competition from American and other foreign banks. At present Penley is about third or fourth in the second division of merchant banks. My aim is to get it up into the first division within three years. That means that we have to raise our standards of technical performance, profitability, and customer service. Could I have your views please?

There is no beating about the bush here. Pritchard uses the language of the English football league standings table to express his aim in shorthand form. Even to stand still, the standards have to be much higher, requiring considerable teamwork in the context of modern banking with increasingly complex tasks. Aftercare services also needed to be upgraded, with a technical and administrative staff of high order. Despite routine and somewhat unexciting office work, it was necessary that everyone feel as though they were one of the "star players" of the bank. A formidable challenge facing the new chief executive!

Penley's began recovering from its financial doldrums over the course of the 1980s and the future looks increasingly promising into the decades ahead. The key, as Pritchard was quick to see and exploit, is to appeal to the workers as a team of professionals committed to working together for the good of the company. If a sense of teamwork and mutual dependence can be instilled in a group, whether an international bank or a project team, the executive or project manager has laid the necessary groundwork for turnaround and ultimate success.

# 12

## Team Building *

*Where we all think alike, no one thinks very much.*

—W. LIPPMAN

THE DIFFICULTIES INVOLVED in building and co-ordinating an effective team are daunting and inattention to these demands has caused many implementation efforts to fail (Wilemon and Thamhain, 1983). What often makes this set of duties so frustrating for many project managers is that they have received extensive training in the technical aspects of their jobs, but often have little knowledge of the "human" side of their responsibilities. Specifically, the efforts involved in building and maintaining cooperation among a team of disparate individuals have been and remain a considerable challenge. Many managers, uncomfortable

---

* Portions of this chapter were adapted from J. K. Pinto (1994), *Successful Information System Implementation: The Human Side,* Upper Darby, PA: Project Management Institute.

225

with these duties, often are willing to turn a blind eye to their execution, perhaps under the mistaken belief that the rest of the team are professionals willing to put the implementation effort first and bury past conflicts and animosities.

Unfortunately, as was discussed in the chapter on organizational politics, the reverse is often the case. While nominally being members of the team, usually composed of people from different functional departments or with varying degrees of technical training, individuals still retain loyalties to the concerns and interests of their own functional departments. Consequently, in addition to harboring prejudices about members of other functional groups, team members will also often view their primary responsibility as being to their own functional group, rather than the implementation team. This, then, is the challenge that is faced by project managers: how to take a disparate group of individuals with different backgrounds, attitudes, and goals and mold them into a "team" in every sense of the word.

## CHARACTERISTICS OF EFFECTIVE TEAMS

A great deal of research has investigated the qualities that effective teams possess and the degree to which those same qualities are missing from less effective groups. Although much has been written, there are a great many aspects of successful teams that these sources share in common. Briefly, the most common underlying features of successful implementation teams tend to be 1) a clear sense of mission, 2) an understanding of interdependencies, 3) cohesiveness, 4) trust among team members, and 5) a shared sense of enthusiasm. Each of these factors can be examined in turn.

1. *A clear sense of mission.* As Chapter 4 on critical success factors demonstrated, one of the key determinants of implementation success is a clear project mission. Further, that sense of mission must be mutually understood and accepted by all team members. In fact, research on the 10-critical-success-factor model of Pinto and Slevin (1987) not only demonstrated the existence of this factor,

it also showed that it was the number one predictor of project implementation success among the 10 critical factors. Team members need a purpose around which to rally. They must have some sense of the overall goals that drive the project implementation. Our experience with project implementation successes and failures has very clearly differentiated the efficacy of team performance in both the presence and absence of overall goals. A further key point is that it is not enough for the implementation team leader to know the goals; this knowledge must be shared by all concerned parties.

A common, but often tragic, mistake made by many managers, particularly those who are insecure about their authority vis à vis the project team, is to segment the team in terms of their duties, giving each member a small, well-specified task but no sense of how that activity contributes to the overall project implementation effort. Such an approach is a serious mistake for several important reasons. First, the project team is the manager's best source of troubleshooting for problems, both potential and actual. If the team is kept in the dark, members who could potentially help with the smooth development and transfer of the project by participating in other aspects of the implementation effort are not able to contribute in ways that may be most helpful. Second, team members know and resent it when they are being kept in the dark about other features of the system's implementation. Consciously or not, when project managers keep their team isolated and involved in fragmented tasks, they are sending out the signal that they either do not trust their team or do not feel it has the competence to address issues related to the overall implementation effort. Finally, from a "firefighting" perspective, it simply makes good sense for team leaders to keep their people abreast of the project's status. The more time spent defining goals and clarifying roles in the initial stages of the team's development, the less time will be needed to resolve problems and adjudicate disputes down the road.

2. *Understanding the team's interdependencies.* This characteristic refers to the level of knowledge that team members have and the importance that they attach to the interrelatedness of their

efforts. Interdependence is the degree of joint activity among team members that is required in order to bring the project to completion. In many situations, an implementation team leader may be required to form a team with members from various functional areas within the organization. For example, a typical project implementation at a large computer manufacturer could conceivably require the development of a team that included members from computer science, MIS, software engineering, diagnostics, documentation, accounting, and administration. As the concept of differentiation suggested, each of these individuals brings to the team his or her preconceived notions of the roles that everyone should play, the importance of their various contributions, and other parochial attitudes. Developing an understanding of mutual interdependencies implies developing a mutual level of appreciation for the strengths and contributions that each team member brings to the table and is a necessary precondition for team success. Team members must become aware not only of their own contributions, but also how their work fits into the overall scheme of project implementation and, further, how it relates to the other, necessary work of team members from different departments.

**3.** *Cohesiveness.* Cohesiveness, at its most basic, simply refers to the degree of mutual attraction that team members hold for each other and their task. In other words, cohesiveness is the strength of desire all members have to remain a team. In considering political behavior, we discussed the concept of WIIFM—that is, the basic question often asked by organizational members prior to volunteering their services, "What's in it for me?" In many ways, cohesiveness is built and strengthened by appealing to WIIFM in the team members. It is safe to assume that most members of the implementation team need a reason or reasons to contribute their skills and time to the successful development of the project. In other words, when asked to serve on the implementation team and *actively contribute* to the process, they will ask what's in it for them. It is important not to feel "betrayed" by any initial lack of enthusiasm on their part, as it is understandable and predictable. Part of the job of project team leader is to give the team a sense of WIIFM.

Further, it directly affects their efforts toward establishing a degree of cohesiveness and solidarity as a project team. Project managers work to build a team that is cohesive as a starting point for performing their tasks. Cohesiveness is predicated on the attraction that the group holds for each individual member. Consequently, managers need to make use of all resources at their disposal, including reward systems, recognition, performance appraisals, and any other sources of organizational reward to induce team members to devote time and energy in furthering the team's goals.

**4. *Trust.*** Trust means different things to different people. For a project team, trust can best be understood as the team's comfort level with each individual member. Further, given that comfort level, trust is manifested in the team's ability and willingness to squarely address differences of opinion, values, and attitudes and deal with them accordingly. Trust is the common denominator, without which ideas of group cohesion and appreciation become moot.

Consider the situation of any project implementation effort involving personnel from a variety of departments. Conflict and disagreements among team members are likely and perhaps even desirable. "Trust" is embodied in the belief of various team members that they are able to raise issues of conflict and disagreement without concern for retaliation or other sanctions. Because intragroup conflicts are so frequent within project teams, the manner in which they are dealt with is often a determinant of the group's ultimate success or failure. In our experience, managers make a big mistake in trying to submerge or put off disagreements and conflict, believing that they are counterproductive to group activities. In a sense, these managers are correct: No one *wants* conflicts among members of their team. On the other hand, we would argue that they are missing the larger picture, which is that these conflicts are inevitable. *The mark of managerial success lies in not dampening conflict but the manner that conflict, once having arisen, is handled.* It is through establishing trust among team members that conflicts and other disagreements over procedures or activities can be most effectively discussed and concluded with a minimal loss of time and energy. We will focus on the problem of project team conflict to a much greater degree in a future chapter.

5. *Enthusiasm.* Enthusiasm is the key to creating the energy and spirit that drive effective implementation efforts. The point that the implementation team leader needs to keep addressing is the belief among team members that they can achieve the goals set for them. This point is best illustrated by an example that one author recently witnessed. A project team leader had been tasked with installing an information system in the planning and development office of a large city government. Despite his initial enthusiasm and energy, he was becoming increasingly frustrated with his project team members, most of whom had been assigned to him without his input in the decision. His chief concern was the constant litany of "We can't do that here" that he heard every time he offered a suggestion for changing a procedure or trying anything new. One Monday morning, his team members walked into the office to the vision of the words, *"Yes we can!"* painted in letters 3 feet high across one wall of the office. (Over the weekend, the team leader had come in and done a little redecorating.) From that point on, the motto "Yes we can!" became the theme of the implementation team and had a wonderful impact on adoption success.

This story illustrates an important point: Enthusiasm starts at the top. If the team senses that the leader is only going through the motions or has little optimism for system success, that same sense of apathy is quickly communicated to the team and soon pervades all its activities. The team cannot be fooled. It senses when managers truly believe in the project and when they do not.

## STAGES IN GROUP DEVELOPMENT

The importance of molding an effective implementation team is further supported by the work of Tuchman and Jensen (1977) who argue that the group development process is a dynamic one. Groups go through several maturation stages that are often readily identifiable, are generally found across a variety of organizations, and involve groups formed for a variety of different purposes. These stages are illustrated in Table 12.1.

## *Stage 1: Forming*

The first step in group development consists of the stage where there is no group but instead a collection of individuals. Forming consists of the process or approaches used in order to mold a collection of individuals into a coherent team. Team members begin to get acquainted with each other, talk about the purposes of the group, how and what types of leadership patterns will be used, and what will be acceptable behaviors within the group. In essence, forming constitutes the "rule-setting" stage in which the ground rules for interaction (who is really in charge and how members are expected to interact) and activity (how productive members are expected to be) are established and mutually agreed to. It is important that this step be completed early in the group's

**TABLE 12.1. Stage in Group Development**

| Stage | Defining Characteristics |
|---|---|
| 1. Forming | Members get to know each other and lay the basis for project ground rules. |
| 2. Storming | Conflicts begin as members come to resist authority, demonstrate hidden agendas and prejudices. |
| 3. Norming | Members agree on operating procedures, seek to work together, developing close relationships and a commitment to the implementation process. |
| 4. Performing | Group members work together to accomplish their tasks. |
| 5. Adjourning | Group may disband either following the installation or through group member reassignments. |

life in order to eliminate ambiguities further down the implementation process. In many instances, the role of the team leader will be to create structure in these early meetings, as well as set the tone for future cooperation and positive member attitudes.

## Stage 2: Storming

Storming refers to the natural reaction to these initial ground rules as members begin to test the limits and constraints placed on their behavior. Storming is a conflict-laden stage in which the preliminary leadership patterns, reporting relationships, and norms of work and interpersonal behavior are challenged and, perhaps, reestablished. During this stage, it is likely that the team leader will begin to see a number of the group members demonstrating personal agendas (do not forget WIIFM) and prejudices. These behaviors are bound to create a level of hostility and conflict among team members that the leader must be prepared to address.

It is also important to point out that the process of storming is a very natural phase through which all groups go. One of the worst things that the leader can do when confronted with storming behavior is to attempt to suppress that behavior through ridicule ("Why don't you both start acting like adults?") or appeals to professionalism ("We are all on the same side") in the hope that members will be shamed or coaxed into dropping the conflict. This approach almost never works because it simply pushes the conflict below the surface. Consequently, team members who have not been allowed to resolve difficulties during an active storming phase may begin engaging in a campaign of guerrilla warfare against each other, constantly sniping or denigrating each other's contributions to the implementation effort. Taken to its extreme, unresolved conflict can sink the implementation process as it reduces the group's efforts to ineffectiveness.

Project team leaders should acknowledge storming behavior for what it is and treat it as a serious, but an ultimately *healthy* sign of team growth and maturation. One of the most productive behaviors that they can engage in is to provide a forum for group members to air concerns and complaints, without indulging in judgmental behavior. The team leader who acts as a problem solver and coach is likely to be far more effective in building a productive team than the manager who views all intragroup conflict with alarm and actively seeks to suppress it in the mistaken hope that if ignored, it will simply go away.

## *Stage 3: Norming*

A norm is most often defined as an unwritten rule of behavior. Norming behavior in a group implies that the team members are establishing mutually agreed to practices and attitudes. Norms serve to help the team determine how it should make decisions, how often it should meet, the degree of openness and trust that team members will exhibit toward each other, and how conflicts will be resolved. Research has shown that it is during the norming stage that the cohesiveness of the group grows to its highest level. Close relationships develop, a sense of mutual concern and appreciation emerge, and feelings of camaraderie and shared responsibility are in evidence. The norming stage establishes the playing field on which the actual work of the team will commence.

## *Stage 4: Performing*

It is during the performing stage that the actual "work" of the implementation team is performed—that is, the implementation plan is executed. It is only when the first three phases have been properly dealt with that the team will have reached the level of maturity and confidence to effectively perform its duties. One of the most common mistakes that occurs among novice project managers is to push the team immediately into the work of the implementation plan. Typically, this approach consists of holding an initial meeting to get acquainted, parceling out the work, and essentially telling team members to get started with their piece of the process. The reason that this approach, although quite erroneous, is so often used is the impatience of top management and the team leader to be "doing something." The real fear that these project managers exhibit is based on their expectation of retribution from top management and is articulated by the belief that top management expects results. Naturally, this assumption is correct, to a degree. However, bear in mind that what top management is expecting is a successfully developed and implemented project. Their rightful concern is with results, not process. A more seasoned manager, while taking the time to develop a productive implementation team, is also communicating with top management to keep them informed on the progress of team development as part of project implementation. As Graham (1992) so aptly stated:

*It is only when top management knows nothing of what a manager is doing that they assume the manager is doing nothing.*

## Stage 5: Adjourning

Adjourning recognizes the fact that implementation does not last forever. At some point, the project has been developed and transferred to its clients and the team is disbanded to return to its other functional duties within the organization. In some cases, the group may downsize slowly and deliberately; for example, as various elements of the project come on-line, a team that contains a cost accountant may no longer require that individual's services and he or she will be reassigned. In other circumstances, the team will complete its tasks and be disbanded completely. In either case, it is important to remember that during the final stages of the implementation process, group members are likely to be exhibiting some concern about their future: where will they be reassigned and what their new duties will be. Project managers should be sensitive to the real concerns felt by team members and, when possible, help to smooth the transition from the old team to new assignments.

In addition to presenting the stages in group development, we have also attempted to describe some of the leadership duties for project managers that are a necessary part of their jobs. The "moral" of this message for project managers is to pay particular attention to the stage that the implementation team is currently addressing and tailor leadership behaviors to facilitate the attainment of that stage. For example, during the early stages of forming and storming, project managers can be most effective when they play the dual roles of developing task assignments and nurturing and influencing interpersonal relationships. In other words, they need to foster a combination of work and people skills as they set the agenda for the implementation effort within the context of the human interactions that are bound to lead to conflict and disagreement. On the other hand, later in the team's implementation efforts, the leader can begin to develop a more exclusively task-oriented style. If you assume that the leader has spent adequate time developing the team, by the performing stage, he or she can devote time almost entirely to creating a work-related atmosphere. Finally, in the adjourning stage of the project, leaders should again be aware of the end in sight and use their people skills as the implementation project starts to "ramp down" toward completion. It goes without saying that this combination of people and task skills is difficult to develop. Further, it is even more difficult, particularly for new project managers, to know when to differentially employ them. Nevertheless, the mark of successful team leaders is often their acknowledgment that the team development process is dynamic; their leadership style can and *must* change at appropriate points to address the relevant issues that surface. These issues are discussed in detail in Chapter 8.

## DETERMINANTS OF CROSS-FUNCTIONAL COOPERATION

Throughout this book, we have painted a picture in which many project implementation teams are staffed by a skilled but disparate group of organizational members. Because these members come from a variety of different backgrounds and, further, are inculcated with certain beliefs and value sets once they join a functional department, the challenge of creating a viable, cohesive team out of these different individuals is often daunting. So far in this chapter, we have examined the characteristics of effective teams, as well as addressing how team attitudes and behaviors change across various, identifiable stages in group maturation. However, we have not yet examined the basic concern of many project managers: Exactly how does one begin to create cohesion, trust, enthusiasm, and other characteristics of winning teams? In other words, what are some of the tactics that managers can employ to encourage the type of effective team development that will aid in project implementation? The purpose of this section is to report on some of the factors under a project manager's control that can help foster cross-functional cooperation among project team members.

The factors discussed below were uncovered as part of a recent research project investigating the causes of cross-functional cooperation on project teams (Pinto, Pinto, and Prescott, 1993). The study affirmed the importance of a set of factors that can help encourage cross-functional cooperation and further offered some managerial implications that will be discussed below (see Figure 12.1).

• *Superordinate goals.* Every organization and, indeed, every manager has more than one goal that guides activities and actions. Often, project managers are faced with trying to resolve situations in which implementation team members from different functional areas perceive conflicting goals for an implementation effort. For example, consider the implementation of MIS technology in a local government. For this project, accounting's primary goal is to minimize cost, whereas engineering's primary goal is to enlarge the range of applications in the hope of increasing client satisfaction and, therefore, use of the system. In order for this implementation effort to be successful, one functional area may be required to sacrifice, or at least compromise, its primary goals. Aware of these areas of potential cross-functional conflict, managers charged with the responsibility for implementation success are continually looking for ways of developing goals that increase, rather than detract from, cross-functional cooperation.

A superordinate goal refers to an overall goal or purpose that

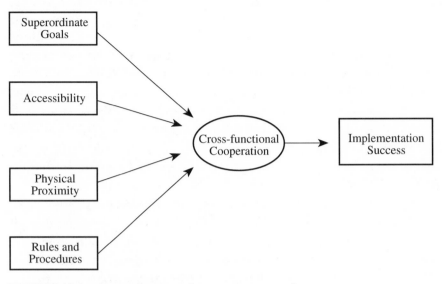

FIGURE 12.1. Antecedents and consequences of
cross-functional cooperation.

is important to all functional groups involved, but whose attainment requires the resources and efforts of more than one group
(Sherif, 1958). The superordinate goal is an addition to, not a re-
placement for, other goals the functional groups may have. The
premise is that when project team members from different functional areas share an overall goal or common purpose, they tend
to cooperate toward this end. To illustrate, let us return to the
example of a project to implement MIS in a local government. A
superordinate goal for this project team may be "to develop a
high-quality, user-friendly, and generally useful MIS that will enhance the operations of various city departments and agencies."
This overall goal attempts to enhance, or pull together, some of
the diverse function-specific goals for cost-effectiveness, schedule
adherence, quality, and innovation. It provides a central objective
or an overriding goal toward which the entire project team can
strive.

• *Rules and Procedures.* Rules and procedures are central to
any discussion of cross-functional cooperation because they offer

a means for coordinating or integrating activities that involve several functional units (Galbraith, 1977). For years, organizations have relied on standard operating procedures to link together the activities of organizational members. Rules and procedures have been used to assign duties, evaluate performance, solve conflicts, and so on. They can be used to address formalized rules and procedures established by the organization for the performance of the implementation process, as well as project-specific rules and procedures developed by the project team to facilitate its operations.

In some instances, project teams do not have the luxury of relying on established rules and procedures to assist them with their tasks. Therefore, they often must create their own rules and procedures to facilitate the progress of the project. Organizational rules and procedures are defined as formalized rules and procedures established by the organization that mandated or controlled the activities of the project team in terms of team membership, task assignment, and performance evaluation. Project team rules and procedures, on the other hand, refer to the degree to which the project team must establish its own rules and procedures to facilitate the progress of the project. It is likely that greater levels of cross-functional cooperation will result from the establishment of these rules and procedures.

• *Physical proximity.* Both the literature and common observations seem to suggest that individuals are more likely to interact and communicate with others when the physical characteristics of buildings or settings encourage them to do so (Davis, 1984). For example, the sheer size or spatial layout of a building can affect working relationships. In a small building or when a work group is clustered on the same floor, relationships tend to be more intimate since people are in close physical proximity to each other. As people spread out along corridors or in different buildings, interactions may become less frequent and/or less spontaneous. In these situations, it is harder for employees to interact with members of either their own department or other departments.

Many companies seriously consider the potential effects of

physical proximity on project team cooperation. In fact, some project organizations relocate personnel who are working together on a project to the same office or floor. These organizations contend that when individuals work near each other, they are more likely to communicate and, ultimately, cooperate with each other.

- *Accessibility.* Although physical proximity is important to the study of cross-functional cooperation, another factor—accessibility—appears to be an equally important predictor of the phenomenon. Separate from the issue of physical proximity, additional factors can inhibit the amount of interaction that occurs between organizational members, such as an individual's schedule, position in an organization, or out-of-office commitments (Peters, 1986). These factors often affect accessibility among organizational members.

For example, consider a public-sector organization in which a member of the engineering department is physically located near a member of the city census department. Although these individuals are in close proximity to one another, they may rarely interact because of different work schedules, varied duties and priorities, and commitment to their own agendas. These factors often create a perception of "inaccessibility" among the individuals involved. Accessibility is defined as an individual's perception of his or her ability to approach, communicate, or interact with another organizational member.

## IMPLICATIONS FOR PROJECT MANAGERS

The results of Pinto, Pinto, and Prescott's (1993) research study suggest some pragmatic implications for project managers who are interested in increasing cooperation among project team members.

1. *Cooperation is a vital element in implementation success.* Cross-functional cooperation can truly result in higher levels of project implementation performance. In other words, to follow the research model in Figure 12.1, Pinto, Pinto, and Prescott found

strong support for the link between cross-functional cooperation and successful project outcomes. Although this result should not be surprising to most project managers, the strength of the relationship between cooperation and implementation success has important implications. It suggests, for example, that because cooperation is so important for project success, factors that facilitate cross-functional cooperation will also greatly enhance the likelihood of successful project implementation. In other words, cooperation is more than an element in project success; it is often the key link in helping mangers develop a project team that is both capable and motivated to successfully develop and implement the project.

**2. Superordinate goals are a strong predictor of cross-functional cooperation.** Pinto, Pinto, and Prescott's study clearly demonstrated the importance of superordinate goals for attaining cross-functional cooperation among project team members. In fact, superordinate goals were the strongest individual predictor of cooperation, suggesting that their importance for project success cannot be overestimated. The implications for project managers reinforce the necessity of establishing overriding goals, goals toward which the entire implementation team as a whole must work. Superordinate goals are only useful if they require the combined efforts of different members of the project team. If any one individual or subgroup can independently attain the goals, they are not helpful in fostering cooperation. Further, these goals need to be clearly specified and laid out. Excessively vague goals can result in increased confusion, rather than clarity. Finally, the project manager needs to continually reinforce the pursuit of these goals.

It is important, however, to note that superordinate goals are not intended as a substitute for other project goals. By their definition, superordinate goals are overriding and are intended to complement, rather than replace, other specific project team goals. Consequently, project team members from different functional areas may still hold some of their own specific departmental goals, while also being committed to the overall project or common goal of the project.

**3. Set up policies to ensure that team members remain accessible to each other.** An important way to promote cooperation among members of the project team is to ensure that they remain accessible to each other, both during and outside of their regular project duties. Accessibility was previously defined as an individual's perception of his or her ability or liberty to approach or communicate with another organizational member. A variety of methods can be used to encourage such accessibility, including establishing regular project meetings, setting up formal channels of communication, and encouraging informal get-togethers, for example, in the hall, over coffee, and at lunch. It is important that team leaders promote an atmosphere in which team members feel they can approach or get in contact with other team members outside of formally developed hierarchical channels or project meetings.

One suggestion for promoting an atmosphere of accessibility surfaced in a followup interview with a project manager. The project manager, in speaking to one of the authors, commented on the need to create a "priority status" for the project:

> "I try to convey a sense of urgency about this project to my team members. I want them to give this project 'priority status.' When something is a priority, then they will find the time necessary to devote to it."

**4. Physical proximity is an important "supplemental" factor for achieving cooperation.** The physical proximity factor was also found to have an important influence on achieving cooperation. These results suggest that in addition to fostering an atmosphere of accessibility, project managers may wish, under some circumstances, to consider relocating team members to improve cooperation. The importance of physical proximity for cooperation stems from the contention that when individuals work near each other they are more likely to interact, communicate, and cooperate with each other. Research on the design of the engineering offices at Corning Glass provides support for this claim. As one individual noted (Leibson, 1981):

Engineers get more than 80 percent of their ideas through direct, face-to-face contact with their peers. They will not travel more than 100 feet from their desks to exchange ideas . . . and they hate to use the telephone to seek information.

**5. *Work to establish standard operating rules and procedures for the project team.*** An additional implication reemphasizes the importance of establishing standardized rules and operating procedures for new system implementation. It has been found that rules and procedures can be quite useful in mandating, or determining, exactly how members of different departments and functional areas are required to interact with other project team members. If managers set up standardized rules of behavior, they can better regulate and facilitate the degree and quality of cross-functional cooperation. To illustrate, consider a policy instituted by one project manager that stated, "All major changes to the project, either scheduling, budgetary, or technical, will require input from and active involvement of project team representatives from each functional department." When adequately enforced, this type of operating procedure is a very simple, yet effective method for promoting cross-functional cooperation.

Because of the relative simplicity of rules and procedures as a tool for encouraging cross-functional cooperation, some organizations tend to overrely on this method while ignoring other techniques that have been discussed, such as project member accessibility, physical proximity, or the creation of superordinate goals. It should be noted that, although it is true that each of these factors has been found to lead to enhanced cross-functional cooperation, we are not suggesting that project managers choose the technique, or factor, that is most available or easiest to implement. To truly create and maintain an atmosphere in which cross-functional cooperation can occur on the project team, it is highly advisable to make use of a combination of all the aforementioned factors, including superordinate goals, accessibility, and rules and procedures. Used individually, they may each be helpful to the project manager. Used in conjunction with each other, they represent a significantly more powerful tool for creating a cooperative business climate and, consequently, aiding in project success.

## CONCLUSIONS

The purpose of this chapter has been to discuss some of the important issues in developing and maintaining effective implementation teams. Team building and development is an important and ongoing challenge for project managers because, although often time-consuming, it can reap large dividends. This chapter has developed a basis for understanding the factors that characterize successful teams. Further, the various stages of team development have been argued to be not only an important, but healthy sign of implementation team performance. Finally, in an attempt to offer some usable advice to project managers, this chapter concluded with some practical advice on promoting cross-functional cooperation among team members by discussing the results of a recent study that investigated this phenomenon.

Both experience as well as research and anecdotal evidence have long pointed to the fact that the project implementation process is difficult and complex. Many issues and factors go into creating a project team atmosphere that is conducive to successful project implementation. Among the most important elements to be considered are those of team development and cooperation among project team members, particularly when the implementation team is composed of members from various functional departments. It is our hope that in this chapter, some practical approaches to fostering better cross-functional cooperation have been suggested to managers.

# 13

## Project Management and Conflict

*Madness is the exception in individuals but the rule in groups.*

—Nietzsche

PROJECT MANAGERS FACE conflict as part of their daily life from a number of sources, both internal to the project team itself and external, in dealing with other project stakeholders (Posner, 1986; Thamhain and Wilemon, 1975, 1977). Indeed, one study estimated that the average manager spends over 20% of his or her time dealing with conflict (Thomas and Schmidt, 1976). Most project managers would likely suggest that the 20% figure understates the case! Consequently, because so much of a project manager's time is taken up with active conflict and its residual aftermath, it is important that we examine this natural process within the project management context.

This chapter is intended to more formally explore the process of conflict, examining the various sources of conflict for project teams and managers, developing a model of conflict behavior, and fostering an understanding of some of the most common methods for deescalating conflict. We will argue that many conflicts develop out of a basic lack of or unwillingness to understand another party's position. Further, as we will show, once conflict does occur, either within or outside the project team boundaries, if project managers are aware of the various action alternatives they can employ, there is a real opportunity to not only defuse conflict, but also learn valuable lessons from the conflict episode. Learning these lessons well can go a long way toward making project managers better at their job.

## WHAT IS CONFLICT?

Conflict is best defined as the process that begins when one party perceives that one or more others have frustrated or are about to frustrate a major concern of theirs (Thomas, 1992; Pondy, 1968). This definition contains two important elements. First, it suggests that conflict is not a "state" per se, but a process. As such, it has a dynamic aspect that is very important. Conflicts evolve (Thamhain and Wilemon, 1975). Further, the one-time causes of a conflict may change over time; that is, the reasons why two individuals or groups developed a conflict initially may no longer have any validity. However, because the conflict state is dynamic and evolving, once a conflict *has* occurred, the reasons behind it may no longer matter. The process of conflict has important ramifications that we will explore in greater detail later in this chapter.

The second important element in our definition is that conflict is perceptual in nature. In other words, it does not ultimately matter whether or not one party has truly frustrated another party. The important thing is that the one party *perceives* that state or event to have occurred. Such a perception is enough, because for the first party, the perception of frustration is sufficient to promote a conflict.

## SOURCES OF CONFLICT

There are an enormous number of potential sources of conflict. Some of the most common sources include the competition for scarce resources, violations of group or organizational norms, disagreements over goals or the means to achieve those goals, personal slights and threats to job security, long-held biases and prejudices, and so forth. Many of the sources of conflict arise out of the position of managers or the nature of their work. On the other hand, an equally compelling set of causes stems from the individuals themselves; that is, their own psychological processes can contribute to the level and amount of conflict within an organization. One useful method for determining the causes of conflict is to consider the organizational and interpersonal causes of conflict.

Some of the most common organizational causes of conflict include:

- Reward systems

- Scarce resources

- Uncertainty over lines of authority

- Differentiation

Reward systems refer to the fact that in some organizations competitive reward systems are in place that pit one group or functional department against another. For example, when functional managers are evaluated on the performance of their subordinates within the department, they are loath to allow their best workers to become involved in project work for any length of time. The organization may have unwittingly created a state in which managers perceive that either the project teams *or* the departments will be rewarded for superior performance. In such cases, they will naturally retain their best people for functional duties and offer their less desirable subordinates for project team work. The project managers, on the other hand, will also perceive competition between their projects and the functional departments and develop a strong sense of animosity toward functional managers who they perceive, with some justification, are placing their own interests above those of the organization.

We have talked about the impact of scarce resources at length in Chapter 3 on power and project politics. As you will recall, because organizations are characterized by scarce resources sought by many different groups, the struggle to gain these resources is a prime source of organizational conflict. As long as scarce resources are the natural state within organizations, groups will be in conflict as they seek to bargain and negotiate to gain an advantage in their distribution.

Uncertainty over lines of authority essentially asks the tongue in cheek question, "Who's in charge around here?" In the project environment, it is easy to see how this problem can be badly exacerbated due to the essential ambiguity that exists in terms of formal channels of authority. Project managers and their teams sit "outside" the formal organizational hierarchy in many organizations. As a result, they find themselves in the uniquely fragile position of having a great deal of autonomy but also responsibility to the functional department heads who provide the personnel for the team. For example, when a project team member from R&D is given orders by her functional manager that subsume or directly contradict directives from the project manager, she is placed in the dilemma of having to find (if possible) a middle ground between two nominal authority figures. In many cases, project managers do not have the authority to complete performance evaluations of their team members—the functional department retains that control. In such situations, the team member from R&D, facing role conflict brought on by this uncertainty over lines of authority, will most likely do the expedient thing and obey her functional managers because of their power in terms of eventual performance appraisal.

The final source of organizational conflict, differentiation, was also discussed at length in Chapter 3. Briefly, differentiation suggests that as individuals join an organization within some functional specialty, they begin to adopt the attitudes and outlook of that functional group. For example, a member of the finance department, when asked his or her opinion of marketing, might reply, "All they ever do is travel around and spend money. They're a bunch of cowboys who would give away the store if they had to." Marketing's response would follow along the lines of, "Finance is just a group of bean-counters who don't understand that the company is only as successful as it can sell its products. They're so hung up on their margins, they don't know what goes on in the real world." Now the important point in both of these views is that, within their narrow frames of reference, they are essentially correct: Marketing is interested primarily in just *making sales* and finance is devoted to *maintaining high margins.* However, these opinions are by no means completely true and simply reflect the underlying attitudes and prejudices of members of both functional departments. The more profound the differentiation within an organization, the greater the likelihood of individuals and groups dividing up into "us" versus "them" encampments that continue to promote and provoke conflict.

In addition to these organizational causes of conflict, we need to also consider some of the salient interpersonal causes. Although by no means a comprehensive list, among these interpersonal sources of conflict are included:

- Faulty attributions

- Faulty communication

- Grudges and prejudices

Faulty attributions refers to our misconceptions of the reasons behind another's behavior. When people perceive that their interests have been thwarted by another individual or group, they typically try to determine why the other party has acted as it did. In making attributions about another's actions, we wish to determine if their motives are based on personal malevolence, hidden agendas, and so forth. For example, when one member of a project team has his or her wishes frustrated, it is common to perceive the motives behind the other party's actions in terms of the most convenient causes. In other words, rather than acknowledge the fact that reasonable people may differ in their opinions, it may be more convenient for the frustrated person to assume that the other is provoking a conflict for personal reasons: "He just doesn't like me." This attribution is convenient for an obvious and psychologically "safe" reason; if we assume that the other person disagrees with us for valid reasons, it implies a flaw in our position. Many individuals do not have the strength of ego to acknowledge and accept objective disagreement, preferring to couch their frustration in personal terms.

A second and very common interpersonal cause of conflict stems from faulty communication. Faulty communication implies the potential for two mistakes: communicating in ways that are ambiguous and lead to different interpretations, thus causing a resulting conflict, and unintentionally communicating in ways that annoy or anger other parties. Lack of clarity can send out mixed signals: the message the sender intended to communicate and that which was received and interpreted by the receiver. Consequently, the project manager may be surprised and annoyed by the work of a subordinate who genuinely thought he or she was adhering to the project manager's desires. Likewise, project managers often engage in criticism in the hopes of correcting and improving project team member performance. Unfortunately, what the project manager may consider to be harmless, constructive criticism may come across as a destructive, unfair critique if the information is not communicated accurately and effectively.

The final cause of interpersonal conflict refers to the personal grudges and prejudices that each of us brings to any work situation. These attitudes arise as the result of long-term experiences or lessons taught at some point in the past. Often unconsciously held, we may be unaware that we nurture these attitudes and can experience a genuine sense of affront when we are challenged or accused of holding biases. Nevertheless, these grudges or prejudices, whether they are held against another race, sex, or functional department, have a seriously debilitating effect on our ability to work with others in a purposeful team and can ruin any chance at project team cohesion and subsequent project performance.

## STEPS IN THE CONFLICT PROCESS

Regardless of the triggering cause, once conflicts, either intra- or inter-group, have begun, they often follow a rather well-defined pattern that we can begin to explore. This pattern is highly useful for project managers because it serves as a general template, offering conflict dynamics and patterns for project managers to recognize. If they are able to observe the nature of the conflict process as it progresses, they will be in a better position to search for methods to defuse and minimize the conflict or channel its energies into more constructive pastimes. In this section, we will examine the stages in the conflict process and offer some suggestions to project managers on how to most effectively deal with the conflict dynamics that often emerge at these stages.

Typically, there are five recognizable stages in the conflict process, including

- Frustration

- Conceptualization

- Orientation

- Interaction

- Outcome

**1. *Frustration.*** The first step in any conflict process refers to the triggering event that set one or more people at odds. As we have suggested in our original definition of conflict, this event is referred to as perceived frustration. Frustration comes in many forms and approaches. Earlier, we identified several sources of frustration and possible conflict and classified them into two categories: organizational and interpersonal. The important point to remember is that frustrations occur in everyone's life on a daily basis. Therefore, there must be some reason why we choose to respond to certain frustrations in a confrontational manner rather than others. Often, this choice is predicated on our perception of how important the issue is to us. For example, although under normal circumstances a traffic jam would be a source of frustration, we would rarely deem it serious enough to actively confront the city's administration over the issue. On the other hand, in situations that involve slights to status, promotion possibilities, or public image, we tend to react to frustrations more directly. It is these situations, in which we attach a level of importance to the frustrated goal, that we are liable to respond in an aggressive and competitive manner.

**2. *Conceptualization.*** Conceptualization means defining the issues underlying the source of conflict. When we analyze why a conflict is occurring between ourselves and our team or with another party, an interesting psychological process begins to occur: We see the conflict through the lens of egocentricity. Egocentricity refers to the predilection of most people to define issues solely in terms of their own concerns. In other words, when confronted with a situation in which we feel frustrated by another individual, we respond in a way that does not recognize the other party's perspective. That is, we perceive that the other person is thwarting us, without considering her point of view or why he is acting in a particular way.

The clear alternative to analyzing frustration in terms of egocentricity is to begin to develop a level of insight into the other party's concerns. There is an old saying that admonishes us to never judge another person unless we have walked a mile in their shoes. The implication of this is that until we are able to understand another person's motives, intent, and past experiences, we cannot objectively address the nature of the conflict episode. Rather, we will continue to be inclined to simply respond with an egocentric approach that only further solidifies the lines that separate the rival party's positions. Attempting to gain this insight into the underlying issues involves refusing to capitulate to the initial sense of frustration with another party and searching for reasons *why* that person or group operates the way it does. It is this search for the answer to "why" that can defuse many conflicts before they escalate. It requires the project manager or team member to be able to forgo the appeals of egocentricity in order to try and analyze the problem from the other party's perspective. Depending on the nature and degree of the conflict, this rational objectivity can be very difficult, but it is an activity well worth the effort. If we are able to halt conflicts at this stage, many of the problems that will continually plague the project team throughout the remainder of project development can be halted before they become too destructive.

**3.  *Orientation.*** Orientation refers to the outlook we begin to adopt once a conflict episode continues to escalate. Thomas (1992) and Ruble and Thomas (1976) have argued that conflict orientation generally involves operating along two separate dimensions of concern: 1) the degree to which one party seeks to satisfy its own concerns, and 2) the degree to which a party seeks to satisfy the other person's concerns. Figure 13.1 shows Ruble and Thomas' (1976) conceptualization of this two-dimensional model of conflict orientation. They argue that we make implicit trade-offs in our willingness to seek our own gains versus our willingness to satisfy the other party to the conflict. They further posit that the underlying motive driving these two dimensions is our desire on one hand to be assertive and gain maximum advantage and on the other hand to be cooperative with the other party in order to maintain satisfactory relationships (Kilmann and Thomas, 1977).

Within this two-dimensional model of conflict orientation and behavior, Thomas suggests that five distinct and recognizable types of conflict behavior are potentially possible. Figure 13.2 shows each of the five conflict-handling styles. The decision of which type of behavior to engage in resides solely with the party who is conceptualizing the nature and reasons for the conflict. The five conflict-handling styles are competing, accommodating, avoiding, compromising, and collaborating.

*Competing* behavior is basically assertive and uncooperative. Someone adopting a competing style has no regard for satisfying the other party's concerns, viewing conflict as a win–lose proposition in which he or she has resolved not to lose. Competing behavior is often used by insecure or power-hungry people who will use

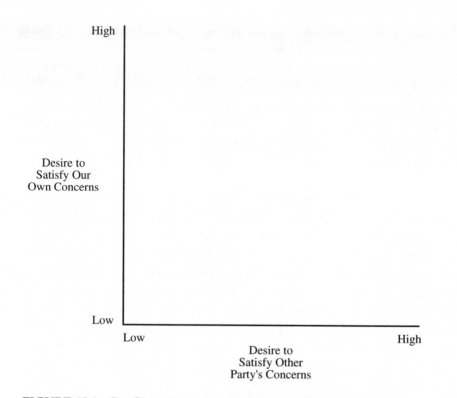

FIGURE 13.1.  Conflict orientation (Ruble and Thomas, 1976).

every technique or trick to get their way. It is ironic to find that individuals who are high on the competing dimension have great difficulty in operating under any other style, no matter what the nature of the conflict. For example, highly competitive people take issues of resource allocation or the results of a game of gin rummy with the same degree of intensity. They often cannot distinguish between "important" and "unimportant" conflicts; indeed, the very creation of a concept such as an unimportant conflict is alien to their way of thinking.

At the opposite extreme from competing behavior is the *accommodating* style. As Figure 13.2 shows, accommodators enter conflicts from the perspective of seeking to first satisfy the other party's concerns. Accommodators foster nonassertive and cooperative styles, usually in an effort to be true "team players." They

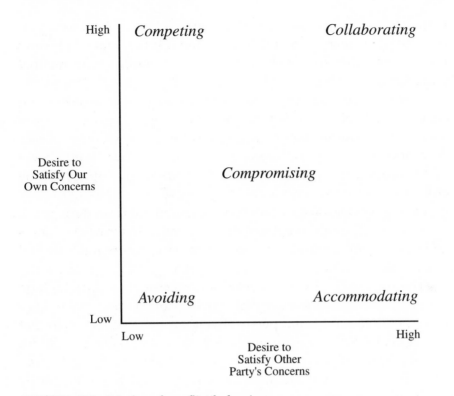

FIGURE 13.2. Modes of conflict behavior.

are quick to look for ways to either defuse a situation or allow the other party to win. The accommodating style can be very useful when the issue of concern is seen as much more important for the other side than the accommodator. It may serve as an important goodwill gesture or a basis for "storing up" favors that the manager may need at a later point. The obvious problem with overuse of the accommodating style is that it tends to create passivity in a project manager, a state that can deprive subordinates or peers of useful viewpoints and contributions.

The *avoiding* style is one that is at the same time unassertive and uncooperative. Individuals who rely on the avoiding style manifest no desire to either satisfy their own concerns or those of the other party to the conflict. Avoiding tends to be an effective method for sidestepping a conflict that one party does not seek. It is the style of organizational diplomats and politicians who perceive that they can accomplish much more if they operate behind the scenes rather than out in the open, in conflict with another party.

*Compromising* behavior falls somewhere between assertive and cooperative behavior. It represents a desire by one party to satisfy some of their concerns and a willingness to give in on other points. A compromiser sees conflict as a win–lose situation, but believes that in order to get something, it is necessary to give up something else. A compromising style tacitly acknowledges the importance of making concessions in order to gain something from the conflict. As a result, although compromisers see conflict in terms of winners and losers, they generally feel that each party can win a little and lose a little.

The final style of conflict behavior, *collaborating,* rates high on both assertiveness and cooperativeness. Collaborators view conflict from a very different perspective than most managers in that they reject the win–lose argument that most of us believe underlies conflict. They always seek a win–win solution to conflict situations. In order to achieve such an outcome, collaborators readily work with the other party to see if it is possible to find a solution that fully satisfies both sides. This sort of joint problem solving requires a great deal of flexibility, creativity, and precise communication between the parties to the conflict.

A collaborating style is usually necessary when the issue at hand is simply too important to be solved with a compromising approach. For example, in situations in which project leaders are seeking to make major product specification changes or determine resource allocation, they may be faced with two or more distinct alternatives. Rather than vainly attempt to satisfy these disparate viewpoints by offering a compromise that will please no one and do nothing to further the development of the project, these managers may seek to hold a series of project team meetings in order to get all positions on the table where they can be addressed in a problem-solving session. The results of this problem-solving meeting may be a new strategic focus for the project with new tasks and responsibilities for each team member. In this example, the problem underlying the conflict could not be ignored. Further, simply allowing one team member to dominate the others with a competing style could potentially result in an incorrect decision. The best alternative for the project manager is to seek, in active collaboration with the project team, a solution that offers a win–win alternative.

Because no one conflict-handling style is appropriate in every situation, insightful project managers will seek to develop flexibility in their approaches in dealing with conflicts, either their own or those of team members within the group. The benefits of a collaborative style are that, unlike competing or avoiding, it emphasizes group relationships. That is, using this style offers a method for enhancing communication and creative problem solving. In doing so, a collaborating approach can bring a team in conflict closer together, rather than driving them farther apart by solidifying the conflict situation.

**4. Interaction.** Once a conflict episode escalates, a number of different exchanges begin to occur between the two parties in conflict. This exchange process is referred to as the conflict interaction step. Although there are many potential actions that conflicting parties can take during this process, we will focus on some of the more common dynamics of group conflict during the interaction stage.

One common occurrence that usually takes place early in the conflict process is reinforcement through stereotyping. When we perceive that another party is frustrating a goal we value, we may respond by attributing his or her intransigence to convenient (and often incorrect) motives. For example, in a budgeting disagreement with the project cost accountant, a project manager may react by saying, "What can you expect from a group of unimaginative bean-counters?" This reaction, although common, underscores the potential for reinforcing the disagreement by creating a self-serving stereotype of the other party. Under this process, all opponents are selfish, willfully ignorant, or malicious because these attributions allow us to hold the high ground in the dispute. At the same time, we attribute honorable motives to our own behavior.

Through stereotyping other cultures, races, or the opposite sex, we create a convenient cause for our discontent without being forced to reexamine our own motives as a potential contributing cause of the conflict. The irony is that, as the name of this process suggests, when we initially perceive ourselves in a conflict, rather than attempting to defuse or suppress this tension, our first inclination is to reinforce the conflict, making it that much more difficult to correct.

The second process that often occurs during the interaction phase is that conflict begins to heighten feelings of positive identification with our own group. There is a natural tendency, when we perceive ourselves in conflict with an external stakeholder, to close ranks and become more single-minded in our attitudes and dispositions. As a result of that process, it is very common for groups to develop a superiority complex vis à vis the other group. This superiority complex feeds our natural inclinations to regard our own position as sacrosanct and justified as opposed to our "devious" and "maliciously inclined" opponents.

On a national level, this positive identification dynamic occurs quite frequently. To cite a recent historical example, in the early 1980s, just prior to the Falkland War between Great Britain and Argentina, the country of Argentina was in a state of tremendous political turmoil. Crowds in Buenos Aires and other large cities continually protested the right-wing rule of the military junta that controlled the government—right up until Argentina invaded the Falklands, creating a convenient external foe in the form of Great Britain. Literally overnight, the crowds that had been demonstrating against the government outside the Casa Rosada in downtown Buenos Aires became vast throngs supporting the actions of their leaders. This is another example of the positive identification that frequently occurs in the face of external conflict.

A final dynamic during intervention refers to our exaggerating the positive nature of our own group and its members, while also seeking to distort and exaggerate differences between our group and the opponent. In other words, once we find ourselves in a conflict situation, there is a real pressure to conform to group norms, swallow internal differences in the face of outside aggression, and deny any degree of similarity with members of the opposing group. This separation serves to further solidify differences that prevent easy solutions to conflicts because they make it much harder for groups to seek common ground. In fact, we actively avoid the potential for identifying commonalties, preferring to focus on the differences and reasons why we are justified in maintaining our beliefs.

**5. *Outcome*.** The final step in the conflict process is the outcome, during which time the two parties have come to some agreement in terms of resolving the conflict. The possible methods that were used to resolve the disagreement will be discussed in more detail below. For our purposes, it is important to bear in mind that no matter what the outcome—agreement, disagreement, or tacit agreement to let the issue drop—there will be residual emotions and ill will from the process. It seems an obvious point but it bears repeating that people simply do not forgive and immediately forget conflict episodes, particularly when the issues were significant or the emotional commitment of either party brought the conflict to a personal level. Project managers must be cognizant of the likely detritus of conflict. Playing down or smoothing over the problem when it has been "resolved" may be overly simplistic and ignores the potential for further tensions.

A final point about the outcome stage is to remember the difference between short- and long-term outcomes. There is a familiar concept known as winning the battle and losing the war. When a manager wins a conflict, there is a strong potential for the other party to remember these experiences and look for retribution opportunities. This result is particularly true in the case of a manager who is prone to rely solely on the competing style in dealing with conflicts. As we had suggested, a competing approach that is based on assertiveness and unconcern for the other party is likely to create bad emotional feelings on the part of the other party. Whether that party wins or loses the conflict, he or she is likely to remember the event and seek ways to repay the other group (Robbins, 1978).

## METHODS FOR RESOLVING CONFLICT

A number of methods for resolving inter- and intragroup conflict are at the project manager's disposal. Before a decision is made about what approach will be employed, it is paramount that project managers consider a number of relevant issues pertaining to the conflict (Tjosvold, 1993). For example, will the project manager's siding with one party to the dispute alienate the other person? Is the conflict professional or personal in nature? Does any sort of intervention have to occur or can team members resolve the issue on their own? Does the project manager have the time and inclination to mediate the dispute? All these questions play an important role in determining how to approach a conflict situation. We suggest that project managers learn to develop flexibility in dealing with conflict, assessing and prioritizing the situations in which it is appropriate to intervene and those in which the sounder course is to adopt a neutral style.

As Table 13.1 demonstrates, we find it helpful to categorize possible conflict resolution methods in terms of three fundamental philosophies: avoidance, defusion, and confrontation. Each approach has its benefits and drawbacks and, more important, each may be an appropriate response under certain circumstances. Let us consider the different approaches in turn.

Avoidance techniques suggest that the project manager ignore the causes of the conflict and allow it to continue under controlled circumstances. Avoidance is a conflict-handling approach that requires the project manager to adopt a position of neutrality and, indeed, passivity, while the parties to the conflict work out their differences on their own. One simple example of avoidance is *non-attention*. Nonattention suggests that the project manager simply look the other way and allow the parties in conflict to come to their own resolution without the project manager stepping in. Mark McCormack (1989), in his highly entertaining work, *What They Still Don't Teach You at Harvard Business School*, points to a situation in which two of his vice-presidents had developed an antagonism based on personal dislike rather than professional reasons. He sug-

**TABLE 13.1. Methods for Resolving Conflict**

*Avoidance*
- Nonattention
- Physical separation
- Limited interaction

*Defusion*
- Smoothing
- Compromise

*Confrontation*
- Problem solving

gests that when conflict is of a personal and emotionally charged nature, a prudent manager will often refuse to intervene, sending signals that this sort of interaction is unacceptable but otherwise expecting the warring parties to work out their differences.

Other examples of avoidance techniques include *physical separation* and *limited interaction.* These approaches are similar in that they essentially suggest that project managers with subordinates in conflict should find ways to keep their people out of each other's way. When they must get together, for project status meetings, the project team leader plays the role of referee, making sure that the conflict is kept at bay throughout the course of the meeting. Needless to say, these techniques, along with nonattention, suggest that the project manager refrain from seeking the source of the conflict and instead pay attention to ensuring that the fallout from subordinate conflict does not impact on the project's development. This may be a forlorn hope, however, as frequent or intense conflict can force team members to expend a tremendous amount of energy in worthless pursuits. Consequently, a project manager's decision to adopt an avoidance tactic in the face of subordinate conflict should be made with due consideration of the implications of allowing the conflict to continue. Such a decision should not simply be the result of the project manager's distaste for conflict intervention or inherent laziness.

The second set of conflict resolution techniques are called defusion approaches. These tactics are based on the desire to buy time until both parties have a chance to cool down and deal with the conflict in a more "rational" manner. Note that as in the case of avoidance techniques, the defusion approaches also do not seek to determine the underlying causes of conflict. Rather, they are intended to address the unintended consequences once a conflict situation exists. One type of defusion technique is referred to as *smoothing.* The smoothing approach involves the project manager playing down group differences and emphasizing commonalties. Under this approach, it would be common to hear a project manager say, "Come on, people. We are all on the same side here. Let's get together to work on the project." Smoothing represents appeals to professionalism or the group's commitment to higher goals (the organization, the project, etc.).

A second defusion technique is compromise. Compromise has already been examined in this chapter and refers to the implicit assumption that in order for one party to the conflict to win on some points, it must be willing to give up others. The compromise approach is classic "give and take" management and, as with smoothing, does not require the project manager to plumb the root causes of the conflict. It simply arbitrates the process once it is underway.

The final conflict resolution method is confrontation, best represented by *problem-solving meetings.* Unlike the other two sets of conflict resolution methods, confrontation requires project managers to seek and expose the causes underlying the conflict. Each source, whether personal or professional, is identified and discussed at length, so that all parties to the conflict have the opportunity to put their issues out on the table where they can be addressed and resolved. Problem-solving meetings are difficult; they require a project manager to have patience, strong nerves, and poise. When a manager seeks the causes of a conflict, it is akin to attempting to understand other individuals' underlying motives and goals. Frequently, the parties to the conflict are initially loath to open themselves up and examine their basic causes. Hence, the problem-solving process is often a lengthy one, accompanied by high emotions, intransigence, and obstructions from the parties concerned. As we noted in our chapter on team building, a good example of problem-solving meetings frequently occurs during the storming phase of team development. Although an important part of group development, the process can be difficult to manage. Successful problem-solving meetings are necessary for future project team operations, but they contain an element of risk. If they are not handled well, they will not work. Indeed, a poorly run problem-solving meeting can actually solidify conflict and ill feelings between group members, making future cooperative activities highly unlikely.

The important point to bear in mind concerning the nature of resolving conflict is that each of the above approaches may be appropriate in different situations. We do not suggest that a problem-solving session is always beneficial or warranted, nor would we argue that nonattention is always "lazy" management. Project managers have to learn to understand their own preferences when it comes to handling conflict. Once we have achieved a greater sense of self-awareness about our own predilections, we will be in a far better position to resolve our own conflicts constructively as well as deal more effectively with subordinate conflicts. As we argued previously, the key is flexibility. It is important to not lock into any particular conflict style or favor one resolution tactic to the exclusion of all others. Each has its strengths and drawbacks and can be an important part of the project manager's tool chest.

## CONCLUSIONS

A number of noted writers on project management have pointed to the inevitability of conflict within the project development process (e.g., Adams and Barndt, 1988; Chan, 1989). Conflict comes from a variety of sources and exists for a myriad of reasons. Nevertheless, it is essentially impossible for a project manager to run a team and develop a project without having to confront a number of conflicts along the way. In this chapter, we have sought to develop a framework for the organizational conflict process, examining some of the common causes of conflict and arguing that the unique nature of project-based work makes it a natural environment in which conflicts will develop. Because of the inevitability of project team conflict, project managers need to be aware of the basic conflict process and understand how to deal with conflicts once they arise. We proposed a model of the conflict process, arguing that when project managers understand the common steps, they will be in a better position to defuse the conflict or use it constructively to further the project's goals. Conflict has a strong potential to delay and even kill a project unless managers learn how to recognize its characteristics and harness the energy in appropriate channels. Conflict is inevitable, it is not disastrous. Indeed, the degree to which a conflict disrupts a project's development depends on the project manager's willingness to learn enough about conflict to deal with it effectively.

# 14

## Meeting Skills for Project Managers

A COMMON COMPLAINT that we encounter in our consulting work worldwide is the lack of productivity coming from project team meetings. Often, team members and their manager/leader express identical degrees of frustration with the amount of time that is wasted in meetings, mistakenly concluding that the act of holding meetings is itself a waste of time. We, however, argue that meetings *are* important and a prerequisite for project success, provided some important guidelines are followed in how project managers run them. In reality, meetings are usually successful or unsuccessful precisely to the degree that project managers are willing to take charge of them, rather than allow them to spin out of control.

Surprisingly, contrary to normal expectations, harmony in a group and its meetings can serve to make the process less effective. This is the finding of an in-depth research study, as detailed later on in this chapter. On the other hand, as in the case of traditional functional management, an autocratic approach to project management that constitutes rule by fiat is no solution either. In both alternatives, dissent at meetings and elsewhere must be encouraged, in order to stimulate fresh and novel ideas and thus arrive at the most optimum solution among the various alternatives available. The nature of team chemistry and meeting performance is somewhat paradoxical. The teams that ultimately perform well often begin the project with lower opinions of their respective groups, in sharp contrast to the teams that did not perform well. Conversely, there is greater agreement and faster consensus-building among the members of low-performance teams than among those of high-performance teams. These findings are intriguing and should be kept in mind by project managers to ensure better success in project meetings.

## LISTENING: THE MOST VITAL BUT FORGOTTEN AND NEGLECTED SKILL

Listening is a key skill; it is not only basic, it is *fundamental*. Executives extol its virtues but do not seem to practice what they preach. Results of numerous surveys show that well over half of our time is spent in some form of listening, but, unfortunately, it is often done so poorly that the time is almost wasted. What is the result? Half-understood instructions, erroneous actions, misdirected projects. As a result, most of the meetings that we attend prove counterproductive and are, we suspect, a sheer waste of time. And all this, just because *we do not really know how to listen!*

Listening well is a fundamental activity in the communication process because it implies a two-way flow of information. Many novice managers make the mistake of assuming that communication consists simply of a "speaker" and "listeners," implying that communication is unidirectional. In reality, as anyone who has ever addressed a group of people at a meeting knows, the communication process, even with only one person actually talking, flows in both directions. Listeners constantly communicate their interest level, understanding, enthusiasm, disinterest, and boredom, without actually saying a word. As we will explore in this section, *active listening* (i.e., engaged and open listening) is a skill that requires practice, so that listeners understand how to better achieve a high level of communication with others attending the meeting. Some effective listening aids include (Burley-Allen, 1982):

- Show keen interest.

- Overcome language barriers.

- Interpret body language clues.

- Ask questions constructively and nonthreateningly.

- Get others to listen to you.

Nonverbal factors have been found to be far more important than the verbal (words) alone. It is common experience that in the communication of attitudes and feelings, body language and tone of voice play a far more important role than mere words. It is, of course, not easy to quantify these, but one such attempt, in observing the relative importance of each source of communication, assesses their relative importance thus: body language, 55%; voice (inflection, tone, and mannerisms), 38%; and words (actual message content), 7%! One of the authors pioneered the introduction of a full-day program on listening and in the process conducted a field research study on the subject. Its findings (Kharbanda, 1983) were most revealing indeed; for example, most of us are not even aware that average listening efficiency is as low as 25%. Merely knowing this seems to act as a "shock" to many project team members and compels them to make a conscious effort to be better listeners. In due course, this seminar has become one of the most popular the company offers. In particular, a short 1 to 2 hour session on listening skills preceding a 2 to 5 day seminar on a serious and technical subject has been found to pay rich dividends.

Proper listening goes a long way toward dealing with conflict, handling emotionally charged situations, solving problems, and confronting someone effectively—thus preventing the everyday misunderstandings and costly mistakes, both at the workplace and at home, that result from poor listening. President Kennedy, a superb listener, was noted for exhausting people by genuinely listening to them talk and clarify any doubts or concerns he might have on a topic. In this way, he succeeded in clearly understanding complex problems without revealing his own position, thereafter (it was hoped) making the right decision. Perhaps the president was fully conscious of listening "tricks" such as (Spiro, 1992):

- Sit up but in a relaxed way.

- Choose a place where there are no obvious physical barriers.

- Maintain eye contact and generally signal that you are interested.

- A well-run course with plenty of practice can be a great help.

Some more listening "tips" have been provided by Shields (1984) and Vining and Yrle (1980). For example, ask questions to show your interest, give the speaker the benefit of the doubt, try to look beyond awkward voice or body mannerisms, and so forth. It is abundantly clear that listening helps bridge the gap between one mind and another, one person and another—a gap that may actually be widened by words without listening (Levin, 1989). Make sure to listen as if your life, your career depended on it. *It well may!* Listening to others holds the key to getting others to listen to us. As someone once cogently observed: No good idea ever entered a head through an open mouth. Besides, our lives would be longer and richer if we were to devote a greater part of our time to listening. In general, most people both inside and outside of work situations spend far too much time talking and too time little listening. If the reader were to consider how he or she spends the bulk of their time "listening," it is no wonder that, of what is said, far more goes unheard/unheeded than is assimilated.

Typically, a busy executive spends 80% of his or her time listening to others through meetings, unplanned chats, appointments, and telephone calls and yet most do not hear half of what is said. In fact, as we noted previously, the average listening efficiency is a miserable 25%! What a criminal waste of time and money. At a typical executive's salary, if we assume a figure of $60,000 per year, some 60% (0.80 × 0.75 = 0.60) or $36,000 is wasted due to poor listening. Is it any wonder, then, that many if not most meetings are not simply perceived as a sheer waste of time but, in fact, *are* next to worthless? Most listening is casual/ marginal, people tend to hear but *not* listen. Managers need to take time to listen for suggestions, information, complaints, and feelings. At the same time, they must look for meaning behind the message, main ideas, pros and cons, and key words. Active listening will prepare you physically and mentally for the appropriate solution. Proper homework before the meeting and rapt attention to what is said could make all the difference between a project's succeeding and failing. The choice is ours!

We tend to take listening for granted. We cannot communicate effectively face to face, unless speaking and listening are developed in tandem. Further, listening cannot be practiced the same way that we practice speaking. There is, however, an opportunity for speakers and listeners to exchange roles (Anderson and Lynch, 1988). Listening is *not passive,* as reading is; listening is *active,* in that the listener plays a direct, dynamic role. Friendly casual and social conversations are undemanding, as compared with active listening that is most demanding and requires a considerable amount of practice, training, and effort. Some additional suggestions to consider for active listening when engaging another individual in conversation include:

1. *Rephrase.* Restate what the other person has said.

2. *Clarify.* Ask pointed questions aimed at gaining an understanding and new information.

3. *Summarize.* Brief assessment of what has been said.

4. *Feedback.* Give the speaker feedback on your understanding of what he or she has said.

5. *Goals.* Finally, we must establish listening goals and then strive hard to achieve them.

Sometimes, we would do well to remember that we were listeners long before we became speakers. Even three-day-old babies prefer listening to speaking, but with age our preferences seem to change dramatically. According to an expert in the field of communications, Norbert Weiner (Burley-Allen, 1982):

> Speech is a joint game between the talker and the listener against the forces of confusion. Unless both make the effort, interpersonal communication is quite hopeless.

If you are a skilled listener, more people will remember you and respond to you more favorably. Consequently, adept listerners are usually better able to sell their ideas, cut down problem-solving time, and streamline working relationships. Listening is the greatest asset in meetings. In effect, a listener conveys to the speaker: You are important. No wonder, a person who is truly understanding, who takes the trouble to listen to us, often cannot help but influence our attitudes, often without employing anything more for argument than the eloquence of his or her listening abilities. For those who are still not convinced, consider what Harry Overstreet (Burley-Allen, 1982) says:

> If in all our practices of life, we could learn to listen, if we could grasp what the other persons are saying as they themselves understand what they are saying, the major hostility of life will disappear for the simple reason that misunderstandings would disappear.

Effective listening does take time and effort, but it is an easy way to acquire information and ideas that can be of use in everyday life, both in meetings and other work-related activities as well as outside the workplace, particularly at home. Deep, attentive, and appreciative listening can be most satisfying to not only the speaker but also oneself; it can resolve differences of opinion far more effectively than talking. It can bring more people around to your point of view as they experience the satisfaction of being listened to. It is easier to shine as a good listener than a good talker.

The project manager/leader certainly needs to be a compulsive listener. This is the only way in which he or she can really help his or her team to succeed in its mission. If our present century is noted for a type of management that often talked down to employees, it is hoped the next century will be remembered for managers who are good listeners: managers who leave their offices from time to time and walk around to see what is happening and listen to what is being said (shop talk). Project team members, and particularly the leader, must be completely familiar with the details of a project, and this is possible only through active and effective listening—hard work but it can pay enormous dividends. The project leader and team *can listen* their way to project success. Simple, but true!

The Midland Bank (in the United Kingdom) used to take pride in calling itself "the listening bank." It was fond of proclaiming, "We understand how important it is to listen!" (Sperry, 1983). A series of two-page advertisements in popular and prestigious magazines such as *Fortune* proclaimed:

> Most of an executive's time is spent in listening. Yet it's the thing he's least qualified to do.

Proctor and Gamble pioneered the use of a toll-free telephone number for its customers to phone in their complaints and suggestions. The company was "bombarded" with calls, but in the process received a host of useful ideas. Some of these ideas proved to be a major source of product innovation, resulting in the introduction of new and novel products. Likewise, Digital Equipment Corporation capitalized on this technique in relying on its customers to find new uses for minicomputers. It proved not only financially inexpensive but also most effective in generating a host of captive customers for new and innovative products. The long-term success of IBM has been to a large extent attributed to its ability to listen to its customers, rather than ride the crest of its technical excellence.

## UNDERSTAND THE PROBLEM, FIRST AND FOREMOST

Effective meetings require structure and clear pacing. That is, a casual approach by the project leader or an unwillingness to take charge and keep the process on track usually results in mediocrity. There are often clear signals when a meeting starts to drift: People begin to talk with those around them so that the meeting breaks up into a series of coalitionlike discussions, people begin to sit back and show obvious boredom, some individuals begin to dominate conversation, and so forth. All these are sure signs that the project leader has begun to lose effective control of the process. Unfortunately, once a meeting has begun to drift, it is often difficult to steer back on course unless the project leader is willing to take a firm hand.

Paradoxically, however, overcontrol may not be the answer either. Some members of the team are reticent by nature and will overinterpret a project manager's efforts to keep the meeting structured as an implicit command to keep quiet and do as they are told. The key is to strike a balance between allowing the meeting to run its course with little direct intervention and direction and overcontrolling to the point where it seems to team members that their opinions do not matter. Leaders must, first of all, understand themselves and opt for a simple and economical approach. Meetings should be for the purpose of solving a specific problem (Prince, 1970). As the meeting chair, the project leader must establish a clear step-by-step procedure and also learn to keep sensitivity and aggression focused on the problem and *not* the personalities concerned. But unfortunately, as Siegfried and Englemann (1966) note

> The human animal is the only one on earth so intelligent that it can actually learn to be stupid. . . . The inherent problem-solving capacity is, tragically, the best kept secret of our age . . . each person needs to understand in his own individual way . . . a damaging myth about problem-solving meetings: you must have concensus about the problem. . . . Consensus is impossible and even undesirable in the understanding of most problems. . . .

An effective meeting model includes two problem-solving activities: *understanding* and *solving*. Two elements usually govern an individual's behavior in a meeting: 1) Members see a meeting as a contest, competition, win–lose situation; and 2) any slight slur damages the delicate self-image he or she may have. When meetings are viewed as contests, team members often feel the need to try and outdo each other, demonstrating that they are well in control of their activities and minimizing any problems so as not to appear to require assistance. Obviously, this approach results in many problems being suppressed by team members who do not want to appear to the rest of the team as incompetent: a potentially dangerous situation for project performance.

The other problem that can develop in meetings are team members who delight in attempting to deflate or criticize each other. In these situations, meetings quickly become antagonistic as members adopt defensive modes and refuse to communicate. In either case, due to the project team leader's unwillingness to provide interpersonal signals and structure for the process, meetings lose their utility. Another important and related lesson emerging from intensive research in this area is that a group cannot work effectively unless the individuality and respect of each member are carefully protected.

## GOLDEN RULES FOR SUCCESS AT MEETINGS

The first and foremost three golden rules for ensuring success at meetings are listen, listen, and *listen!* Most of us love to talk. And that is at the root of most problems at meetings, rendering them totally ineffective. Carl Rogers, the clinical psychologist, has hit the "nail on the head" by saying that we fail to listen because of our natural tendency to evaluate, approve, or disapprove what has just been said, and in the process we lose the speaker and what they are saying. There is even less communication in case of an emotional encounter.

To get the real message, one has to go beyond the spoken words, considering intentions, feelings, and even intuition and hopes. This should be seen as an opportunity to contribute, advance, and add to the creative sum of an emerging idea—leading to one's satisfaction. Sometimes, sensitive individuals are selected by the meeting leader to do nothing other than observe the responses, body language, and inflection of other team members, solely for the purpose of trying to understand not only what members are saying, but more important, what they are attempting to communicate.

Each individual has changing roles in a meeting. The conventional one is to help solve someone else's problem (as expert), and at the second level, he or she may take on a leadership role. It is important to remember, however, that the process of soliciting ideas can create its own tensions. With an individual's ideas come opposition and antagonism, and once personalized, a meeting can degenerate into a collection of competing individuals instead of remaining a constructive team. *Make sure the meeting has a designated and well-understood leader.* To minimize and avoid resentment, it is useful to clarify the respective tasks of the leader and meeting members, or sometimes to even make everyone a leader by turn. Chances of success are dramatically reduced if there is no functional meeting leader.

Project managers need the sensitivity and appreciation of other personalities and viewpoints in order to make maximum use of each team member's input and style to generate diverse possibilities for creativity. At the same time, however, leaders should realize that each person's instinct is for self-preservation; in other words, until an atmosphere of trust and comfort has been established, it is impossible to expect team members to stick their necks out too far. Leaders must never compete with the team members overtly, as this behavior will invariably stifle conversation and creativity. They need, rather, to develop the patience to listen to team members closely. The leader's challenge lies in learning to understand what others say, without making evaluative judgments; in effect, seeking value rather than allowing subordinates to go on the defensive.

Diversity among team members can serve as an important catalyst for team success. On the surface, it is understandable why many project managers become nervous when they are faced with a diverse group of team members, comprising many functional backgrounds, races, and even nationalities. However, as a recent article in *The Economist* (1993) reported, the positive results of "managed diversity" among team members often far outweigh the potential for problems. The article's conclusion was that diversity may be costly in the short run, in terms of additional time spent in the storming and norming phases of team development, but it can pay off over time, as the team works together on a project. Quoting directly from the article:

> ... Large companies are built on hundreds, even thousands, of 'teams' whose members are increasingly diverse. To exploit that diversity ... groups of workers need time to surmount their differences and to learn to cooperate ... with patience comes creativity.

Participants, of course, are the heart of a meeting and can make a useful contribution, especially in the presence of a skillful leader. They must be encouraged but they also need to be disciplined. If the team is stumped, it may be reactivated by the leader. In a larger sense, each individual is a one-person team, considering the many roles he or she may play in the course of a day: parent, teacher, boss, buyer. Meetings are the basic communication tool throughout the business world, and one of the most highly successful corporations, 3M, has learned to approach meetings in a most professional way after having realized that because of poor planning and inefficiency, millions of dollars were being wasted every year in unproductive meetings. So intent did 3M become on improving the productivity of its meetings that it eventually developed a training manual with guidelines for effective meeting skills. Initially produced for in-house use, an expanded version has been published for the benefit of the business world. Some of the key questions to be asked before a meeting is arranged are shown in Table 14.1 (3M Meeting Management Team, 1987).

Another useful guideline for meetings is the agenda: setting one in advance and following it. Although developing a meeting agenda is, in reality, a commonsense approach to streamlining

**TABLE 14.1. Meeting Checklist**

---

- Is the meeting really necessary?

- Who should attend it?

- When and where should the meeting be held?

- How long should the meeting be?

- What is the best room arrangement?

- How to effectively present your ideas to the group?

- When to use visuals and what makes a good visual?

- How can I make meetings stimulating, inspiring, and productive?

---

meetings and improving the likelihood of sticking to the issues at hand, it is surprising how many project managers do not use them. As consultants, we hear the same excuses time after time, "They take too much time to prepare," "I don't like to lock myself into anything—I want the meeting to stay flexible," and "Too much happens that can't be foreseen by an agenda." To an extent, these are understandable points. However, when we consider how the meetings run by these same project managers often evolve, it is obvious that far too much time is wasted in minutia, side issues, or having to put off decisions until more information is collected.

Meetings are intended to exchange important project information and solve problems. When the meeting leaders establish an agenda and circulate it prior to the meeting, they enable team members to prepare and collect relevant information and maintain their focus. It is often only in cases where agendas were not prepared or not followed that meetings devolve into wasted time that, as one project manager put it, "Generate lots of heat but shed no light."

It is abundantly clear that meetings are closely linked to excellence in management, though they are seldom seen as such. Business is highly complex, much like a mammoth jigsaw puzzle. A specific meeting represents just a tiny piece of this puzzle, but for the final picture to be perfect, each piece must not only be perfect, it must fall at precisely the right place. Meetings are, no doubt, a critical part of a project, indeed of any business-related activity. Just as an example, effective decision making results from a series of meetings. And preparatory to each one of these, managers must acquire the relevant information, explore various possibilities and capabilities, rub ideas together, marshall the facts, and at the end of this exciting process, make decisions.

No wonder, then, that the quality of each meeting contributes greatly to the quality of the business operation, and in the context of our present subject, to the success of a project. A major element of excellence in business management is, undoubtedly, the effectiveness and quality of meetings. In presenting its book to the corporate world, the 3M editorial board makes an honest confession that developing a guide for meeting skills seems like "carrying coal to Newcastle." But then 3M adds, very wisely, that it seems Newcastle these days is indeed in need of coal! Two vital elements in assessing organizational excellence in the business world have been recognized as

- The quality of a business' workers

- The quality of how they communicate

The latter, though deceptively simple, is indeed extremely complex and difficult. To put it simply and bluntly, it means how well the executives meet and work together; that is, its people and their interplay that promote the company's attitude and policies, leading to a certain atmosphere, character, outlook, and eventually achievement. It is no doubt that the excellence achieved at 3M is a result of a company-wide respect for people, their ideas and creativity, and with a very serious concern for how they work together. Herein lies the "magic" and secret of 3M's phenomenal success.

## HARMONY IS NO MAGIC SOLUTION

Project managers often make the mistake of seeking unity and agreement for major project decisions too quickly, without allowing for all relevant information to be presented and argued. Further, many of these same managers are made intensely uncomfortable by team disagreements, seeking to quell or inhibit honest exchanges of opinion in the fear that they will somehow destroy the cohesion of the group. Both of these attitudes, though on the surface understandable, have the potential for doing long-term harm to the ability of the team to work together in an atmosphere of trust and comfort. As a result, the ironic implication is that limiting argument in the name of "harmony" can actually work against the team's successful development of its project.

Fostering an atmosphere that encourages team member dissent can be threatening, both to project managers and their team. Few team members are willing to adopt a challenging position without sound supporting reasons. However, it is important that the act of dissenting not overshadow its consequences: Dissent *is* important, precisely because of the positive effects that come from regularly challenging group positions. Published literature is replete with debates about the proper structure and behavior of effective project teams. The findings appear to be rather paradoxical. For example, an extensive research study (Brown, Klastorin, and Valluzzi, 1990) observed the behavior and performance of 44 members of 14 project teams who worked on the same complex computer-simulated project. A very detailed survey was administered to the team members four times during the life of the project. The findings suggest that the initial ratings of group attributes were good predictors of later success. The teams that ultimately performed well began the project with somewhat lower opinions of their respective groups, in sharp contrast to those teams that ultimately did not perform well.

The survey further assessed individual opinions about group attributes. Teams were divided into groups of high and low performers, based on the vital criteria of total project cost at the end of the simulation. At the project inception stage, the low-performing (i.e., high-cost) teams attributed more positive characteristics to themselves than the high-performing teams (i.e., low-cost). The most significant differences between the two occurred with respect to the quality of decision making. Strangely, the poor performers felt that they were making the best-quality decisions. Further, the average intrateam peer contribution ratings were highest in the teams with the poorest performance; the teams with the lowest performance had the lowest variance in intrateam peer ratings. In effect, there was greater agreement among the members of the low-performance teams than those of the high-performance teams. Further, an individual's perceptions of his or her contributions were in keeping with those of the group.

These results seem to contradict the common belief that harmonious groups with camaraderie among their members are the most effective ones. It seems that getting along too well, particularly at the start, may keep a group from becoming sufficiently task-oriented. Project teams with high intragroup harmony fail to carefully examine and criticize constructively each other's decisions. Clearly, this research is significant and represents an important contribution. Also it is rather unique since it extended to the observation of changes over time.

These findings may not be so surprising, however, in light of research done by Janis (1982) on a concept known as "groupthink." Groupthink implies the desire of the team to maintain good relationships above all other concerns, even the desire to make the best or most accurate decisions. Janus found that groups suffering from groupthink routinely prevent dissenting viewpoints, discourage questions, and work to achieve consensus without allowing free and open debate, perhaps in the belief that from debate comes bad feelings among group members. Needless to say, research such as that cited above demonstrates quite clearly that teams suffering from groupthink and an excessive desire for harmony are typically much poorer performers than those that encourage dissension and differences of opinion in order to get all alternatives out in the open.

What is the moral of the story? It may be beneficial for a group not to begin in perfect harmony: The presence of conflict and strife indicates that some members are going through the process of presenting and evaluating different points of view. But lest the group get bogged down in trying to accommodate too many points of view at once, it is essential that an effective leader, while listening to and acknowledging all viewpoints, takes charge and keeps the group from becoming a free-for-all affair. The results of this research, obviously, have great bearing in determining the success of a project or otherwise.

Part *4*

# Some Success and Failure Stories

*I*n this section, we have assembled some relevant examples of project successes and failures to illustrate in a practical way the impact that effective leaders and teams can have on project success. All the case studies present a similar message in regard to the roles managers play in keeping a project on track, addressing unforeseen problems, and maintaining solid working relationships with all important stakeholders. One other unique characteristic of these examples is that they were purposely chosen from a number of international locations. Rather than simply presenting a number of cases from the United States, all relating to similar types of projects, we have specifically sought diversity, both in location and the type of project to be developed. Regardless of the country or type of project, the basic message is still the same: The project leader truly is the individual who can act as a driving force for project success.

# 15

# Case Studies*

*Examples draw when precept fails*
*And sermons are less read than tales.*

—PRIOR

IN THE FOLLOWING chapters, we have included several real-life case studies from around the world, of successful project managers and how they managed their roles and projects. Interestingly enough, such examples were rare in the literature, and we had to seek them largely from our own experiences, as well as the in-house newsletters and brochures published by contractors operating worldwide. Despite their having achieved astounding successes in the face of heavy odds in remote corners

---

\* Some of the examples used in this chapter were adapted from O. P. Kharbanda and E. A. Stallworthy (1990), *Project Teams: The Human Factor*, Manchester, UK: Blackwell.

of the world, many of the contractors needed coaxing to share their valuable know-how.

Mega-projects are notorious for enormous time and cost over-runs. For this reason, special attention is being paid to them, in particular with reference to that one person, the *project manager*, who can often make all the difference. Some of the classic examples of project failures in this area include nuclear power plants; the Concorde aircraft development; and, to some degree, even the Channel tunnel that made headlines as it headed toward comple-tion. With a price tag of over £15 billion, the cost of just one day's delay, in terms of interest and loss of profit, is estimated at $10 million! Among some of the spectacular success stories described here are the IBM 360 System and Ford Taurus project. Unfortu-nately for General Motors, it was not able to capitalize on the merits of teamwork, perhaps due to the absence of the right leader. Its story offers an interesting counterpoint to Ford's success. Also included is a short discussion of construction projects and the challenging Falkland Airfield Project.

## BEWARE: MEGA-PROJECTS

Mega- or macro-projects, loosely defined as those costing $1 billion and more, pose their own problems. The risks involved are great, of course, but in addition, major projects are more prone to failures than success. Success, as we have repeatedly pointed out, is gener-ally measured in terms of time, budget, quality, and user satisfac-tion. In down-to-earth terms, success may be judged as follows:

- Does the project perform as originally intended?

- Does the plane fly as envisaged and is it commercially suc-cessful?

- Is the power station performance as intended?

- Does the refinery make money?

- Was the project profitable for the consultant and contractor?

- Was the "plug pulled" (terminated) when the project seemed headed for disaster?

The subject of mega-projects has become so fundamental and significant that it has warranted the formation of several international bodies, for example,

American Society for Macro-Engineering
Japan Institute of Macro-Engineering
La Association Española de Macroingenieria
Major Projects Association (MPA)

MPA, based at Oxford, United Kingdom, undertook a two-year exhaustive study on the preconditions of success in such projects. The results of this study are described in some detail by Morris and Hough (1987) and its major findings appeared as a preview in Morris (1987). Some of the major preconditions for success in macro-projects (as indeed for projects of any size!) are

- Good positive attitudes by owner, contractor, and others.

- Comprehensive and clearly communicated project definition.

- Good planning, clear schedules, and adequate backup.

- Full attention to quality assurance and auditing.

- Proper management of urgency and scheduling.

- Proper recognition of external factors.

- Political and community support when required.

- Full financial analysis, also necessary financial support.

- Appropriate project organization, contract strategy/terms.

- Effective leadership, teamwork, resources, and communication

- Highly visible, simple, and friendly project controls.

- Recognize that projects are built by people and none are perfect.

We would strongly recommend the Morris and Hough works, as well as another classic and more recent monograph (Kharbanda and Stallworthy, 1984, 1992) on the subject of project failures. Medley (1991) has discussed the failure and success of aided projects in developing countries. One vital factor for project success needs to be specially highlighted in the context of our present subject. This relates to strong managerial commitment, particularly at senior levels. Success usually results from

- Focused attention

- Motivated staff

- Identified key issues

- Exhibited strength in times of conflict

- Good judgment in the making of decisions

Needless to say, our project manager plays the central role in all these activities. As we have suggested, he or she is indeed the "kingpin", though *not* the king!


## IBM SYSTEM 360: A LANDMARK

The development of this project is a classic success story used in business schools to demonstrate that teams can, indeed, achieve wonders. If we were to sum up the primary reasons for the success of IBM 360, surely a major landmark in the field of computers, we would point to the fact that the company manifested complete faith and trust in its employees as people. This faith and trust in people extend, of course, to the project teams that are set up to achieve specific objectives.

IBM was "born" in 1924 as the successor of CTR (Computer-Tabulator-Recording), a company founded by Charles Flint in

1910. The man who set the tone of the company, however, was Thomas J. Watson, Sr. His basic philosophy, which has become part of the "company culture," was and still is (Sobel, 1984):

A company is known by the men it keeps. We have different ideas, and different work, but when you come right down to it there is just one thing we have to deal with throughout the whole organization —that is the man. . . . A team that won't be beat can't be beat. . . . Everybody in this company is the supervisor of someone else . . . no man is big enough to instruct everybody how to do his work.

Though this was said over 70 years ago by Watson, it is valid even today. The emphasis at IBM rests on teamwork and the importance of giving both the individual and team full opportunity to use their skills in order to achieve success. This is, of course, our central theme here—revolving around the one person who is all in all.

The system 360 project leader, Frederick Brooks, had a competent and large support team. Peters and Waterman (1984) tell us that the team met only once a week for a half-day to review progress, but contact between team members was continuous and intense. The minutes of such meetings were circulated within a few hours, and every member of the team had instant access to all the information that he or she required. This sharing of information carried right through to the programmers, who received copies of material from every group within the project team. In addition, there were annual two-week sessions, at which all outstanding major problems were resolved. Everyone attending the weekly meetings had the authority to make binding decisions on behalf of their departments. Brooks continually emphasized the necessity for open communications. With a giant project team and much larger than usual task force, there had to be a field structure, which was reorganized regularly, but all team members had access to all the information necessary for their work.

This project cost more and took longer than was expected. However, do not forget that we are describing a development project in a high-technology area, with many unknowns. In its anxiety to preempt competitors, IBM proclaimed as early as 1962 that the system would be available by April 1964. Even at that point in time, the system was still being developed and development costs were escalating. However, although the first 360/40 computers were installed a year later than promised, they proved to be an instant success. Before the end of that year, other models in the series—the 360/30s, 50s, and 60s—had also appeared and there was a record backlog of orders for these outstanding machines. Production problems were surmounted and the transition from what was called "second generation" to "third generation" computers went very smoothly indeed. Within two years, the 360 series accounted for nearly half the total sales of IBM at home and the series was also making great strides abroad, with sales far ahead of those of any of its competitors.

Although the competition was well aware of what was happening and was developing its response, no one was ready to enter the market when the 360 appeared. The development of a new generation in computers is both expensive and time-consuming, and it was thought that such a major technological advance would take at least 10 years. IBM got there in less than half that time, thanks to intensive teamwork! The 360 series was the dominant factor in the growth of IBM in the 1960s, propelling the company to even greater successes in the years following.

## FROM VIRTUAL MONOPOLY TO FINANCIAL WOE

Everyone knows that IBM is no longer the legendary colossus that it once was. Indeed, the last few years have been damaging to the company's image and financial standing. Although we do not deny the upheaval IBM has seen, it also seems apparent that it has the talent and resilience to survive its present crisis. As testimony to its acumen, we wish to offer a brief case study of how IBM first entered the field of personal computers.

In July 1980, William C. Lowe, manager of the entry level systems unit at the IBM plant in Boca Raton, Florida, advised the

Corporate Management Committee (CMC) that IBM should explore the PC market. Judging by past disasters, Lowe knew that this development could not succeed within IBM's normal culture and heavy external aid was essential. Lowe conceived the basics for the project and assembled 13 planning engineers for "Project Chess," the development of a PC prototype. Within a month, Lowe received the CMC's preliminary approval for the project and guided the team through the October 1980 "checkpoint" when the final go-ahead was given. Anticipating his own departure for higher office within IBM, Lowe lined up Philip "Don" Estridge to take over for him.

Estridge turned out to be the right man in the right place at the right time. He was a charismatic leader and the corporation had the insight to "turn him loose" (Heller, 1994). The project was considered a venture capital investment, freed from time-consuming reviews and clearances. In about a year's time, IBM started shipping the PCs. Thus, IBM entered this lucrative market at a tremendous speed. The initial expectation was to make and sell a quarter of a million units throughout its life. In reality, the IBM PC became the most popular personal computer in history, serving as the industry standard throughout much of the 1980s. The total risk to IBM from the project: $14 million, a mere five hours' revenue for the computer giant!

There is no doubt that the project team concept is almost always the answer, whatever the size of the company. Problems, whether they are direct manufacturing problems, or involve the introduction of a new product, are best formulated as a project, with a stated objective, to be achieved within a budgeted cost and stipulated time. Then a group of people should be nominated, with a leader, to produce the answer—and they often will!

A few other examples from the United States illustrate how teams have achieved wonders, particularly under the right leadership. R. G. Boerg Corporation, a footwear manufacturer, organized its 300 employees into teams of 8 to 12 people, each team being responsible for the manufacture of a specific product, starting with the appropriate raw materials. In addition, these teams participate in overall company decision making. This resulted in a complete transformation of the company, according to an employee (Kharbanda and Stallworthy, 1990):

> "Before, everyone was on his own and no one cared about helping the fellow employee. Now everyone is dependent upon everyone else. I know that in my case I think twice before taking a day off, because I know that if I do, it will affect my team."

In the case of the semiconductor giant, Intel Corporation, the word *team* appears in its statement of operating philosophy (Harris, 1985):

> Teams are an integral part of the Intel work ethic environment. Team performance is critical to the accomplishment of Intel objectives. . . . Team objectives take precedence over individual objectives. This principle is applied in day to day operations and is fundamental. [Any] changes are made in a manner to optimize team results, rather than to maintain individual career paths.

## FORD'S PROJECT TAURUS ACHIEVED WONDERS

Lee Iacocca is often credited with having turned Chrysler around practically single-handedly and Sir Michael Edwardes is believed to have accomplished the same for British Leyland. But the fact is that both men led the teams within their respective company that actually affected the turnaround. As team leaders, they received most of the credit, particularly in the media, and emerged as heroes, or "company doctors," a term now popular for persons who cure sick companies. Both these stories have been well documented by, among others, Kharbanda and Stallworthy (1987). However, we maintain that no one person can achieve such wonders alone: A team is a *must* for this process and, further, it must be led by a leader of exceptional qualities, as we demonstrated at length in Part 2 of this book.

The same thinking applies to the turnaround at Ford, symbolized by its successful Taurus/Sable project. The name of the then-chief executive, Philip Caldwell, is often mentioned as the one who inspired the production revolution that took place, but there was also his successor, Donald Petersen, and the company's president, Harold Poling. This team of three and certainly many more played a part, each contributing his or her individual skills in order to ensure the success of the project as a whole. Because this was so, the term "team Taurus" was used to describe everyone connected with this particular project (Peters, 1989). Ford is known to excel in the area of team product development. It seeks to remove the barriers between design, engineering, production, marketing, sales, and purchasing. However, the Taurus team went far beyond that, while creating a car that excelled in design and quality. The development cost was practically halved by maintaining simultaneous action on a number of fronts, instead of adopting the normal sequential process.

In cases of normal sequential development of a car, designers create a conceptual design that is then developed by engineers. Manufacturing and purchasing then set up the necessary tooling and select the best suppliers on the basis of competitive tendering. Production is then taken in hand and other departments, such as marketing, legal, and dealer service, become involved. Finally, the customer enters the picture. Should there be any hitch in this program, the problem is referred back to the designers. Of course, the further along this process of development that the project has gone, the more expensive any change becomes. Once the tooling has been completed, changes become very, very expensive indeed; hence, change at this late stage must be avoided if at all possible.

In the case of project Taurus, all the relevant disciplines were brought together as a team and the various steps taken simultaneously as well as sequentially. The team included production, sales, and marketing people right from the beginning. Even the dealers were consulted at a very early stage, in order to establish what the market needed in a user-friendly car. Insurance companies were consulted on design features that would minimize the effects of accidents and reduce the cost of repairs. Legal and safety advisors gave advice on likely trends in the law, so that the design would conform right from the start. Here was real teamwork in action, with several multidisciplinary teams working in tandem. The production team was providing valuable input long before the car went into production. In the words of Lew Veraldi, the Taurus team project leader (Peters, 1989):

> "We went to all the stamping plants, assembly plants, and put layouts on the walls. We asked them how to make it easier to build. We talked to hourly people. . . . It's amazing the dedication and commitment you can get from people. . . . We will never go back to the old ways because we now know so much [about] what they can bring to the party."

A unique procedure was adopted with regard to suppliers. Instead of choosing the lowest tenders, as is the usual practice, the Taurus team identified the suppliers who were offering the highest quality and then sought their advice on the development of an economic design, with the understanding that they would be the sole preferred supplier. This had the effect of incorporating such suppliers into the "team": They became yet another team involved in the project. More important, these suppliers had a real commitment to the project's success. Indeed, one supplier, the family-owned company of A. O. Smith, makers of automotive subframes and the like, went so far as to offer the services of its own drafting department to prepare initial designs for Ford's approval. Such cooperation provided extremely valuable cross-fertilization of ideas at the conceptual stage, where changes can be made without much extra cost. Not only were there substantial savings in cost and design time, but major production contracts were being negotiated and set up some three years ahead of production, with the duration of the contract some five years. This also led to cost economies.

But progress really lies in constantly seeking improvement. Ford did achieve a sort of record in the case of the above project, but the indomitable H. Ross Perot, known for "calling a spade a spade," observed: "It takes five years to develop a new car in this country. Heck, we won World War II in four years."

## A Lesson General Motors Is Learning the Hard Way

It seems that not all companies are able to apply the principle of teams to their operations. General Motors employed pilot schemes using teams instead of assembly lines. This approach seemed to succeed in the early 1970s, but later experience proved so disappointing that General Motors management concluded, "Group experiments may suit some people but not all."

The General Motors Assembly Division handled Chevrolet vans. Over the years, this had become a fairly straightforward product, built on an assembly line. However, as an experiment, four people were trained to build a van in a separate building, with the assistance of an engineer. The average time on the assembly line was 8 man-hours per van, but the team initially took 13 to 14 man-hours per van. However, continuing experience reduced this to $1^1/_2$ man-hours per team member, and the process seemed very competitive, as indeed we would expect. But it seems that some of the team members preferred working on the assembly line, and considerable juggling within the labor force had to occur to assemble a team that preferred teamwork. The team concept could have been extended to the entire plant, but the workers did not want it. Why?

One potential answer was that the job on the assembly line was fairly simple, one that lent itself to a comfortable style and rhythm whereby workers could do their jobs in their own way and at their own pace, without really having to think, or exert themselves. But with a team, each person has a number of different things to do, and the entire psychology of the job changes. The individual has to carry much greater responsibility and instead of having to contend with perhaps three work elements, he or she may well have to deal with some 20 to 30 elements. It seems the employees at General Motors did not like this extra responsibility. There were also practical problems associated with the handling of all required parts. What would the mechanics be of bringing together some 15,000 parts at one location, to allow the van to be built? The chairman of General Motors is reported to have summed up the situation with which the company was faced as follows (Kharbanda and Stallworthy, 1990):

> "I don't ever foresee the end of the assembly line. We may use different approaches to sub-assembly, to break down the job so that it can be done more effectively. But our experience in the plant is this: the greatest difficulty we have with our employees is not because the job is repetitive so much as the fact that we have to change the job, which we frequently do because of product development or new investment."

It may be that with certain types of manufacturing, there are a critical manpower level and an optimum approach, but in this situation, we suspect it was General Motors management that was at fault. It failed to inspire its employees with the concepts of pride, involvement, and commitment: It is these factors that are the essence of successful teamwork. Another quote from Roger Smith, the former CEO of General Motors, is indicative of management's inability to create a vision that was inspiring to workers. Commenting to *Fortune* magazine in February 1989 on the failure of a major, billion dollar retooling effort aimed at improving productivity, Smith reflected on what he would do differently. He mused:

> "I sure wish I'd done a better job of communicating with GM people. I'd . . . make sure they understood and shared my vision for the company. . . . If people understand the why, they'll work at it. I never got this across. There we were, charging up the hill right on schedule, and I looked behind me and saw that many people were still at the bottom, trying to decide whether to come along."

Each country has its own special proverbs, and India has one that brings us a lot of wisdom in a few words. Although quoted earlier, it bears repetition. It says: *"Ek, ek or do giara."* Freely translated, this means: "One is one, but two is eleven." Is not that what teamwork is all about?

## THE CONSTRUCTION INDUSTRY THRIVES ON TEAMWORK, BUT . . .

The construction industry is largely project-based, and it provides an ideal example of how teams can achieve wonders. A major British construction company, Taylor Woodrow, has a logo strongly suggestive of teamwork. It consists of a number of men pulling on a rope. Further, its house magazine is entitled *Team Spirit.* John Laing International, another British construction company, places great emphasis on teamwork. John Armitt, the deputy managing director, presented a paper at a British Institute of Management conference in 1985 with the title, "Creating commitment in project-based industries." Commitment is, of course, the essence of successful teamwork.

Each construction project is unique, its success requires creative solutions, and teamwork provides just the right environment for this to occur. But the company must be fully committed to a "team-centered" structure. The construction industry has as its raison d'être the construction of permanent, highly functional, and very visible results. When possible, the families of workers can tour the site to see what has been achieved by their "bread winners." All this induces a sense of pride in the task at hand. On the site itself, workers should be able to identify the rest of their primary work group, know their foreman, and understand their immediate objective. It is the responsibility of management to ensure that tools and materials are available as required—in essence, to give the teams the means to allow them to succeed and to then stand aside.

Teamwork lies at the heart of every construction project. No one individual can conceive, design, construct, and commission a construction project, however small. Such projects demand the skills of many people, all committed and motivated, who have to be brought together at the right place and in the right sequence. Commitment within a team amounts to having a positive answer to the question: "Are you with us? Is your objective the same as ours?" Of course, there have been many projects, even major ones, where the answers to these questions have been negative. It is thought that financial reward and economic necessity will inspire people to excel, but it does not always happen that way. The Central Electricity Generating Board (CEGB) planned Europe's largest oil-fired power station on the Isle of Grain and sought to have the plant built economically and on time, but it failed. It could not get the 2000-strong workforce to cooperate and share its desire to meet this goal. The problem does not seem to have been a question of monetary reward: The people working on the project were well paid. There was just a complete lack of effective leadership.

## THE FALKLAND AIRFIELD PROJECT

The Falkland Airfield Project is typical of the successful projects completed by the Laing Group. To secure this particular contract, it formed a consortium with Mowlem International Limited and Amey Roadstone Construction Limited, known as Laing-Molem-ARC, or LMA. The joint venture board appointed a bid manager, and extensive discussions between the three companies followed, with a free exchange of ideas on labor, plant, staffing levels, and material resources. Each of the member companies concentrated on a particular aspect of the project, agreed beforehand, and there were weekly meetings to review progress. When the time came for them to submit their tender, a final settlement meeting occurred, which took some two days, with the three chairmen and several senior directors in attendance. The tender preparation team worked until 2:30 a.m. on the day of submission, and everyone seemed committed to winning the project. The successful completion and submission of the tender were a team achievement, and the enthusiasm that is generated in such circumstances can be very infectious and long-lasting (Adair, 1986).

The Falkland Islands are situated some 8000 miles from the home base of these companies, and the construction force had to be completely self-reliant. There were extensive logistics problems, difficult communications, and a complete absence of harbor facilities. There is no doubt that a novel proposal in the LMA tender, that of using a ship as a floating jetty head, contributed significantly to the success of both their tender and the project. As a result, for the length of the project, the freighter MV Merchant Providence remained anchored offshore for this purpose. A Bailey Bridge led from the ship to the shore and road had been built from the docking facilities to the airfield site further inland.

With this project, as with all, the project manager's main task is to win commitment by setting realistic goals and clear targets. Although he has to be a quick decision maker, and some of his decisions may not be popular, he has to lead, and this is best done by example. The quality of the food for his workforce should receive just as much attention as the quality of his concrete. He can gain commitment only by commanding respect, and this is secured by maintaining close personal communication with the workforce. In marked contrast with the previous example of the Central Electricity Generating Board's power plant construction project, there is no doubt that the conduct of the project manager, the team leader, is the key to project success.

Construction projects present a special problem in terms of commitment, since there can be no guarantee of permanent employment. Every project comes to an end, and there may or may not be another project, and further employment, to follow. John Armitt, the project manager on the Falkland Islands Project, was intimately and personally involved in supervising a large UK labor force in the late 1970s, before he came to manage the Falkland Islands Project in 1983. There was no incentive scheme on either of these projects, but much attention was paid to explaining in detail to the workforce all that was entailed. The criteria for recruitment were also clearly established right from the beginning and maintained throughout the project.

With the Falkland Islands project, the essence of project success was speed to completion, and the airport became operational on time because the project management team adopted an unconventional approach. It was innovative, as it demonstrated in particular by setting up the bridgehead, instituting a ferry service to get employees home on leave regularly, and providing a ship charter service for the supply of materials. A similar spirit was inspired in the workforce, with the result that a news feature reporting on the project quoted individual workers on the site as speaking of "fantastic companionship" and saying, "We're all in this together —we're going to win together." The management philosophy called for decision making throughout the organization, expressed in the injunction: "Don't make decisions too easily—but make them!" The fact that the project manager was on site, despite its remoteness, also contributed to the feeling that everyone was on one team, with a common purpose. We are sure that to some extent, the feeling of team spirit was developed by the team's relative isolation, but the important thing is that all the workers operated as a team. Hence, their eventual success: a project built on time and within budget.

Laing holds fairly large staff meetings regularly, when the entire staff in a region get together, and the local director briefs all on the company's current business, its financial status, existing problems, and future prospects. This is followed by general questions and open discussion. These meetings have proved very popular and well worthwhile. It is another step in development of team spirit, giving employees a feeling of involvement and responsibility, thereby strengthening their commitment to the company and its objectives—particularly difficult to achieve in the construction industry.

The essence of successful project management calls for an innovative and creative leader who has the ability to build and inspire a team of equally committed and dedicated members. As we shall see in the following chapter, these examples are by no means isolated or eccentric. More and more, we discover that the laws governing projects point to the team leader as the bellwether for project success, in both theory and practice.

# 16

# More Real-Life Examples*

*The road to learning by precept is long, by example short and effectual.*

—S̲ᴇɴ

IT IS CLEAR that success in projects is *not* merely a matter of luck or good fortune (though, it does help!). It is a matter of careful, detailed application of the basic principles of good project management that have been well covered in the extensive literature on the subject. In this way, the so-called "luck" is assured and not merely left to chance. A project is a dynamic process and to handle it efficiently requires a dynamic project manager and team with a management system that can respond quickly to the changing situation. For this, it is essential that each member of the project team have a good working knowledge of

---

* Some of the examples used in this chapter were adapted from O. P. Kharbanda and E. A. Stallworthy (1990), *Project Teams: The Human Factor*, Manchester, UK: Blackwell.

his or her colleagues' jobs, needs, and responsibilities. But in all cases, it is the project managers who put their own "stamp" on the project through excellent communication with everyone engaged on that project. When problems arise, as they often do, the project manager has to resolve them, in consultation with the team.

The case studies included here are from Australia, India, Indonesia, Japan, Papua, New Guinea, South Africa, Sweden, and Algeria. Each case study brings its own lessons, but the abiding theme is that of success through teams with good leadership.

## JAPAN EXCELS IN TEAMWORK

Japanese organizations enjoy a legitmately strong reputation for excelling in teamwork, a trait that has largely contributed to their spectacular success since the mid–1940s. Their basic philosophy is that teams can achieve wonders and team objectives should be ambitious, but attainable. Maude (1978) outlines a number of characteristics of Japanese teams:

- Each member understands clearly his or her role and responsibilities.

- All team members share the same values and goals.

- There is frank, candid, and continuous two-way communication.

- Team members have diverse skills and experience.

- Grievances are sorted out, resulting in high morale and low staff turnover.

- The leader constantly stresses the task's successful completion.

In Japan, gaps in salary and perquisites between the chief executive and those who work on the shop floor are perhaps the smallest in the industrialized world. This has been a major factor in inculcating the team spirit, also in building high staff morale, re-sulting in ever-increasing productivity. In the United States, the chief executive of the Nissan plant at Smyrna, Tennessee, wears company-issued overalls at work, even while conducting VIP visi-tors around the plant. Actions speak louder than words, and even a seemingly small factor of uniformity in dress means a lot to the average worker on the shop floor and ensures that all will work with enthusiasm and recognize that they have a cause in common with management—they are members of the same team! This has an almost magical effect on the workforce (Peters, 1987). Honda is known worldwide for its motorbikes and more recently for its cars. The company has risen to its present position of market dominance over a number of years, and many articles have been written about its phenomenal success, and the reasons for it. The underlying causes appear to be those of quality and productivity, factors that depend on both the performance of workers and quality of man-agement.

It seems that the rigid organizational structure present in a great many companies is not conducive to success, and this is most certainly not present at Honda. It has no clear-cut organization or company chart, but does ascribe to the project team concept. Just to illustrate the motivation that can exist in a properly inspired and led workforce, the story is told of the Honda worker who, returning home from work each evening, never failed to straighten up the windshield wipers of every Honda car that he passed. With such strong feelings of loyalty, workers will inevitably be continu-ously striving for ever-higher quality. How to instill such loyalty and devotion to duty is another matter. People matter, and it seems that the singular success of the Japanese is due to, not complex management systems, but their attaching proper importance to their most vital resource: those actually working on a project.

Although it is important not to "mythologize" Japanese man-agement strengths or generalize this prowess across all companies and industries, we often find that Japanese managers are essen-tially team builders. They lead rather than manage and do this by a process of consensus. This approach is so much better than passing down instructions without discussion. There is therefore free and honest communication up and down the management structure, and this inculcates a family relationship, with its warm, cooperative atmosphere and strong team spirit. Physical factors also contribute to this concept. Offices with an open plan not only demonstrate that there are no barriers, but they encourage the interchange of ideas and information between colleagues, senior and junior. As we have mentioned above, one material example of this concept of equality is further fostered by managers and workers alike wearing identical overalls.

## PUBLIC SECTOR PROJECT: A SPECTACULAR SUCCESS

The Kudremukh iron ore project, in southern India, is an outstanding example of a successful project and one, too, in the public sector! It is one of the largest mining and beneficiation projects in the world, developed in hilly terrain under the most severe climatic conditions. In that area, the heavy monsoon rains last for some four months, and for most of the year, there are strong winds and much fog. Indeed, it is said that the Bhadra river valley, where the Kudremukh community is situated, has the unwelcome distinction of being the third wettest place known on earth. In the monsoon season, the average rainfall is some 6000 millimeters (233 inches). In 1980, the year in which the Kudremukh plant was established, the rainfall was exceptional even by local standards, exceeding 9500 millimeters, with 417 millimeters (17 inches) in one 24-hour period, yet another record. However, thanks to proper project planning, this $650 million venture, with a capacity of 7 million tons per year of iron ore pellets, was completed under a very tight construction schedule: Only 40 months were allowed to mechanical completion. In addition, the project was completed within budget. The basic reasons for this were said to be teamwork par excellence, which translated into:

- Carrying out detailed design and construction simultaneously.

- Undertaking a number of independent activities in parallel.

- Delivering equipment to site whenever possible fully or partially assembled.

- The full use of standardization and modular design.

The project office was set up in November 1975, with a small project team of personnel from MECON (Metallurgical and Engineering Consultants (India) Limited), HSCL (Hindustan Steelworks Construction Limited), and SAIL (Steel Authority of India Limited). These were all public sector organizations. Then there was the operating company KIOCL (Kudremukh Iron Ore Company Limited) and MET-CHEM (Canadian MET-CHEM Consultants), the mining associate and engineering construction firm called in from overseas to assist. So the principle of teamwork was established, with individuals nominated from their companies to form some three teams—the government advisory team, operating company team, and overseas consultant's team—to develop the project and bring it to fruition. A total of some 80 contracts were signed for civil and structural work both at Kudremukh and Mangalore, the port from which the iron ore pellets were to be shipped abroad. At peak, in October 1979, MET-CHEM had a total of 40 expatriates supervising the construction, supported by some 400 Indian personnel at site. There were also a number of outside agencies employed for surveying, quality control, and similar work. When we consider the difficult terrain, harsh climate, and inaccessibility of the site, completion within the time schedule established was a real challenge. But that challenge was met and overcome (Mirchandani, 1983).

As with any major project, there were serious problems to be encountered and resolved, and it is here that teamwork came into its own. Decisions had to be made forthwith, if the situation was to be saved. Some of the equipment came from Calcutta, but floods delayed delivery. Other equipment came from Canada, and delivery was threatened by a dock strike in North America, necessitating the diversion of the equipment to other ports not affected by the strike. Then one Indian manufacturer experienced serious labor problems and hovered on the brink of failure. This situation was only redeemed by the transfer of the unfinished equipment to another fabricator overnight under a stay order from the Madras High Court. Despite these setbacks, the plant was completed on time and within budget, the several emergencies having been handled with decisive, resolute, and immediate action. There is no doubt that this project has been an outstanding success, thanks to project direction given by the dynamic chairman and managing director, K. C. Khanna. He inspired his teams to commit wholeheartedly to what he saw as a national cause. Expectations were high, but they were met!

## TECHNOLOGY TRANSFER BETWEEN MULTINATIONAL TEAMS

The government of Indonesia has continually striven to develop its own natural resources and also to ensure that it will ultimately be self-sufficient in terms of not only food and energy, but also in relation to the design and operation of the plants it needs. This goal demands continuous and intensive technology transfer, with the training of large numbers of people. An American firm, M. W. Kellogg, has been closely involved in this process of technology transfer in Indonesia since 1971, the year in which self-sufficiency in fertilizer production became a national objective. To achieve this objective, a new Indonesian engineering and construction management company was established in Jakarta, P. T. Kellogg Sriwidjaja (KELSRI), as a joint venture between the Indonesian government and M. W. Kellogg.

Meanwhile, by 1978, M. W. Kellogg had completed its fourth large-scale ammonia-urea plant complex in Indonesia. Built for P. T. Pupuk at Kujang near Dauwan in central West Java, the complex utilizes natural gas feedstock provided by the national oil company, Pertimina. Not only this plant, but the previous three plants had all been completed well on time and within budget, as demonstrated by the following table:

| | Months to Completion | | Project Cost | |
|---|---|---|---|---|
| | Target | Actual | Target | Actual |
| | (in months) | | (in $ millions) | |
| PUSRI II | 30 | 34 | 67 | 77 |
| PUSRI III | 32 | 31 | 166 | 165 |
| PUSRI IV | 30 | 26 | 157 | 130 |

There is no doubt that the success of the PUSRI projects has been due to teamwork, with complete cooperation between the owner, a nationalized company, and the contractor, who had come from overseas. The various plants are said to be working very well, completely under local control. Indeed, it was reported that in 1983, Indonesia set a world record in urea fertilizer output with over 100% capacity utilization with some of its plants. The knowledge brought to the country from abroad has been avidly assimilated and applied. This attitude is crucial to teamwork. There must be a willingness to listen and learn, and this openmindedness must begin right at the top, with the chief executive.

Another project, Asahan, is different only in that it demonstrates cooperation between a different pair of countries: Indonesia and Japan. The massive Ashahan project consists of the construction of two power stations, a 100-mile transmission line, and a three-line aluminum smelting plant. In addition, a substantial infrastructure had to be developed, including roads, water supply, communications facilities, housing, and schools. The completion of this major project, accomplished with the full cooperation of the Japanese government, was the realization of long-cherished goals for both countries. Japan benefited because it secured a cheap and steady source of aluminum, whereas Indonesia gained from the subsequent social and economic development in North Sumatra.

This sense of mutual interest was transferred to the respective project teams, so that every member shared a sense of enthusiasm and commitment. Project managers should recognize the powerful positive influence that such personal involvement brings and therefore take continuing and active steps to inform their workforces as to the ultimate aims and benefits of the project in which they are engaged.

## A CHALLENGING PROJECT COVERED IN A FULL-LENGTH BOOK

The Ok Tedi Gold and Copper Project, costing some $2.5 billion, involved the mining, processing, and shipping of more than a billion tons of copper ore that had been found beneath an isolated mountaintop in northwest Papua, New Guinea. What is more, the copper deposit lay under more than two million troy ounces of high-grade gold ore, which naturally enough was to be mined first, yielding some million troy ounces of gold bullion. All this ore was located on the top of a mountain in the middle of a rain-forest near the Equator. It is said to be one of wettest places on earth, with some 8 meters (311 inches) of rain falling annually. The ground is unstable and landslides are commonplace. The whole area is covered by nearly impenetrable forest. The project's peculiar title, "Ok Tedi," comes from the Papuan word *ok*, which means river, and the river Tedi ran adjacent to the project site (Pintz, 1984).

The materials and supplies for the project, which came from all over the world, entered Papua, New Guinea at Port Moresby. There they were transferred to barges and shipped some 300 miles across the gulf to the mouth of the Fly River, and then a further 500 miles up that river to the town of Kianga. There was then an additional 100 miles to go, up the steep mountain road that led to the project site. This road had to be specially built as part of the project; it was literally carved out of the forest. The project team had to contend with not only the site conditions, but also the labor force employed on the project. Some of the local people working on the project had never seen a wheel until 20 years ago, much less sat in the cab of an enormous bulldozer. Thus, there had to be an intensive training effort, first in the classroom and then on the job. However, despite the high proportion of "green" staff, the accident rate was kept to a minimum: less than that normally encountered on construction sites in the United States.

This was a project demanding an innovative spirit from all concerned, especially those who were, in effect, isolated from the world at the project site. That such an innovative spirit, so crucial to effective teamwork, prevailed is well illustrated by some comments on the project by the main contractor's project manager (Bechtel, 1985):

> "This was a project that you like to tell people you worked on. It was a mega-project, a one-of-its-kind challenge, something that provided much more than just a new mining project. There's a tremendous amount of satisfaction when you complete something that seems so difficult. It's just a hell-of-a-good feeling for all of us to see this job come together knowing what we accomplished to get it there."

It is clear that the project manager has spoken from his heart— this is the stuff of which project managers are really made. Let us conclude by saying it for him: "We did it!" It was manifestly a completely cooperative effort from a well-coordinated team, working far from home. And paying compliment where it is due, the project manager may well point to his team and say, "They did it!"

## INTERNATIONAL TEAMS AT WORK

The Sasol project in the Republic of South Africa is an outstanding example of the way in which companies from several different continents were able to team up and so complete an important task. The name "Sasol" stands for South African Coal, Oil and Gas Company when that company name is written in Afrikaans, the Dutch-related language of the Republic of South Africa. The plant —in effect two plants, Sasol Two and Sasol Three—was built to produce liquid fuels, including gasoline, from coal, which South Africa has in abundance. Sasol One came on stream back in 1954, and Sasol Two was started in 1975. The Fluor Corporation, of Irvine, California, was appointed as managing contractor and the plant was to be located at Secunda, some 150 kilometers east of Johannesburg in the eastern Transvaal. The plant, together with Sasol Three, occupies a total area of some 15 square kilometers (15,000 hectares). The scope of the involvement of international companies other than Fluor is demonstrated by the following list of major overseas engineering contractors employed to supply specialist equipment and services (Kharbanda and Stallworthy, 1986):

Badger, Cambridge, Massachusetts, United States
Deutsche Babcock, Oberhausen, Germany
Fluor Mining & Metals, Redwood City, California, United States
L'Air Liquide, Champigny, France
Linde, Munich, Germany
Lurgi, Frankfurt-am-Main, Germany
Mobil, New York, United States
Universal Oil Products (UOP), Des Plaines, Illinois, United States

So successful were these contractors in completing Sasol Two on time and within budget, that the contracts for Sasol Three were awarded to them even before Sasol Two had been completed and commissioned. This indicates a high degree of confidence in both the process and contractors who had been building Sasol Two. Sasol Three was to be largely a "carbon copy" of Sasol Two, using the existing drawings and temporary facilities already available. With two projects now being handled effectively as one, further economies resulted in terms of both cost and time. As a result, Sasol Three came on stream very quickly after Sasol Two, early in 1982. The total investment in the two projects was on the order of $6.5 billion with the U.S. dollar equivalent to 1.15 Rand, as it was then.

How was the project managed? The construction site was divided into six zones, each zone in turn being subdivided into areas. This resulted in a total, for Sasol Two, of more than 60 construction areas, each of which was handled separately, with its own project team, critical path network, and the like. A similar process was used for Sasol Three. So all in all, there were some 120 separate projects, each handled autonomously, with its own project team. It is very evident from the project's ultimate success that this system of project management was very effective, and once again, we have demonstrated the value of establishing small teams. We have said that the optimum number of personnel for such teams is on the order of 10, and this seems to be proven in practice. Larger teams are by no means so effective. But in the case of the Sasol project, we have an example of not only effective teamwork on site, but also teamwork across continents, with companies speaking different languages cooperating together. This represents teamwork at its best!

## VOLVO: TEAMS MAKE ASSEMBLY LINE OBSOLETE

Henry Ford revolutionized car manufacturing in 1914 with the introduction of assembly line concepts replacing the team approach. History is now repeating itself with teams replacing the assembly line at Volvo's plant at Uddevalla in southwest Sweden; this is widely acclaimed as a breakthrough and Volvo may well become the forerunner of future auto factories. Roger Holtback, Volvo's car division president, states (Taylor, 1989):

> "We are saying farewell to the traditional assembly line. . . . I hope that one day in the future somebody will be able to stand here and say 'Henry Ford invented the assembly line but Volvo did away with it—in a profitable way'. . . . [After all] it is people who create quality, not technology alone. A robot does a good job only if correctly programmed by humans."

Interestingly, Volvo took to assembly line operations rather late, in 1953 though the company was established in 1926. In the 1960s, the company faced high absenteeism and high labor turnover, with low productivity. In its efforts to make the work more varied, interesting, and attractive, the company based its Kalmar plant on a work-team basis with computer-guided carriers bringing components to the decentralized assembly points. Absenteeism and labor turnover declined and productivity soared. Uddevalla is a much improved version of Kalmar. Full use is also being made of high technoogy in engineering and the computer sciences. Workers are grouped in teams of 8 to 10 in six product plants; the teams are autonomous and responsible for assembly of the complete car, including quality control. About 40% of the workers are women, assembly is done in a stationary position, not moving lines, and special hand tools, ergonomically designed for women, are being used. The noise level is low, natural light and stress-free color designs are on the walls, and there is a conspicuous lack of dirt and odors. More power is continuously being delegated down the line, thereby posing more challenges to the workers and also encouraging creativity. Training is very elaborate, planning and design a cooperative effort between the union and management, and operation occurs on a consensus basis with no supervisors or foremen.

Elsewhere in the world, the trend is to use cheap, unskilled labor in Third World countries to build volume via assembly line operations, but Volvo is convinced that there will always be a market for a high-quality handmade car built in a humane way and to the latest environmental standards. On the whole, Volvo's is a most commendable effort, one being keenly watched by entrepreneurs, social scientists, and others all over the world.

## EVEN BIG CAN BE BEAUTIFUL!

One of the world's largest managing contractors is the American firm, Bechtel. Its strength lies in the project management field and it is said to employ literally hundreds of project managers. From time to time, the sayings and doings of some of these project managers are highlighted in its in-house magazine. One of its issues featured the project manager responsible for the world's largest liquid natural gas (LNG) project in Algeria, and he is quoted as saying (*Bechtel Brief*, 1979):

> "The role of a project manager is essentially to keep an objective view of the whole project—its trends, problems and activities—from an informed viewpoint. It's important that the project manager does not become, for example, the engineering manager or the construction manager on the project, but stands back and ensures that engineering and construction are properly performed and managed."

Interestingly, this is the same project that was awarded in 1973 to the Chemical Construction Corporation (Chemico), one of the major contractors of that time. The project was so badly managed, with the discovery of kickbacks and other illegal payments being made all around, that the original contract was canceled in November 1975 and awarded to Bechtel (Kharbanda and Stallworthy, 1984). Bechtel succeeded where Chemico failed, mainly because of the new project manager who knew his job and was made of entirely "different stuff"—though there were other factors as well. Another project manager, with more than 30 years of experience behind him, describes himself as a firm believer in "cooperative management" and explains it thus (Kharbanda and Stallworthy, 1987):

> "Generally, people are interested in performing well and cooperating if they are treated like human beings and not criticized unnecessarily. . . . You've got to compliment people on their good efforts and performance, you've got to work with them, put forth the effort to help them work well with one another. If you're going to get the job done well, it will be through teamwork and cooperation, not through fighting with one another."

Another project manager emphasizes the importance of listening (which we have dealt with at length in a previous chapter), also that people really want to feel they are part of a team. How do you do this? Briefly, he notes (Kharbanda and Stallworthy, 1987):

"You have to be a good listener and respect the thoughts and ideas of the project team members. Then you have to be able to evaluate this input and provide appropriate direction. You have to be able to recognize capability in individuals and give them every opportunity to use their initiative. The younger people of today are going to be the managers of the future and we must help them gain experience. Technical training is essential, but I don't think you can be highly technical or theoretical and be a good project manager on that basis."

In the above quotations, we have a variety of recurrent themes, all of which have come up before as we have pursued the role of the team leader. Words and phrases such as "learning," "initiative," "experience," "being a good listener," "teamwork," and "cooperation" recur constantly. These are the essential elements in a good team, led by an effective project manager.

# 17

## *All Have One Goal*

*It is not enough to take steps which may some day lead to a goal; each step must be itself a goal and a step likewise.*

—GOETHE

PROJECTS, OF COURSE, have invariably one goal comprising four components: completion on time, within budget, to specification, and of the quality necessary to satisfy the client. In fact, a great deal has been written about success in management, but unfortunately not enough about failures and disasters. Lessons are to be derived from both, but particularly from failures. A recent edition of the annual *Cumulative Book Index*, which lists all the books published worldwide in the English language during a year, enumerates over 100 titles relating to success and associated topics, but less than 10 relating to failure. Failures offer valuable lessons for managers, if only they will listen and learn. Consider Otto von Bismark's dictum:

> Fools you are . . . to say you learn by your experience. . . . I prefer to
> profit by other's mistakes and avoid the price of my own.

In projects, time and cost have always been two of the most
visible criteria for measuring success. Of course, quality has also
been a third, often hidden, dimension, but it has assumed a new
and added importance in light of the quality "revolution" in manufacturing. Some of the process plant contractors, such as Kellogg
in the United States and Foster Wheeler in the United Kingdom,
seem to have adopted the total quality management (TQM) concept enthusiastically. Their commitment to quality is turning into
an everyday reality with a clear shift in focus from purely product-
and systems-oriented to customer-driven. This trend is also reflected in a cultural change, with project people using the language
of TQM on a day-to-day basis. It is also helping to reinforce the
team approach that is so vital to success in projects (Nicholson,
1991).

## FAILURES OUTNUMBER SUCCESSES

Plans and projects *can* and *do* fail, no matter how careful we are.
Although projects can fail for a number of reasons, ranging from
acts of God to unexpected personnel transfers, some basic reasons
for failure include poorly defined goals, poor estimates, poor planning, and lack of adequate troubleshooting mechanisms to correct
difficulties in a timely fashion (Pinto and Mantel, 1990). All these
causes of failure are within the control of the project manager and
demonstrate failure on the part of management. The root cause of
failure is seen to be management ineptitude and flaws in the project organization, allowing mistakes of various kinds to go uncor-
rected. Usually, these problems are interlinked, a fact well
demonstrated by the Challenger disaster.

The investigation commission found that a serious flaw existed
in the decision-making process for the launch and further stated
that the decision to launch was based on "incomplete and sometimes misleading information, a conflict between engineering data

and management judgments, and a NASA management structure that permitted internal flight safety problems to bypass key Shuttle managers," representing gross misjudgment on the part of management (*Spaceflight*, 1986).

In projects, time is indeed of the essence. Though time is money, comparatively, overrun in time is far more serious than overrun in cost. Just to convey a sense of both's relative importance: A project that is on budget but brings its product to market 6 months late is said to earn about 33% less profit over 5 years. However, for projects that are on time, but cost 50% above budget, the profit drop is a mere 4%. Of course, each project and each situation are unique, and the findings above are based on certain assumptions. These are meant only to convey a feeling for the subject, no more. In general, speed in completing a project, especially in the high-tech area, can make all the difference between success and disaster. Examples that readily come to mind include (Kharbanda and Stallworthy, 1984, 1992) the Rolls Royce RB 211 engine; Concorde supersonic aircraft; and nuclear power plants. A contemporary project, the Channel tunnel, may well join these projects; so far it has proved so disastrously expensive that some of the companies engaged in its construction went bankrupt and even ceased to exist!

## LET US HEED SOME WORDS OF WISDOM

Jack Mason, a Professor at the University of Houston, has developed a course that his students have dubbed "Failure 101." It deals with innovative ideas, some initially proclaimed even ridiculous. Students learn about, among other things, "slow, stupid failure" and "intelligent, fast failure." Although real lessons are often best learned in the workplace, the classroom is certainly the right place to start talking about key issues, particularly in the case of project failure. Although real-life lessons may have greater impact, they are far too costly to use as a training device!

We have suggested at various points that the decisive sub-issues relative to project success are time, cost, performance, and use and satisfaction. A project may be "95% complete" in terms of both money and time, yet half the work can still be left to do. Software projects are particularly notorious in this respect, for example, 90% of the work is completed in 90% of the time, the rest takes another 90%! Then there is also what we call the "99% syndrome." A project may be almost finished for a year or even longer, while the taxi meter is still running and costs are being incurred on a major scale. When a new project overruns its budget, the project manager must seek the real causes before prescribing remedies. Never forget the almost universal law:

> Ninety percent of the time things turn out to be worse than you expected. Of the other ten percent, you had no right to expect too much.

And above all, always remember friend Murphy, an electronics engineer, whose power of observation made him famous through the now recognized and universal *Murphy's law.* The lesson to be drawn from this law? We must never make the assumption that people will act reasonably, sensibly, or competently. This factor in human behavior the project manager—and indeed, all the members of the project team—must never forget. Finally, a random sampling of some "treasures" on the subject are presented here. We hope the message is loud and clear:

- Work smarter *not* just harder.

- Try to change situations, not people.

- Good leaders set a direction, *not* strategy; they shun excessive meetings/reports.

- Leaders create something of value that did not previously exist.

- Ideal team: open, blunt, and argumentative—much like a successful football team *but* its members caring about each other.

## PROJECT MANAGERS MUST CALL THE TUNE

Functionally, project team members report to a project manager, but administratively they report to their functional head, who also appraises their performance and recommends promotion, future work assignments, and so forth. An extensive study (Katz and Allen, 1985) has examined the relationship between project performance and the relative influence of project and functional managers. The study concerned to 86 R&D teams in nine technology-based organizations, but seems quite relevant to projects in general. Analysis of this study's results shows higher project performance when influence over salaries and promotions is seen as balanced between project and functional managers. Peak performance, however, is achieved when this influence rests with the project manager and influence over purely technical matters lies with the functional manager.

Katz and Allen's article also discusses some of the other factors considered important in developing a better perspective on the matrix structures and relationships. It is clear that balanced authority seldom exists along each dimension of managerial influence. Since the data in this study are cross-sectional, one cannot be sure what happens to a project team as its members continue to interact throughout the different innovative phases of a project. With higher project performance, project managers may come to be seen as more powerful and influential within an organization. However, such relationships are important enough to be the subject of further research. Although the creation of a formal matrix structure is relatively straightforward, albeit expensive and time-consuming, more research is needed to understand the different staffing requirements and specific kinds of leadership and management systems necessary to influence and effectively support matrix relationships in R&D organizations. Katz and Allen's study and its findings are significant enough to warrant similar research on construction and like projects.

## HIGH TECHNOLOGY IS NOT ALWAYS THE ANSWER

Success is usually measured in relation to the fulfillment of preset time and cost targets, and much of the literature on this subject deals with the techniques used to achieve those targets. As an example, information technology (IT) is playing an ever-increasing role in this area, with a host of computer systems, hardware as well as software, to cover various aspects of project management. Nevertheless, we maintain that ultimately it is the human factor in a project, far more than the tools or techniques, including IT, that determines success. McMorris and Gravely (1993) maintain that although computers have provided us with an ability to collect "mountains" of data, it still requires human intervention to analyze and interpret the same information for appropriate action. IT can help considerably in project administration and control, but it also has a negative aspect. With more and more work now being done at home and other places remote from the office, there is less emphasis on the human factor, a factor we consider most vital. Fortunately and very significantly, current trends in IT are making the worker central to the production process. A high-tech production/manufacturing facility at Lockheed, for example, claims to bring the employee "back into the manufacturing equation."

We are convinced that people, rather than materials or money, are by far the most valuable resource in every walk of life. Just one person, the leader, can make all the difference, but to achieve anything, that leader has to be supported by an effective team. It is the team, far more than single individuals or techniques, that successfully translates the initial concept into a working reality. Fortunately, there is a distinct trend worldwide to include business management in the training curricula for existing professions, including finance and engineering. Until recently, there existed in the educational field, a fascination with "method," rather than the basic philosophy of people management. We repeat: What is really required in the present uncertain and fiercely competitive business environment is sound leadership. Such a message is coming from many quarters and must be heeded. Our case studies show that this is already happening.

## PROJECT POSTAPPRAISAL CAN PAY LARGE DIVIDENDS

A project once completed is usually filed away—especially if it has been a failure. This is a pity, since valuable lessons remain, if the team engaged on the project takes the time to conduct a postappraisal. The best time for this is, of course, just after completion, when one's memory is fresh. One of the best examples of postappraisal of projects is provided by British Petroleum (Gulliver, 1987). It established two similar projects for converting gas into a component of high-octane gasoline. One project was in Australia; it was completed on time and below its budgeted cost. The other occurred in Rotterdam; it was completed a year late and the budget exceeded. The obvious conclusion: The Australian project was successful and the Dutch project a failure. However, a closer look at the two projects did not confirm such a conclusion.

The Australian project involved import substitution and was designed to help that country cope with a prevailing adverse balance of payments. Although the project was completed earlier than expected, the economic situation in Australia had already changed radically, with gasoline demand much lower than projected. Hence, the plant had to be run at lower capacity, thus greatly reducing its profitability. On the other hand, the Rotterdam plant, although characterized by time and cost overruns, gave a return on investment much in line with what had been initially forecast, because market demand for the product in Europe continued to be strong. So, we see that what was actually required was better market-forecasting techniques. This contrasting experience in two different countries, providing such unexpected results, led British Petroleum to set up a formal postproject appraisal (PPA) unit at its London headquarters. Its sole purpose is to help the company learn from its mistakes and, of course, to try and repeat its successes. Appraisal of over 80 British Petroleum projects worldwide has helped to provide some guidelines, such as:

- More accurate formulation of investment proposals

- More objective approval procedures

- More efficient execution of projects

As a result of following these guidelines, British Petroleum's return on investment in most projects is now similar to, and sometimes higher than, the figure originally forecasted. This, along with other improved management practices, has naturally led to a considerable boost in British Petroleum's profits. A PPA should ideally assess the following:

- Why was the project taken up at all?

- Is the project producing in accordance with the design?

- Is the demand for the product at the forecast level?

- Was the project completed on time and within budget?

- Does the project fit into the company's overall corporate strategy?

Ideally, PPA team members should not be the sole appraisers of their projects; otherwise, the evaluation will not be truly objective. It is good management policy to centralize and formalize this activity, while bringing in additional experts not directly involved in the completed project. This is a procedure employed by British Petroleum, so that the lessons do reach those most concerned, wherever they are. PPA members are also in a position to provide very useful input to project planners, helping them to formulate sound proposals. Such interaction across the various disciplines involved in a project, such as engineering, finance, production, and marketing, can reap enormous dividends.

## GO EAST, YOUNG MAN

To survive, Japan has adopted, adapted, and improved Western quality control techniques until they have reached superlative levels of effectiveness (Price, 1984). The Japanese have excelled because they have taken the basics of management, including the fact that human beings are the key, to heart and put them into practice. It seems to be a philosophy of life that fits neatly into the Japanese culture and business environment, and this has made its acceptance much easier. There is no doubt that the importance given to the individual has helped the Japanese get where they are today. Some hundreds of books have been written about the Japanese management practices, but one area in the field of project management, namely, management accounting practices, has not attracted much attention. These have contributed much to the "miracle" in Japan; briefly these are (Kharbanda and Stallworthy, 1991):

- Cost is everybody's business, not just the accountant's.

- Design to cost, against the conventional practice of costing the design.

- In the case of new projects or products, enter first. The profits will follow.

- In the workplace, teamwork is at the crux of boosting morale and productivity.

In Japan, accounting procedures are used for controlling a company's activities, not merely measuring what is happening. This means that accounting is used to reinforce management strategies, thus creating a direct link between accounting practices and corporate goals. The result has been that accountancy in Japan plays an "influencing" rather than a mere "informing" role, as is almost invariably the case in the Western world (Munday, 1991). And yet the number of accountants per million of population seems to be one of the lowest in the world, 0.05, compared with over 1.0 in the United States, Britain, India, and many other nations. This represents an apparent paradox, but it works well. The "trick" is that in Japan, engineers are encouraged to become accountants as well, a two-in-one entity! Other distinguishing features of Japanese management practices include:

- Implementing projects quickly to enter the market *first*

- Slow decision making (by consensus), but quick execution of *their* decision!

To explain the Japanese miracle, many observers in the West have tended to undermine the Japanese emphasis on the individual and the use of teams by instead ascribing success to the active role of the Japanese government and, more specifically, the Ministry of International Trade and Industry (MITI). But this is an oversimplification and even wrong, since Japanese companies are equally successful abroad as well! Nearly 10% of both managers' and workers' time in Japan is spent on continuing education: Education is a continuing process, not a "one-time" effort. This is the only way to keep up with new technology, new concepts, and the continuously changing environment; it is therefore a policy that should be pursued by every project manager. He or she ought to give their project team members every opportunity to attend relevant courses, even while they are working on site on a project.

*Part* 5

## *Where Do We Go from Here?*

*T*he final section of this book examines various answers to the question, "Where do we go from here?" We offer some thoughts on the future of project management in Chapter 18. Obviously, gazing into our "crystal ball" with any sort of accuracy is a difficult task, and we are forced to make some projections based on the current state of the world in terms of the future potential for project management. Nevertheless, there are some exciting trends in motion around the globe that offer tremendous possibilities for the rapidly continuing expansion of project management techniques.

Chapter 19 focuses on the new breed of project manager. We will examine not only the types of skills that future project managers are going to need in order to be successful, but also project management as a viable, stand-alone profession. As we will demonstrate, project management does meet the standards generally recognized for the establishment and maintenance of a profession.

Finally, Chapter 20 is our attempt to summarize in a meaningful way some of our more salient points. We offer some concluding principles that, we hope, will guide the reader as he or she learns the art and science of project management.

# 18

## The Future Is Uncertain

WHAT IS THE future of project management? Clearly, we have no more prescient a crystal ball than others, but we can offer some suppositions based on our experience and the state of the industrial world as we near the millennium. We are convinced that the importance of project management for organizational success will grow rather than wane in the years to come. In this chapter, we will discuss some of the reasons why we see a proliferation in project management and subsequent increasing demand for project management skills in the years to come. Finally, we will suggest that companies need to become more systematic in their approach to developing project managers who have the tools and abilities to get the job done.

In the larger context of international business, attempts to make projections regarding the future are often met with skepticism, wariness, and even amusement, as in cases when prognosticators are confronted with their guesses years later. Peter Drucker, the well-known management consultant and writer, is particularly leery of organizations becoming overly infatuated with the future, arguing that those who forecast the future and make strategic decisions on the basis of probabilities and present-day trends are generally unlikely to succeed in the long term (Drucker, 1992). Nevertheless, the future does hold out some tremendous opportunities in addition to its threats and uncertainty. For project management organizations, in particular, there are some encouraging signs that point to the likelihood of a tremendous upsurge in market demand for their services and techniques.

## THE AGE OF PROJECT MANAGEMENT

"The Age of Project Management," as we have chosen to title this section of the chapter, derives from the title of a recent article by a well-known project management scholar (Cleland, 1993). He paints a convincing portrait of the state of project management in the international sphere and demonstrates the basis for supposing that project management will increase in importance in years to come. Some of the reasons why project management techniques will gain in popularity are 1) dramatically shortened market windows and product life cycles, 2) rapid development of third world and "closed" economies, 3) increasingly complex and technical products, 4) heightened international competition, and 5) the environment of organizational resource scarcity that has led to downsizing and streamlining operations. Let us consider each of these reasons in turn.

   **1. *Shortened market windows and product life cycles.*** Evidence of the turbulent changes affecting the business world is the degree to which product obsolescence has been advanced. Traditionally, in many industries, product launches could be carefully crafted and planned because companies knew that they had a comfortably wide window of opportunity to develop, test, and market new products. For example, the IBM system 360 that so revolutionized mainframe computing continued as a viable product for nearly a decade. A more recent example concerns the IBM personal computer, the PC. This benchmark 64K RAM microcomputer, launched in the early 1980s, continued to be the industry standard for almost five years. One has only to contrast those examples to more recent PC product announcements and launches to realize that such lengthy product life cycles, particularly in the computer hardware and software industries, are a thing of the past. Indeed, the technology is advancing so rapidly today that year-old PCs are often literally passé.

What these and other examples point to is the impact that market timing has made on new product development. One of the authors recently spent several months working with a large computer manufacturer's project teams. Their strategic planning and new product development departments routinely prepare for new product delivery and system modification introductions that are sometimes two years into the future. For example, it was common to hear hardware engineers and project managers developing time frames for future product delivery that had to occur within a three-month market window. If the project was late, it was useless because a rival would have exploited the opening and offered a substitute product.

These time-to-market pressures and shortened product life cycles have had a significant impact on more and more organizations as they seek to counter such threats through the use of project teams. Cross-functional teams and project management techniques have had a major impact on a number of companies and their ability to deliver new products within significantly shorter time frames. For example, in 1989, Honda was touted for its "superfast" approach to new product innovation. Using team approaches, Honda had shortened the time frame for new automobile development from five to three years. Although a significant achievement, Honda's team approach was just the beginning of innovative process changes in the automotive industry. By 1994, Chrysler CEO Robert Lutz was able to announce that the Viper platform (cross-functional) team had designed, developed, engineered, and produced a new prototype in 18 months.

Other examples abound. Motorola's order-to-finished-goods

manufacturing cycle for its pagers has been shortened from three weeks to two hours. Hewlett Packard can now produce electronic testing equipment in five days, compared to the former four-week processing time. These innovations have come about through a realization that dynamic changes in the business environment are forcing companies to become more aware of the need to move products to market at a faster and faster pace, both in order to take advantage of market windows and allow for technological changes that render products obsolete at an increasingly rapid pace. Embedded in this realization has been the increased use of project teams and project management techniques to maximize organizational resources and creative processes while giving development teams the freedom from bureaucracy and red tape that can often stifle innovation.

**2. *Rapid development of third world and closed economies.*** One of the astounding by-products of the opening of the former Soviet Union, Eastern Europe, and Asian communist countries has been the explosion in pent-up demand within these societies for all manner of consumer goods and infrastructure development. Wherever one turns in examining the developing sectors of the international economy, it is easy to discover examples of such projects either underway or about to be initiated. Vietnam has recently opened its borders to a number of foreign corporations and initiated a massive program for infrastructure and industrial expansion. The People's Republic of China, although nominally the world's largest communist state, has been increasingly eager to encourage consumerism and "pockets" of capitalism within its largest cities. Further, project management groups from major industrial construction firms in the United States, Europe, and Japan are in serious negotiations with the Chinese government for a number of large-scale development projects of every sort.

Eastern Europe, likewise, stands poised to take advantage of project management in its drive to modernize industries in the wake of a democratic revolution that has replaced the former, command economies with market-driven capitalism. Old, inefficient factories are being closed and torn down or upgraded to turn out new products. Although there are very real limits on funding for the revitalization of its industries, the nature of Eastern European economies is such that capital development is likely to continue, albeit slowly at first, for several decades.

Despite the current recession in international economies, the construction industry continues to boom in Asia, which now accounts for over 60% of worldwide construction and continues to grow rapidly. This development has been a positive windfall for Japanese, European, and American contractors (*Asian Review,* 1994). An October 26, 1989, *Wall Street Journal* article described the enormous capital expansion program underway in Japan, a program that is expected to grow at a double-digit pace well into the 1990s. It is likely that project management will continue to play a key role in this expansion, within not only the borders of Japan but also other countries that manufacture and market Japanese products (Cleland, 1991).

A recent issue of the *Asian Wall Street Journal* (April 18, 1994) carries a 14-page supplement entitled, "Asian Infrastructure—Asia Transforms Itself." The article goes to some length to examine many of the most pressing demands for major infrastructure development and expansion. It is clear that although huge spending on infrastructure in Asia is imperative, the governments of these countries simply cannot meet the enormous costs associated with such mega-projects. Consequently, this situation offers enormous opportunity for the private sector, both local but particularly international companies, to exploit these needs.

To illustrate the level of development currently being undertaken in these Asian countries, consider some of the examples summarized below, each representing a mega-project forecast to, at minimum, cost in excess of $1 billion.

The following is just a cursory list of some of the more exciting mega-projects that are currently being developed in the Asian world. Perhaps even more intriguing is the list of the largest contractors for these projects. We had suggested that the rapid development of these countries offers some lucrative possibilities for private companies, including European and American heavy construction firms. Among the top 10 contractors for these projects

| Country | No. of Projects | Cost Range ($ Billions) | Largest Project |
|---------|-----------------|-------------------------|-----------------|
| China | 7 | 1–77 | Dam and hydropower station |
| Hong Kong | 3 | 1–20 | Airport |
| India | 2 | 1–2 | Enron power plant |
| Indonesia | 4 | 1–2.5 | Coal-fired power plant |
| Malaysia | 5 | 1–5.6 | Dam and hydropower station |
| Philippines | 1 | 1.3 | Elevated rail system |
| Singapore | 4 | 1–5 | Power station |
| South Korea | 6 | 1–20 | Superhighway system |
| Taiwan | 5 | 5–17 | Mass rapid transit system |
| Thailand | 4 | 1.5–4.3 | Airport |

are Bechtel Corporation, M. W. Kellogg, John Brown/Davy, Fluor Daniel, and Brown and Root. As more companies turn to the developing markets of the Pacific Rim, it is likely that new names will be added to this list.

Several of the projects listed are being rushed through to completion at a rapid pace, as they are desperately needed by their clients, the governments of the countries. In moving these projects through the pipeline quickly, two differing approaches are very much in evidence. One model, referred to as BOT, involves the following steps: 1) build, 2) operate, 3) transfer, as the contractor completes the facility, brings it to an operating mode, and then transfers ownership to the client. The other variant, called BOOT, refers to these four steps: 1) build, 2) own, 3) operate, and 4) transfer, in which the contractor takes intial ownership of the facility or project as part of a licensing agreement before eventually turning it over to the government as it is purchased. The latter, in particular, is an exciting concept that has already been translated into reality in several locations (see, e.g., Kharbanda and Stallworthy, 1992).

**3. *Increasingly complex and technical products.*** Many of the products that are being created today in a variety of industries, from children's toys to automobiles, are becoming more technically complex to develop, manufacture, and use. Technologically driven innovation presents a tremendous challenge for organizations in the areas of engineering and design, production, and marketing. As a result, many organizations are relying on project teams composed of cross-functional groups to create and market these products in as efficient a time frame as possible.

Rework cycles are expensive (Cooper, 1994) and often come about through poor internal communication between functional departments, all of whom are expected to cooperate in bringing a new product to market. In many instances, the new product introduction process consists of a series of "cycled loops" from one functional area to another. For example, consider a simplified case in which a new electronics consumer product is slated for introduction. Typically, we would see some sort of causal chain set in motion, in which engineering would first design the product and send its specifications to production. The production department, presented with the design details, may object to certain aspects of the products (perhaps due to manufacturing process limitations that do not allow for all the features engineering originally included in the product) and will then return the product plans to engineering for rework.

Following this "loop," engineering may or may not make enough modifications to satisfy production. Perhaps a couple of iterations of this loop will be needed before production is sufficiently agreeable to the design and begins prototype development. At this point, in many organizations, marketing is finally brought on board and given the opportunity to comment on the prototype. Depending on its experience with and knowledge of other competing products in the marketplace, this department may offer suggestions that will once again cycle the product back to engineering for additional rework, all the while holding up development and new product launch.

The reader can readily see how unwieldy such a causal chain is when an organization is faced with the pressures of new product introduction. Consequently, many companies are now scrapping such a new product introduction strategy and employing cross-functional teams from the beginning of the process, believing, with ample supporting evidence, that allowing all relevant departments immediate access to and ability to influence new product designs will significantly shorten the time to market delivery.

**4. *Heightened international competition.*** Competition drives innovation. It is only in the face of replaceable products that organizations are compelled to upgrade, alter, or develop new and innovative products of their own. In the past, American manufacturing had the economic playing field to herself for a variety of reasons, many associated with the impact of World War II on other industrialized nations and the slow industrial advance of developing countries. During this period, U.S. companies had enormous domestic markets to exploit, leading to a sense of hubris that sowed the seeds for later problems. On the other hand, foreign manufacturing was in its infancy and suffering from the teething problems associated with new start-up companies: poor quality, lack of name recognition, uncertain marketing strategies, and so forth. Although truly a golden age for American business, clearly this was not a state that could continue indefinitely, in spite of many companies' belief that, in fact, it would.

It was not until the late 1960s that any appreciable inroads were made into "traditional" American markets such as automobiles. However, during the 1970s, the oil shocks and Japanese manufacturing skills combined with lower unit prices served to seriously threaten many strategic and consumer U.S. industries, such as steel, computers, electronic data systems (copiers), and electronic consumer goods (television). These economic attacks, although painful, offered a mixed blessing in that they served to finally shake many U.S. companies out of the inertia and sense of complacency into which they had sunk.

In many industries, domestic "counterattacks" have been spurred on by the increased use of project management. One of the fortunate side-effects of the pressures placed on American firms was the development of innovative processes for survival in a new, international marketplace for which they were under-equipped and that they did not foresee with accuracy. Project management has a long history in certain industries, such as airframe development at Boeing and McDonnell-Douglas. However, one of the effects of the end of American corporate lethargy was convincing other companies, many of whom had no experience in project management, to regard it as a new and useful tool for competitive advantage. One of the more appealing aspects of our project management teaching and consulting experiences has been the number of companies in a diverse array of industries that are experimenting with project management for the first time. Properly trained and schooled in its techniques, these firms stand to reap substantial benefits within the international marketplace through speedier product development and greater efficiency of operations.

**5. The environment of organizational resource scarcity.** Obviously, organizations have never existed in a truly munificent environment in which resource acquisition presented no challenges or concerns. Companies have always been forced to operate in pursuit of a variety of scarce resources: money, trained personnel, plant and equipment, and so forth. Nevertheless, the uncertain economic conditions of the current decade have led to a new management philosophy, an age of belief in the need to "do more with less." The practical result of this new approach has seen many organizations downsizing and streamlining operations in pursuit of cost savings and efficiency.

From an operations perspective, the impact of such corporate downsizing has been to create increased demands on those who remain to perform as effectively as possible within a resource-scarce atmosphere. In this regard, several of these organizations (e.g., Kodak) are relying to greater and greater degrees on project management to provide the dual benefits of rapid product development and time to market within greater cost controls and budgetary limitations. These companies, some using project management for the first time in a formal manner, have discovered one of the important features of these techniques: Their use gives project teams the ability to be both externally effective in getting products to market as well as internally efficient in their use of organizational resources.

Project management is predicated on the ability to use resources carefully: In effect, the techniques are themselves "resource-constrained." Consequently, in an atmosphere of efficiency and streamlining operations, project management is a valuable tool for companies to exploit, as many currently are doing.

The above are some of the more compelling reasons why we are likely to continue to witness an increased interest in and use of project management in international businesses. As Cleland (1991) noted, the strategic thrust of many businesses and, indeed, many countries points to a continued drive to improve, upgrade, modernize, and develop their infrastructures, markets, and capital and natural resource bases. In this context, the benefits of project management are substantial and clearly able to provide these countries and their business organizations with a powerful tool for effective and efficient operations.

At the same time that we can look with hope to an expansion in the use of project management, it is perhaps ironic to point out the dangers in creating overly optimistic expectations about project management as a business technique. It is true that project management is the management of change versus traditional functional management, which often solidifies the status quo. As a result, project management is ideally situated to serve as a platform on which many organizations can achieve the degrees of flexibility and efficiency needed for long-term survival and prosperity. Because much is expected from the project management movement, it is also helpful to consider some words of warning on how to avoid the "flash in the pan" sobriquet so often ascribed to the latest management technique. As Barnes and Wearne (1993) write:

> Project management is the management of uncertainty, and its future must itself be uncertain . . . no technique with a distinctive name achieves what its enthusiasts hope for it or lasts as long as they expect. The same could be true of project management itself.

Although our concerns are perhaps overstated, they nevertheless strike an appropriate note of caution that must be considered.

The worst future for project management would be to create a new organizational "buzz word" out of the technique, leading too many companies with too high expectations to begin jumping on the bandwagon in hopes of achieving quick and painless solutions to their problems. Like any other useful management tool or technique, project management will work to the degree that organizations employing it do so in a measured and thoughtful way, understanding its strengths and limitations. Overly ambitious programs without the necessary level of commitment and support could do the worst possible damage to the project management profession, by turning the techniques into simply another "faddish" approach that was tried by ill-informed and unprepared companies, failed predictably, and was dismissed as ineffective.

## CONCLUSIONS

In an area of soaring costs, rapidly increasing complexity, and diminishing natural resources, organizations find themselves having to make do with less and less. Corporate profitability and long-term survival are predicated on their ability to continue to grow, offer the public new and innovative products and services, and find competitive niches that enable them to survive and prosper. It is within this context of diminishing resources, cost cutting, streamlining operations, and slashing overhead and excessive personnel that project management techniques can offer a lucrative form of competitive advantage for those firms that have taken the time to learn and use it well.

Project management, a philosophy and technique based on the ideas of performing to maximum potential within the constraints of limited resources, offers a logical and attractive method for increasing profitability in a number of business areas. Further, the rapid expansion of Asia, Eastern Europe, and Latin American economies will continue to drive a concomitant expansion in development, building, infrastructure repair and improvement, as well as within the industrial sectors of their economies. Many, if not most, of these pushes for expansion will be fueled by project management techniques.

With the future so potentially bright for expanding the role of project management on a worldwide basis, the only potential clouds on the horizon concern the ability of more and more governments and businesses to perform these techniques well. As we have noted throughout this book, the lack of formal training for many future project managers is worrisome and must be corrected, particularly through the development of a common skill set and body of knowledge. The rise of project management as a profession is likely to be a key element in these countries' ability to use the techniques to their maximum potential. As a result, we have devoted the next chapter of our book to examining the professional project manager, understanding the nature of creating and maintaining a professional body of project managers—so key to continued development and industrial expansion around the world.

# 19

## *The New Breed*

*The new man is always in a new time, under new conditions; his course is the facsimile of no prior one, but is by its nature original.*

—CARLYLE

THERE IS CURRENTLY a wave of qualitative change in the nature and particularly the practice of management. The watchword seems to be that a really effective supervisor must lead rather than merely manage. This philosophy is indirectly leading to an emphasis on workplace leadership and subordinate relations shifting from material values to something higher. The nomenclature varies, of course, depending on where the subject is discussed and who is writing on the subject. Nevertheless, even across cultural boundaries, there is an interesting convergence of opinion as to what values are shaping the leadership dynamic in modern business. To illustrate, writing on the management process from the perspective of running Indian corporations, Aga

(1994) notes that, "Profits is not just a set of figures, but of values." In the context of Western business, Hawley (1994) writes that the key questions for today's managers can no longer simply be classified in terms of tasks and structure, but must also encompass the idea of "spirit." The common thread running through many of these ideas is that leadership has a value-laden component that must be addressed head-on rather than ignored.

Based on the discussion of the last chapter, it should be clear that in today's dynamically changing project management environment, skilled project managers will be in even greater demand. Organizations must begin taking the necessary steps to "develop" these project managers in order to gain the most benefit from employing project management techniques for new product and process development. What will this new breed of project managers be like? How will they develop the skills that set them apart from project managers of the past and give them the ability to run their projects to a higher level of proficiency? This chapter addresses the question of the "new" project manager, one who understands the roles and responsibilities he or she inherited. Companies must do a better job of managing the training process for project managers, eliminating the idea of the "accidental" project manager from our lexicon. This chapter will make some educated guesses on how we can accomplish these goals.

## CREATING A PROJECT MANAGEMENT PROFESSION

An important part of the alternative to accidental, or ad hoc, project managers lies in the creation of a formalized profession. Webster's dictionary defines a profession as a vocation or occupation requiring advanced education and training and involving intellectual skills. From this definition, we can see that society contains a wide variety of professions and, by extension, professional groups. Doctors, lawyers, engineers, geographers, computer programmers, and accountants are just a few of the large number of professional groups. These occupations serve as a distinguishing symbol for their members and identify them to the rest of society at large.

Project managers, too, are currently in the process of formalizing their professional legitimacy.

In determining the criteria that characterize all professions, five attributes generally emerge (Obermeyer and Pinto, 1994). These attributes serve as the primary method for identifying and characterizing members of a profession as well as distinguishing between professional groups. In other words, although both a doctor and lawyer are professionals, both are not members of the same professional group. The following discussion analyzes the five distinguishing characteristics of professions and more specifically, addresses how, in establishing themselves as a professional body, project managers fulfill these criteria.

**1. *A unique body of knowledge.*** This first attribute of a profession refers to the importance of organizing, documenting, and codifying a distinct set of principles and concepts that apply to such a body. These principles, as they are established, can then be studied through formal education and training programs. For example, an accountant will quickly recognize the initials GAAP and understand that they refer to "generally accepted accounting principles," his or her profession's formal statement of policy and practice. This unique body of knowledge is often taught in either university settings or formally sanctioned training programs.

In 1979, the Project Management Institute initiated the creation of a "project management body of knowledge" (PMBOK). Although continually undergoing refinement and additions as new techniques and principles are developed, the PMBOK serves as a collection of the concepts and unique knowledge that anyone wishing to become a project manager would be expected to amass. It is important to note the above point: The PMBOK is continually being updated and refined. No profession creates an absolute standard of professional knowledge that is inviolate. As technology advances, science discovers new methods and knowledge, and new theory is created, the profession's body of knowledge must acknowledge these changes and incorporate them into its lexicon. To illustrate, the original PMBOK, developed less than two decades ago, is in the process of undergoing its third formal updating and revision. When a profession is no longer willing to appreciate changes within its body of knowledge, it suffers a serious loss of moral authority over members.

**2. *Standards of entry*.** Not just anyone can become a doctor or lawyer. Likewise, the desire to become an engineer or accountant should not be confused with the *right* to join these professions. All professions have some form of training program, often followed by a practical apprenticeship or training program to learn the profession in a hands-on, experiential manner. Further, many professions also use a formal examination as a strong barrier to entry for prospective entrants. For example, in becoming a university professor, most institutions would expect the applicant to have completed a terminal degree (such as a Ph.D.) in his or her field. As part of that process, the aspiring professor must complete several years of schoolwork, sit for comprehensive examinations, and undertake a piece of original, independent research that is published as a dissertation. Understandably, these rigorous barriers to entry serve to "weed out" all but those who have both a genuine desire and the talent to succeed in this profession.

Because project management is still an evolving profession, there are currently no strong barriers to entry for new project managers. In other words, the profession is still highly inclusive and open to prospective project managers. However, steps are being made by the governing body of the Project Management Institute to create and enforce a standard of entry for professional project managers through the development of a formal certification examination. These tests have been administered by the governing body of the Project Management Institute since 1984. There are currently over 2000 certified project managers worldwide and the number is growing rapidly every year. Further, since the systematic push to develop a formal education program for project managers, 20 universities worldwide have instituted masters-level degree programs in project management, with more undertaking this program of study every year. Although the requirements to become a project manager in most corporations are still ad hoc and informal, the standards for entry into the project management profession are gradually taking on a level that will improve the quality of future generations of project managers. We have come far, but we have far to go.

**3.** *A code of ethics.* Codes of ethics typically comprise a profession's ethical standards. Their purpose is to make explicit expected behaviors and prevent inappropriate actions from professional members. The Hippocratic oath, administered to medical doctors, is an example of a traditional code of ethics in that it establishes a standard of conduct regarding patients and the sick. The code of ethics in any profession should serve as a method for creating self-monitoring and policing mechanisms in order to regulate and/or proscribe professional behavior.

Project management borrows most of its ethical standards from the engineering disciplines (Adams, 1994). That is, depending on the type of project being undertaken, there are often some standard ethical expectations associated with its progress, for example, full-disclosure reporting of construction data or standards of performance for the output to the intended clients. More recently, part of the certification process for project managers involves being aware of project management ethical standards and some of the recent textbooks on project management include sections on or codes for ethical behavior (Obradovitch and Stephanou, 1992). These steps are important because they begin to codify an established set of expectations for project management as a general profession, rather than relying on engineering standards that may vary from project to project.

**4.** *Service orientation to the profession.* Service orientation implies a willingness on the part of organization members to improve the profession through their labors. In effect, this idea refers to the commitment level of members of a professional group to the organization and their desire that through their efforts, the organization, and ultimately the profession, will become better. An interesting aspect of professional affiliation is that it is often the case that a professional's commitment to her profession is stronger than her commitment to an employer. For example, an engineer's affiliation with the Institute of Electrical and Electronic Engineers (IEEE) may have a stronger impact on that individual than his relationship with the company that employs him.

Since the mid–1970s, we have witnessed tremendous growth in the number of members of major project management organizations worldwide. The Project Management Institute, Internet (in Europe), the Australian Institute of Project Management, IEEE, the Engineering Advancement Association of Japan, and other professional bodies now claim thousands of members all over the globe. Project managers are joining these groups in recognition of the expanding influence and legitimacy that they have over the profession of project management, regardless of the types of projects being undertaken or the companies for which members work. Along with the increase in membership has come a concomitant commitment of time and energy in performing the actions and services necessary to maintain the viability of these groups. The strength and impact of project management professional organizations are not waning, but expanding at a steady pace.

**5.** *A sanctioning organization.* Managing the creation and "health" of a professional organization is a taxing process. The role of an officially designated sanctioning organization is to actively monitor and regulate the activities of that organization: communicating and interacting with companies, registering and controlling chapters and individual members, sponsoring professional seminars and training programs, setting standards and enforcing compliance, encouraging research and development activities, and promoting publications and the open exchange of ideas. As we have indicated, there are a number of sanctioning bodies operating in the project management field, the largest of which is the Project Management Institute. This organization actively engages in the above set of activities in actively pursuing the agenda of creating and fostering an internationally recognized professional image for project managers.

## THE RISE OF THE PROFESSIONAL PROJECT MANAGER

In creating a generation of professional project managers, Adams (1994) trenchantly notes that unless organizations can establish an alternative project management career path, very little is likely to improve for the majority of accidental project managers. Table 19.1 is intended to illustrate some of the important differences between the common interim, or accidental, project manager and the career project manager. These two job classifications, though informal, clearly differ in some important ways and serve to demonstrate the nature of change that many organizations must be willing to undertake if they are to establish a work environment that allows career project managers to proliferate.

Note that one of the more common characteristics of accidental, or interim, project managers is that they often originate from the technical end of a company. Engineers and technical personnel with hard science backgrounds are frequently put in charge of new projects, particularly in those cases where the project represents the introduction of a new product. For example, within the pharmaceutical industry, it is quite common to make a clinician or research scientist the project manager for a new drug's development and introduction. Likewise, in computer manufacturing organizations, the great majority of project managers for new hardware systems come from electrical engineering or computer science backgrounds. Contrast these backgrounds with the education that career project managers may have: a more broad-based education that comprises elements of management and organizational skills in addition to technical training. These career project managers have an advantage over their accidental counterparts in that they share technical knowledge, but supplement that understanding with the managerial and "people" skills so vital to project management.

The effective management of the creative abilities of professionals and technicians is obviously vital, but work in this area has typically focused on management styles rather than how to meet these groups' motivational needs. An intensive research study ana-

**TABLE 19.1. Alternative Career Paths**

| Issue | Interim Project Manager | Professional Project Manager |
|---|---|---|
| Education | Technical Engineering Hard science | Project area Management Engineering Functional |
| Entry to PM | Accidental | Planned—after qualifying |
| Progression desire | Return to technical field | Remain in project management |
| Advanced education | Unknown, possibly technical | Project management |
| View of PM | Necessary evil, one career step | Interesting, challenging, rewarding |
| Professional orientation goals | Specialist Technical recognition | Generalist Managerial advancement |
| Knowledge or skill required | Technical Detailed In-depth Line managers with management experience | General Broad in scope Professional project manager |

*Source: Adapted from Adams (1994).*

lyzed the motivation of this group in order to isolate its key motivators and learn how to inspire it to perform to maximum potential (Tampol, 1993). The study's findings suggested that, in numerical order, these professionals valued:

| Motivator | % | Preferred Option |
|---|---|---|
| Personal growth | 34 | Significant growth |
| Operational autonomy | 30 | Freedom to work at their own pace |
| Task achievement | 29 | Visible, high performance |
| Money | 7 | Salary and bonus based on personal effort |

Professional and personal achievement is the trigger for motivation. The essential prerequisites include a clear sense of purpose, access to information, and peer contacts. The five main requirements for professional motivation were found to be

- Commitment

- Individual competence

- Facilitative work environment

- Purpose

- Exchange of knowledge

It is also interesting to compare career path progressions for interim versus professional project managers. Most interim project managers view projects as an unwelcome intrusion on their careers —something unpleasant that must be handled with a minimum of bother—and they usually seek nothing else than to return to their functional assignments and responsibilities following the completion of a project. On the other hand, career project managers understand that project management is their functional assignment. They will progress from one project to another. As their skills grow, they will be given increasingly more difficult, strategically important, and complex projects to manage.

Another interesting difference between the interim project manager and the professional lies in the professional goals that each holds. Interim project managers are, by nature, usually technical specialists pressed into service as project managers. Their goal following a successful project is the merited technical recognition they will receive for a job well done. Further, they believe that their career path will remain technical in nature, following the path of scientist to chief engineer. Career project managers, on the other hand, are generalists of necessity. Possessing the necessary technical skills to competently perform their duties, they are not content unless they also develop the managerial and behavioral skills that will allow them to facilitate the project through all its processes, both technical and human. Instead of technical recognition, career project managers seek managerial advancement and they perceive that successful project management is their key to higher corporate office. Their goal is to be the manager of large, strategically important projects, the type of projects on which an organization places its highest priorities.

The career project manager is a special individual who is committed to successfully implementing his or her projects and approaches them for the challenge they offer, not as a temporary purgatory to be endured, but as an important career stepping stone. In order to develop the skills necessary to effectively manage all facets of their projects, career project managers do not disdain managerial and behavioral skills, but constantly seek to improve their abilities to lead their teams. They realize that technical competency will only guide them so far down the path to project success and so they work to supplement that knowledge with advanced education in other aspects of project management. In order for organizations to most effectively tap into their supply of career project managers, they need to consciously work toward creating an environment that encourages these individuals and allows the company to target likely candidates. It is with this purpose in mind that we would propose the following steps as a useful starting point.

## ESTABLISHING A TRAINING PROCESS FOR PROJECT MANAGERS

In putting into operation some of the points made in this chapter, we would argue that it is necessary for companies to establish a formal agenda for the training of project managers. These points, although relatively clear-cut, are an important first step if organizations are to progress from the interim use of "accidental project managers" to a state where project management is an accepted career path.

1. *Recognize that project management is a career option.* An important part of the problem with training project managers to date has been that within many organizations, the perception is that formal training would be a waste of money given the fact that, once their particular projects are completed, most project managers will simply return to their functional duties. Although this point is often true, it begs the larger question of how to ensure that these temporary project managers, once assigned a project, can function successfully. Companies are caught in a classic catch-22 situation in which they need highly trained project managers to run their programs, but due to the temporary nature of projects, are unwilling to invest in their long-term training. Obviously, such a situation cannot continue to exist without having serious negative ramifications on many organizations. Consequently, the first step is for organizations to acknowledge project management as a viable career path, create a job classification for project managers, and invest the needed time and resources in training them to perform their roles successfully. Project management will continue to be "accidental" until we are willing to acknowledge the permanent positive impact it can have on our organizations.

2. *Top management must recognize the importance of projects in achieving strategic goals.* Much has been written on the use of projects as a mechanism for achieving strategic goals (e.g., King,

1988; Souder, 1988). More and more companies are turning to projects as a method for maximizing time-to-market effectiveness and new product innovation while maintaining internal efficiencies of operation. Because of the steady rise in project management, it is high time that top management formally recognized the importance of projects for attaining corporate objectives. A clear signal to the rest of the organization that projects and project managers matter is top management's willingness to publicly acknowledge and encourage the expansion of project management practices and, at the same time, reward project managers for attaining project goals.

**3.** *Begin formal programs of project management training.* In our past project management consulting and training experience, we have often been amazed by the mixed signals sent by top management when it comes to managerial training. Time after time, we have listened to senior executives reassure us that they are sincere in their desire to institutionalize training in project management skills, while at the same time demand that normal organizational operations not be halted or impaired in any way. Essentially, what these executives are seeking is the project management version of a "quick fix." They are hoping to institute a comprehensive program of project management training, but are unwilling to allow any disruption of ongoing work.

A serious investment in time and money is necessary if project managers are to be fully trained in their duties. It would be foolish to decry the continued existence of the "accidental" profession if, at the same time, our training promotes management skill development in an ad hoc manner. Companies need to make good use of professional experts in the field, while at the same time, giving their prospective project managers the time and opportunity to learn their craft. One fruitful avenue that many organizations could explore is the establishment of closer ties with some of the project management sanctioning bodies. Groups such as the Project Management Institute, Internet, and the Engineering Advancement Association offer a variety of programs geared to training prospective project managers in all facets of their responsibilities.

Currently, some 40 to 50 institutions of higher learning offer undergraduate and advanced degrees in areas such as engineering management, project management, engineering administration, and the like. Companies should take advantage of the programs these schools and governing bodies offer or similar seminars taught by reputable experts, rather than investing large sums in untried instructors and training programs that may be of limited value. Further, it makes good sense in creating professional project managers to provide them with strong ties to the relevant professional groups.

Carr (1993) writes that smart training approaches enable organizations to achieve the greatest amount of learning with the least expenditure of time, money, and effort. Training is "smart" not when it tries to improve performance by itself, but when it adopts a *total* approach to performance improvement. In other words, it must be carefully planned, carried out, and later objectively evaluated to see how successful it was. Briefly, the basic guidelines of smart training are:

- Develop training strategically.

- Focus training on improved performance.

- Analyze, design, and select the delivery system.

- Know what the real costs are.

- Manage change—or else!

- The best training is just-in-time training: Put it to use immediately.

- Set specific performance standards and objectives and evaluate against them.

- Evaluate the alternatives.

- What counts is learning, not training.

**4. Promote a formal mentor-subordinate relationship between experienced project managers and newcomers.** A formal "master-apprentice" relationship between seasoned project managers and those just starting out in the field can be of tremendous help in preventing many of the lessons novice project managers learn by making mistakes. Although not all problems or mistakes are foreseeable, an experienced project manager can help in two ways: 1) by foreseeing and warning novice project managers about some of the recognizable problems that could occur, and 2) by providing the guidance to quickly address and correct such problems once they have occurred. In Chapter 4 on critical success factors, we cited past research that showed the primary cause for project failure is the absence of troubleshooting mechanisms once problems develop. A senior project manager often has the experience necessary to show apprentices the steps to take to get a project back on schedule again.

A recent article noted that project management requires, among other characteristics, intelligence, judgment, energy, and persistence (Wearne, 1994). Clearly, formal theoretical training, by itself, cannot provide each of these characteristics to the degree that experience can. In making use of senior management mentors, novice project managers can begin to develop their judgment, enhance their personal energy, and gain the persistence that springs from positive learning.

Another benefit of this formalized mentoring relationship is that it perpetuates new generations of project managers. The skills that senior project managers impart can be passed on from one generation to the next without each new group of project managers having to learn their lessons through experience. As one senior project manager observed, "We all learn from mistakes, but nobody ever said they had to be *your* mistakes." His point was clear; managers passing on their techniques, tricks, and experiences can smooth the road for new generations of project managers.

**5. *Encourage prospective project managers to gain cross-functional experience.*** An extremely valuable technique for helping project managers develop the leadership, and technical and team-building skills that they will require is to give them the opportunities to work in a variety of functional departments prior to their assignment to a project team. In previous chapters, we have suggested that a major cause of team conflict results from divergent viewpoints and attitudes held by team members from different functional backgrounds. One powerful method for combating the debilitating effects of these functional biases is to provide project managers with the skills and experiences to appreciate alternative points of view. Typically, project managers in most corporations come from a specific functional background and are therefore likely to harbor the same sort of intolerances and mindset as other members of their profession. When they are first placed in the role of managing a team of cross-functional members, they often have great difficulty in abandoning their prejudices, simply because they have had little contact with or appreciation of the activities of other functional departments. Transferring future project managers to different departments can be an eye-opening experience. In addition to aiding them in their future team-building activities, it also gives these prospective project managers a more well-rounded experience base for problem-solving with their own projects.

## TOWARD A PROJECT MANAGEMENT CURRICULUM

What are the skills that project managers need to master if they are to operate successfully in the dynamic, global economy of the 21st century? Throughout this book, we have offered our approach to answering this question in suggesting that although the majority of current project managers are adept at the technical aspects of their assignments, they continually run into trouble with their projects because they lack a basic, fundamental understanding of the so-called "softer skills," that is, the human or behavioral elements of project management (Kharbanda and Stallworthy, 1990). A great deal of research investigating the causes of project success and failure has found repeatedly that it is in the managerial aspects of their jobs (leadership, motivation, team building, personal time management) that many project managers go astray. If we are to give career and temporary project managers the skills necessary to successfully manage their projects, we need to go further than simply advising that all prospective project managers become technically proficient and begin exploring some of the more salient behavioral elements of their assignments.

What is the ideal curriculum for the project manager of the future? Certainly, every trainer and consulting firm have made an effort to answer this question and are currently offering their wares to companies around the world. It is not our purpose in this chapter to offer an alternative simply in order to point to deficiencies in current project manager training. Rather, we view the training of project managers as an extremely important undertaking, not one to be taken lightly or attempted without an organization's full understanding of the skills their project managers will need. We would suggest that organizations or potential project managers who are investigating ways of improving their chances for success consider many of the points we have raised throughout this book in the light of a general course for project managers as proposed below.

It is helpful to consider the various subjects a curriculum should address using the general management model originally proposed by Henri Fayol (1949). Fayol analyzed the activities of managers and classified their various responsibilities into four distinct functions: planning, organizing, leading, and controlling (see Table 19.2). We can employ this general model when considering the types of roles played by project managers, as we examine the skill set needed to succeed (e.g., Cleland, 1990).

- Planning is a key aspect of the project manager's responsibilities. Among the various planning activities that project managers must regularly engage in are work breakdown structures, project milestone development and scheduling, budgeting, and other resource planning. In addition to a theoretical knowledge of each of these tasks, a basic understanding of project management software can be extremely helpful. Many of the better-known software packages on the market allow project managers to perform these various operations from their personal computers. Even for highly com-

**TABLE 19.2. Skills Necessary for Effective Project Managers**

*Planning*
- Work breakdown
- Project scheduling
- Knowledge of PM software
- Budgeting and costing

*Organizing*
- Team building
- Establishing team structure and reporting assignments
- Define team policies, rules, and protocols

*Leading*
- Motivation
- Conflict management
- Interpersonal skills
- Appreciation of team members' strengths and weaknesses
- Reward systems

*Controlling*
- Project review techniques
- Meeting skills
- Project close-out techniques

plex projects, software packages designed to run on mainframe computers offer a speedy alternative to manually determining early start and finish dates, expected time to completion, and so forth.

- Organizing refers to determining who is to be involved in the project and what their specific duties will be. One of the chief responsibilities for project managers has to do with team building: creating a cohesive and potent team from a group of disparate individuals with varying levels of motivation. Further, project managers need to understand the nature of project team structure and their relationship to the external project organization in order to have a better sense of how the project team is expected to operate (Larson and

Gobelli, 1989). Further, internal to the project team, project managers must develop their organizing skills for maximizing the efficiency of team members, rather than simply adding or deleting members without considering the impact of these repeated team reorganizations. Another important skill that project managers need to cultivate is creating the team policies and protocols that can lead to better cross-functional cooperation. A recent study demonstrated that project team rules and procedures can have a significant impact on both the degree of cross-functional cooperation a project team attains and its resulting effect on project success (Pinto, Pinto, and Prescott, 1993). The skills related to organizing a project team are crucial for creating the atmosphere that can lead to successful project development down the road.

- We have argued that leadership is the principal role project managers must play in their assignment. Leadership has many different dimensions and meanings. Some of the important leadership skills that all project managers must develop are a basic understanding of the many forms of leadership behavior itself, including an awareness that leadership style demands a large degree of flexibility if project managers are to function at their highest level. Further, project managers must understand the basic theories of motivation for their duties, realizing what they can and cannot do in motivating their employees to perform to their maximum potential. Again, the key lies in flexibility. We need to make project managers aware that there is no "one best" method for motivating subordinates. Rather, they must work to create an atmosphere in which subordinates do not perceive personal costs or risks by committing to the project.

    One of the most difficult lessons for novice project managers to learn is that of appreciating the various personality types found in a project team. It is a natural consequence of human nature that a manager may gravitate toward those individuals who share the same functional background, or have a similar personality. We frequently hear project managers, in referring to a team member, voice complaints such as, "Why can't he be more direct? Why can't he be a better team player? Why can't she stop acting like such a know-it-all?" Although the project managers' frustrations are real, we have often discovered that in fact, underlying many of these complaints is the more basic question, "Why can't he or she be more like me?" All individuals bring with them their personalities to project team work: Some subordinates will work well with you, and others are bound to remain in a constant state of friction. Canny project managers understand that what matters is results and diverse personality types usually conceal diverse strengths. These strengths, once tapped, can be employed for enhancing project implementation success.

• The controlling function refers to any oversight systems or abilities that project managers possess. One of the chief skills that project managers can fruitfully learn is that of conducting meetings. A tremendous amount of a project manager's day is spent in some form of verbal or written communication, usually face-to-face meetings, informal get-togethers, project team or stakeholder meetings, telephone calls, circulating memos, and so forth. One of the chief "time killers" for most project managers is meetings. We all know from experience that meetings can be conducted in a wide variety of ways, some quickly and efficiently, whereas others seem torturously long and ultimately inconclusive. Learning the rudiments of effective meeting skills is a vital aspect of project managers' controlling abilities. Likewise, other methods for project control involve developing review procedures and maintaining good interpersonal relationships with team members so that problems, once they occur, can be dealt with efficiently and effectively.

The above list demonstrates the myriad of managerial responsibilities that underscore successful project management. Certainly, technical skills are important for project managers. No project team likes to initiate a project without confidence in the team leader's abilities to comprehend the technical details of the project. However, the majority of the duties and day-to-day roles played by project managers are decidedly "managerial," or people-oriented. A good technician has the background to become a successful project manager, but unless he or she has taken the time to develop the people and organizing skills that go along with his or her background training, that project manager is almost invariably destined for significant problems at some point during the project's development. Any curriculum that is intended to make project managers better at their jobs must take into consideration the tremendous impact that "people management" has on project success.

## CONCLUSIONS

This chapter has offered a glimpse into the near future of project management, arguing that as project management becomes more of a profession and less of an ad hoc, accidental process, the nature of the professional project manager is bound to change as well. Project managers of the future must become generalists, not specialists. Although having the technical means to succeed, they must strive to develop their managerial skills as well. More projects are lost due to inadequate people management than have ever been defeated for technical reasons. In their quest to improve their abilities to lead projects, project managers have, as a powerful ally, the modern organizations within which they operate. Top management within these companies needs to make a concerted effort to create the training and environment within which project managers can flourish. If these steps are taken, we have the potential to realize, in the near future, a tremendous surge in professional project managers, operating for the benefit of all companies involved in project-based work.

# 20

## To a Successful End

*Conquer we shall, but we must first content
'Tis not the fight that crowns, but the end.*

—HERRICK

PROJECTS AND BY extension, project management, are the wave of the future in global business. This increase in demand for project management as a development technique has, unfortunately, not been met by a concomitant increase in the creation of qualified, highly trained project managers. For better or (usually) worse, too many organizations continue to initiate projects under the direction of individuals who have not been carefully selected or well trained in their assigned tasks. This set of circumstances lengthens the odds against most organizational projects achieving any of their salient objectives: completion on time and under budget, performing to specifications, or acceptance by clients.

What conclusions are we to draw from the material presented in the preceding chapters? If nothing else, it is certain that we have painted a portrait of project management as being a complex, time-consuming, frequently exasperating process. At the same time, it is equally clear that successful project managers are a breed apart. In order to answer the various calls they continually receive, balance the conflicting demands of a diverse set of stakeholders, navigate the tricky political waters of corporations, understand the fundamental process of motivating subordinates, develop and constantly refine their leadership skills, and engage in the thousands of pieces of detailed minutia while keeping their eyes fixed firmly on the project goals, individuals with special skills and personalities are required. Given the nature of their duties, is it any wonder that successful project managers are in such short supply, and once identified, so valued by their organizations?

There is good news for organizations, however; many of these skills, though difficult to master, can be learned (Thamhain, 1991). This point needs to be emphasized: *Project management is a challenge, not a mystery.* Indeed, it was our special purpose in undertaking this book to demystify much of the human side of project management, starting with the role played by the linchpin in the process: the project manager. The problem in the past has been that there have been few sources for either seasoned or novice project managers to turn to in attempting to better understand the nature of their unique challenge and methods for performing more effectively.

In writing this book, we sought to offer a unique perspective on the problem of project management. Rather than addressing the task itself and writing another text on methods for more efficiently running projects, we chose to consider the main actor in the project management drama: the project manager. Although much has been written on how to improve the process of project management, little is known about the sort of skills and challenges that specifically characterize project managers. As we have made the point previously in this book, too many organizations pay far too little attention to the process of selecting, training, and encouraging those individuals tasked to run project teams. The quite predictable result is to continually compound the mistake of creating wave after wave of accidental project managers, forcing them to learn through trial and error with minimal guidance on how best to perform their roles.

It is in consequence of this gap in the project management literature that this book has been written. Managing projects is a challenge and requires a strategy and methodology all its own. Perhaps most important, it requires a project manager willing to function as a leader in every sense of the term. We have addressed a wide range of challenges, both contextual and personal, that form the basis under which projects are managed in today's organizations. It is hoped that readers will find something of themselves as well as something of use contained in these pages.

## POINTS TO REMEMBER

We have reviewed the topics presented in this book to glean some of the more salient issues that project managers need to keep in mind when undertaking a project implementation effort. This set of 12 rules, not appearing in any particular order, offers a convenient way to synthesize much of the material developed in more detail throughout the book (see Table 20.1).

**1.** *Understand the context of project management.* Much of the difficulty in becoming an effective project manager lies in understanding the particular challenges that project management presents in most corporations. Projects are a unique form of organizational work. They force managers to operate in a temporary environment, outside of the traditional functional lines of authority, relying on influence and other informal methods of power to expedite their projects. In essence, it is not simply the management of a project per se that presents managers with a unique challenge; it is also the atmosphere within which they must operate that adds an extra dimension of difficulty. Projects exist outside the established hierarchy. They threaten, rather than support, the status quo because they represent change. It is important that project managers walk into their assigned role with their eyes wide open as to the monumental nature of the tasks they are likely to face.

**2. *Recognize project team conflict as progress.*** One of the common responses from project managers to project team conflict is panic. This reaction is understandable in that project managers perceive, correctly, that their reputation and careers are on the line in the event that the project fails. Consequently, any evidence that they interpret as damaging to the prospects of project success, such as team conflict, represents a very real source of anxiety. In reality, these interpersonal tensions are a natural result of banding together individuals from diverse backgrounds and requiring them to coordinate their activities. Conflict, as evidenced by the stages of group development, is more often a sign of healthy maturation in the group.

The result of differentiation among functional departments (Lawrence and Lorsch, 1967) points out that conflict under these circumstances is not only possible, but unavoidable. One of the worst mistakes project managers can make when conflicts start to emerge is to immediately force them below the surface without first analyzing the nature of the conflict. Although it is true that many interpersonal conflicts are based on personality differences, others are of a professional nature and should be addressed head-on. As we suggested in our chapter on conflict, once project managers have analyzed the nature of the conflict between team members, a defusion or avoidance approach may be entirely warranted. On the other hand, such an approach should not be the result of a knee-jerk reaction to suppress conflict. In our experience, we have learned that even though a conflict is pushed below the surface, if left unaddressed, it will continue to fester. The resulting eruption, which will inevitably occur later in the project development cycle, will have a far more damaging effect than if the original conflict had been addressed early on.

**3. *Understand who the stakeholders are and what they want.*** Project management is a balancing act. It requires project managers to juggle the various, and often conflicting, demands of a number of powerful project stakeholders. One of the best tools a project manager can use is to develop a realistic assessment early in the project identifying the project's principal stakeholders and their agendas. In some projects, particularly those with important external clients or constituent groups, the number of stakeholders may be quite large, particularly when "intervenor" groups are included. Project managers who acknowledge the impact of stakeholders and work to minimize their effect by fostering good relations with them are often more successful than those who operate in a reactive mode, continually surprised by unexpected demands from groups not initially considered.

A final point about stakeholders: It is important for project managers' morale to remember that it is essentially impossible to please all the stakeholders all the time. The conflicting nature of their demands suggests that when one group is happy, another is probably upset. Project managers need to forget the idea of maximizing everyone's happiness and concentrate instead on maintaining satisfactory relations that allow them to do their job with a minimum of external interference.

**4. *Accept the political nature of organizations and use it to your advantage.*** Like it or not, we exist in a politicized world. Unfortunately, our organizations are no different. Important decisions involving resources are made through bargaining and deal-making. Project managers who wish to succeed must learn to use the political system to their advantage. This involves becoming adept at negotiation and the use of influence tactics to further the project's goals. At the same time, it is important to remember that any project representing possible organizational change is threatening, often due to its potential to reshuffle the power relationships among the key organizational units and actors. Playing the political game simply acknowledges this reality and argues that successful project managers are those who can use their personal power and influence to ensure cordial relations with important stakeholders and secure the resources necessary to smooth the client's adoption of the project.

**5. *Leading from the front: The view is better.*** One message we have tried to clearly impart throughout this book is that project management is a "leader-intensive" undertaking. Strong, effective leaders can go a long way toward helping a project succeed in spite of a number of external or unforeseen problems. Likewise, a poor, inflexible leader can often ruin the chances of many important projects ever succeeding. Consequently, it is important for the reader to distinguish between simply operating as the project "manager" and working instead to develop the techniques and qualities of a "leader." Leaders are the focal point of projects. They serve as a rallying point for the team and they are usually the major source of information and communication for external stakeholders. Because their role is so central and so vital, we have talked at length about many of the attributes project leaders must work to develop.

The essence of leadership lies in our ability to use it flexibly. That implies that not all subordinates or situations merit the same response. Under some circumstances, a very autocratic approach is appropriate, whereas other situations will be far better served by the project manager's adopting a consensual style. Effective project leaders seem to understand this idea intuitively: Their approach must be tailored to the situation; it is self-defeating to attempt to tailor the situation to a preferred approach. The worst leaders are those who are unaware or indifferent to the freedom they have to vary their leadership styles. Further, they see any situation in which they must involve subordinates as inherently threatening to their authority. As a result, they usually operate under what is euphemistically termed the "mushroom principle of management." That is, they treat their subordinates the same way they would raise a crop of mushrooms—keeping them in the dark and feeding them a steady diet of manure.

The importance of flexibility in leading was reinforced recently when a midlevel manager, in speaking with one of the authors, asserted, "I'm completely fair. I treat all my subordinates the same." Better-informed readers can immediately see the obvious contradiction. Subordinates are not the same. Why, then, do we make the mistake of treating them as if they were? Until managers learn to vary their leadership styles to meet a wide variety of criteria, they will never begin to realize the potential they possess as team leaders.

A final point about leadership is that an element of flexible leadership behavior is a realistic assessment of personal strengths and weaknesses. It goes without saying that no one person, including the project manager, possesses all necessary information, knowledge, or expertise to perform project tasks on his or her own. Rather, successful project managers are usually those who acknowledge their limitations and work through subordinates' strengths. In serving as a facilitator, one of the essential abilities of an exceptional project manager is knowing where to go to seek the right help and how to ask the right questions. Obviously, the act of effective questioning is easier said than done. However, a point to bear in mind is that questioning is not interrogation; that is, good questions challenge subordinates without putting them on the spot, they encourage definite answers rather than vague responses, and they discourage guessing. The leader's job is to probe, require subordinates to consider all angles and options, and support them in making reasoned decisions. Direct involvement is a key component of a leader's ability to perform these tasks.

**6. Understand what "success" means.** Successful project implementation is no longer subject to the traditional "triple constraint." That is, the days when projects were evaluated solely on the basis of budget, schedule, and performance criteria are past. In modern-day business, with its increased emphasis on customer satisfaction, we have to retrain project managers to expand their criteria for project success to include a fourth item: client use and satisfaction. Project success is a far more comprehensive word than some managers may have initially thought. The implication for rewards is also important. Within some organizations that regularly implement projects, it is common practice to reward the implementation manager when, in reality, only half the job has been accomplished. In other words, giving managers promotions and commendations before the project has been successfully transferred to clients, is being used, and is impacting on organization effectiveness is seriously jumping the gun.

Any project is only as good as it is used. In the final analysis, nothing else matters if a system is not productively employed. Consequently, every effort must be made to ensure that the system meets client needs, their concerns and opinions are solicited *and listened to,* and they have final approval on the transferred project. This implies that the intended user of the project is the major determinant of its success. Traditionally, the bulk of the team's efforts are centered internally, mainly on its own concerns: budgets, timetables, and so forth. Certainly, these aspects of the project implementation process are necessary, but they should not be confused with the ultimate determinant of success: the client.

*7. **Build and maintain a cohesive team.*** Many projects are developed through the use of cross-functional teams. Developing and maintaining cordial team relations and fostering a healthy intergroup atmosphere often seem like a full-time job for most project managers. However, the payoff resulting from a cohesive project team cannot be overestimated. When a team is tasked to work toward project development and implementation, the healthier the atmosphere within that team, and the greater the likelihood that it will perform effectively. The project manager's job is to do whatever is necessary to build and maintain the health (cohesion) of his or her team. Sometimes, that support can be accomplished by periodically checking with team members to determine their attitudes and satisfaction with the process. Other times, the project manager may have to resort to less conventional methods such as throwing parties or organizing field trips for the team. In order to effectively intervene and support a team, project managers play a variety of roles, including motivator, cheerleader, peacemaker, and conflict resolver. All these duties are appropriate in creating and maintaining an effective team.

Even a top-notch leader needs an effective team to truly "bloom." Consider the example of Bill Fletcher, a top-level executive, smart and aggressive, a brilliant planner and strategist. Unfortunately, he is likely to alienate his team by taking all the credit for its success and passing off all the blame when things go wrong (Kaplan, Drath, and Kofodimos, 1993). Though it is good to be driven, it is important not to go too far, lest in the process the project manager destroys him- or herself, the team, and the project. Successful project managers must also be expansive enough to harness their drive for mastery and control for the benefit of the project and the organization. Such managers are willing to acknowledge their mistakes and failings, as well as realize their own limits and the project team's strengths.

**8. *Enthusiasm and despair are both infectious.*** One of the more interesting aspects of project leaders is that they often function like miniaturized billboards. They project an image and attitude that signal the current status of the project and its likelihood for success. The team takes its cue from the attitudes and emotions of its manager. One of the most important roles as the leader is that of motivator and encourager. The worst type of project managers are those who play their cards close to their chests, revealing little or nothing about the status of the project (the "mushroom manager"). Team members want and deserve to be kept abreast of what is happening. It is important to remember that the success or failure of the project affects the team as well as the manager. Rather than allowing the rumor mill to churn out disinformation, team leaders need to function as honest sources of information. When team members come to the project manager for advice or project updates, it is important to be honest. If the manager does not know the answer to their questions, tell them the truth. Truth in all forms is recognizable and most team members are much more appreciative of honesty than whitewash.

**9. *One look forward is worth two looks back.*** A recent series of commercials from a large computer manufacturer had, as its slogan, "We never stop asking 'What if?'" Asking the "what if?" question is another way of saying that we should never become comfortable about the status of the project under development. As we mentioned previously in the chapter on critical success factors, an earlier large-scale study of project failure found that the number one determinant of project failure was the absence of any trouble-shooting mechanisms, that is, anyone asking the "what if?" questions. Projecting a skeptical eye toward the future may seem gloomy to some managers. In our opinion, it makes good sense. We cannot control the future, but if we are proactive, we can control our response to it.

A good example of the failure to apply this philosophy is evidenced with the progress of the Chunnel, linking Great Britain with France. Although finally becoming operational in the fall of 1994, it has opened for limited use some 18 months later than originally scheduled. At the same time, the final cost of £15 billion is likely to be over six times the original estimate of £2.3 billion (O'Connor, 1993). It is instructive to take note of a recent statement by one of the project's somewhat harassed directors who, when pressed to state when the project would be completed, replied: "Now it will be ready when it's ready and not before!" Clearly, the failure to apply adequate contingency planning has led to the predictable result: a belief that the project will simply end when it ends.

**10.** *Remember what you are trying to do.* Do not lose sight of the purpose behind the project. Sometimes, it is easy to get bogged down in the minutia of the development process, fighting fires on a daily basis and dealing with thousands of immediate concerns. The danger is that in so doing, project managers may fail to maintain a view of what the end product is supposed to be. This point reemphasizes the need to keep the mission in the forefront, not just for the project manager, but for the team as well. The implementation goal serves as a large banner that the project team leader can wave as needed to keep attitudes and motives focused in the right direction. Sometimes, a superordinate goal can serve as a rallying point. Whatever technique project managers use, it is important that they understand the importance of keeping the mission in focus for all team members. A simple technique for assessing team members' understanding of the project is to intermittently ask for their assessment of the project's status. Further,

**TABLE 20.1. Points to Remember**

---

- Understand the context of project management.

- Recognize project team conflict as progress.

- Understand who the stakeholders are and what they want.

- Accept and utilize the political nature of organizations.

- Lead from the front.

- Understand what "success" means.

- Build and maintain a cohesive team.

- Enthusiasm and despair are both infectious.

- One look forward is worth two looks back.

- Remember what you are trying to do.

- Use time carefully or it will use you.

- Above all, plan, plan, plan.

---

they should be aware of how their contributions fit into the overall installation plan. Are they aware of the specific contributions of other team members? If the answer is no, more attention needs to be paid to reestablishing a community sense of mission.

**11.** *Use time carefully or it will use you.* Time is a precious commodity and yet, when we talk to project managers, it seems that no matter how hard they work to budget it, there is never enough. Project managers need to make a realistic assessment of the "time killers" in their daily schedule: How are they spending their time and what are they doing profitably or unprofitably? We have found that the simple practice of keeping a daily time log for a short time can be an eye-opening experience. Project managers usually discover that they spend far too much of their time in unproductive ways: project team meetings without agendas that grind on and on, unexpected telephone calls in the middle of planning sessions, quick "chats" with other managers that consume hours, and so forth. Efficient time management, one of the keys to successful project development, starts with project managers. When they proactively plan their days and stick to a timetable, they often find that they are operating efficiently. On the other hand, when they take each problem as it comes and function in an ad hoc, reactive mode, they are likely to forever remain prisoners of their own schedules.

A sure recipe for finding the time and resources required to get everything done without spending an inordinate amount of time on the job or construction site is provided by Gosselin (1993). The six practical, down-to-earth steps to help project managers control their tasks and projects without feeling that they are constantly behind schedule include:

- Create a realistic time estimate without overextending yourself.

- Be absolutely clear about what the boss or client requires.

- Provide for contingencies (schedule slippage or loss of key team member).

- Revise original time estimate and provide a set of options as required.

- Be clear about factors that are fixed (e.g., specifications, resources, etc.).

- Learn to say, "Yes, and . . ." rather than "No, but. . . ." Negotiation is the key.

**12. *Above all, plan, plan, plan.*** This final point proceeds from several of those stated above: The essence of efficient project management is to take the time to get it as right as possible the first time. By "it," we mean to get the schedule right, get the team composition right, get the project specifications right, and get the budget right. There is a truism that those who fail to plan are planning to fail. One of the practical difficulties with planning is that so many of us distinguish planning from other aspects of project development (i.e., doing the work). Top management is often particularly guilty of this offense as it waits impatiently for the project manager to begin doing the work of the project. It often seems that too much planning is guaranteed to elicit repeated and pointed questions from top management and other stakeholders as they seek to discover the reason why "nothing is being done." Experienced project managers know that it is vital not to rush this stage by reacting too quickly to top management inquiries. The planning stage must be managed carefully to allow the project manager and team the time necessary to formulate appropriate and workable plans that will form the basis for the development process. Dividing up the tasks and starting the "work" of the project too quickly is often ultimately wasteful. Steps that were poorly executed are often steps that must be redone.

A complete and full investigation of any proposed project does take significant time and effort. However, bear in mind that by the time an opportunity is fully investigated with overly elaborate or intricate planning, it may no longer exist. We have time and again emphasized the importance of planning, but it is also apparent that there comes a limit, to both the extent and time frame of the planning cycle. A survey among entrepreneurs, for example, revealed that only 28% of them drew up a full-scale plan. Perhaps they rely more on their intuition and "gut" feeling. A lesson here for project managers is that they, like entrepreneurs, must plan, but they must also be smart enough to recognize mistakes and change their strategy accordingly. As is noted in an old military slogan, "No plan ever survives its first contact with the enemy."

The above 12 points are intended to put into simpler terms some of the most important "tips" from this book. Much more can and has been said about each of these topics, and within the preceding chapters they have been developed to a considerable degree. It was our intent to begin to explore some of the numerous roles and challenges that project managers are expected to undertake as part of their professional responsibilities. Project management is an exciting and continually evolving field of work and study. To date, however, although large volumes have been written on methods for improving the *process* of project management, little in comparison is being produced that examines in detail the various tasks, responsibilities, and difficulties that this form of work places on the project manager. This current dearth of information must be addressed in order to prepare a new generation of project managers for the challenges they will face as they start down the path of the accidental profession.

## DIRECTIONS FOR THE FUTURE

*Successful Project Managers: Leading Your Team to Success* represents one of the few efforts to date intended to delineate the problems of not project management, but the project manager. In our research and consulting experiences, we constantly interact with project managers, some with many years of experience, who express their frustration with their organizations due to the lack of understanding of their assigned tasks and responsibilities. Year after year, manager after manager, companies continue to make the same mistakes in "training" their project managers, usually through an almost ritualized baptism of fire. Project managers deserve better. Indeed, the challenges and potential for project management in the global marketplace of the future necessitate a dramatically different mind-set from organizations that will find themselves increasingly dependent on project management techniques in order to profitably operate.

In a recent editorial in the *International Journal of Project Management,* Rodney Turner (1993) reflected on the likely future of project management in the turbulent world of the future. He suggests:

> Through the 90's and into the 21st century, project-based management will sweep aside traditional functional line management and (almost) all organizations will adopt flat, flexible organizational structures in place of the old bureaucratic hierarchies ... new organizational structures are replacing the old ... with flexible ... ones ... managers will use project-based management as a vehicle for intro-

ducing strategic planning and for winning and maintaining competitive advantage.

Turner presents quite a rosy future, a future that is predicated on organizations recognizing the changes they are currently undergoing and likely to continue to see in the years ahead. Within this challenging environment, project management is likely to emerge as a technique that can provide the competitive edge necessary to succeed.

At the same time, there seems to be a sea of change in recent years regarding the image of the project manager. The old view of the project manager as essentially that of a decision maker, expert, boss, and director seems to be giving way to a newer ideal: that of the project manager as a leader, coach, and facilitator. Lest the reader assume that these duties are any easier, we would quickly assert that they are, in fact, much more difficult. As part of this metamorphosis, the new breed of project manager needs to be a natural salesperson who can establish harmonious customer (client) relations and develop trusting relationships with stakeholders (Clarke, 1993). Although we have repeatedly stressed the importance of personal commitment, energy, and enthusiasm, it appears that most of all, successful project managers must manifest an obvious desire to see others succeed.

For successful project managers, there will always exist a dynamic tension between the twin demands of technical training and an understanding of human resource needs. It must be clearly understood, however, that in assessing the relative importance of each sort of challenge for successful project management, the focus must clearly be on managing the human side of the process. Project management is primarily a challenge in managing people. This point was recently brought to light in an excellent review of a book on managing the "human side" of projects (Horner, 1993). The book reviewer noted (and, in fact, lamented) that:

There must be many project managers like me who come from a technological background, and who *suffered* [author's emphasis] an education which left them singularly ill-prepared to manage people.

How can project managers incorporate modern ideals into existing organizations and develop commitment and motivation in team members? Nichols (1994) offers some interesting leads about the priorities that project managers need to adopt, while at the same time paying close attention to the environmental needs and moral imperatives of the corporate mission. She suggests that as part of their project teams, project managers will have to contend with the new "knowledge" professional, an individual who:

1. Constantly questions the values of the company.

2. Feels little loyalty to corporate authority.

3. Longs for connections in a large organization.

Her solution? Nichols argues that the key for managing these individuals in project teams lies in the team leader's ability to create a sense of meaning for the subordinate. It is in establishing that standard of meaning, whether generally accepted by all members of the team or unique to each individual, that the project manager offers his or her team the basis for demonstrating personal commitment.

Leading researchers and scholars perceive the 21st century as the upcoming age of project management (Cleland, 1991). The age of globalization of markets, merging of many European economies, the enhanced expenditures of money on capital improvement both in the United States and abroad, and the rapidly opening borders of Eastern European and Pacific Rim countries with their goals of rapid infrastructure expansion—all offer an eloquent argument for the enhanced popularity of project management as a technique for improving the efficiency and effectiveness of organizational operations. With so much at stake, it is vital that we begin to address immediately some of the deficiencies in our project management theory and practice.

As further evidence of the rise in project management techniques, more and more companies in the developed world are shifting away from mass production operations to "high-performance" workplaces predicated on the use of specialization, task forces, cross-functional teams, and project management to encourage rapid time to market and lower costs. These high-performance workplaces, with their emphasis on "lean production," offer a tremendous environment within which to foster and maintain project management as the technique of choice for achieving the dual goals of internal operating efficiency coupled with responsive external effectiveness.

Project management techniques are well known; however, until we are able to take further steps toward formalizing project manager training by teaching the required skill set, the problems with efficiently developing, implementing, and gaining client acceptance for these projects are likely to continue growing (Thamhain, 1991). Consequently, there is currently a true window of opportunity in the field of project management. It is our hope that this book does not become the last word in project manager training, but rather, represents a first step toward comprehensive programs to create a new generation of highly trained project managers. Too often in the past, project managers have been forced to learn their skills the hard way, through practical experience coupled with all the problems of trial and error (Thamhain, 1991). Certainly, experience *is* a valuable component of learning to become an effective project manager, but it is by no means the only method. This book, in addition to the continuing rise of project management programs at universities around the world, offers corporations another alternative: one that creates a formalized body of knowledge, on not just project management, but how to become a better project manager.

# *Sources*

## PART 1: SETTING THE SCENE

*Chapter 1: Introduction*

Molière, *The Nuttall Dictionary of Quotations*, compiled by J. Wood, London: Frederick Warne & Co., 1961 ed.

Randolph, W. A. and B. Z. Posner (1989), What every manager should know about project management, *Sloan Management Review* 29(4), 65–73.

Davis, J. C. (1984), The accidental profession, *Project Management Journal* XV(3), 6.

Frame, J. D. (1987), *Managing Projects in Organizations*, San Francisco, CA: Jossey-Bass.

Graham, R. J. (1992), A survival guide for the accidental project manager, in *Proceedings of the Annual Project Management Institute Symposium*, Drexel Hill, PA: Project Management Institute, pp. 355–361.

Thamhain, H. J. (1991), Developing project management skills, *Project Management Journal* XXII(3), 39–53.

Steiner, G. A. (1969), *Top Management Planning*, New York: MacMillan, p. 498.

Cleland, D. I. and H. Kerzner (1985), *A Project Management Dictionary of Terms*, New York: Van Nostrand Reinhold, p. 199.

Meredith, J. and S. J. Mantel, Jr. (1989), *Project Management*, New York: Wiley.

Bryson, J. M. and P. Bromiley (1993), Critical factors affecting the planning and implementation of major projects, *Strategic Management Journal* 14, 319–337.

Lord, M. A. (1993), Implementing strategy through project management, *Long-Range Planning* 26, 76–88.

Adams, J. R. and S. E. Barndt (1988), Behavioral implications of the project life cycle, in D. I. Cleland and W. R. King (eds.), *Project Management Handbook*, 2nd ed., New York: Van Nostrand Reinhold, pp. 206–230.

King, W. R. and D. I. Cleland (1988), Life cycle management, in D. I. Cleland and W. R. King (eds.), *Project Management Handbook*, 2nd ed., New York: Van Nostrand Reinhold, pp. 191–205.

*Chapter 2: Stakeholder Analysis and Project Management*

Dill, W. R. (1958), Environment as an influence on managerial autonomy, *Administrative Science Quarterly* 3, 409–443.

Wheelen, T. L. and J. D. Hunger (1992), *Strategic Management and Business Policy*, 4th ed., Reading, MA: Addison-Wesley.

Weiner, E. and A. Brown (1986), Stakeholder analysis for effective issues management, *Planning Review* 36, pp. 27–31.

Mendelow, A. (1986), Stakeholder analysis for strategic planning and implementation, in W. R. King and D. I. Cleland (eds.), *Strategic Planning and Management Handbook*, New York: Van Nostrand Reinhold, pp. 67–81.

Gaddis, P. O. (1959), The project manager, *Harvard Business Review* 37, 89–97.

Cleland, D. I. (1988), Project stakeholder management, in D. I. Cleland and W. R. King (eds.), *Project Management Handbook*, 2nd ed., New York: Van Nostrand Reinhold, pp. 275–301.

## Chapter 3: The Politics of Project Management

Bierce, A., *Dictionary of Quotations*, compiled by E. Berger, New York: Delacorte Press, 1968 ed.

Butler, A. G. (1973), Project management: A study in organizational conflict, *Academy of Management Journal* 16, 84–101.

Graham, R. J. (1989), *Project Management as If People Mattered*, Bala Cynwyd, PA: Primavera Press.

French, J. R. P. and B. Raven (1959), The bases of social power, in D. Cartwright (ed.), *Studies in Social Power*, Ann Arbor, MI: Institute for Social Research, pp. 150–167.

Goodman, R. M. (1967), Ambiguous authority definition in project management, *Academy of Management Journal* 10, 395–407.

Cialdini, R. B. (1993), *Influence*, 3rd ed., New York: HarperCollins.

Thamhain, H. J. and J. R. Gemmill (1974), Influence styles of project managers: Some project performance correlates, *Academy of Management Journal* 17, 216–224.

Pfeffer, J. (1981), *Power in Organizations*, Marshfield, MA: Pitman, p. 7.

Mintzberg, H. (1983), *Power In and Around Organizations*, Englewood Cliffs, NJ: Prentice Hall, p. 421.

Mayes, B. T. and R. W. Allen (1977), Toward a definition of organizational politics, *Academy of Management Review* 2, 675.

Beeman, D. R. and T. W. Sharkey (1987), The use and abuse of corporate politics, *Business Horizons* 36(2), 26–30.

Allen, R. W., D. L. Madison, L. W. Porter, P. A. Renwick, and B. Y. Moyes (1979), Organizational politics: Tactics and characteristics of actors, *California Management Review* 22(1), 78.

Markus, M. L. (1981), Implementation politics—top management support and user involvement, *Systems, Objectives, Solutions* 2, 203–215.

Markus, M. L. (1983), Power, politics, and MIS implementation, *Communications of the ACM* 26, 430–444.

Markus, M. L. and J. Pfeffer (1983), Power and the design and implementation of accounting and control systems, *Accounting, Organizations and Society* 8, 205–218.

March, J. G. and H. A. Simon (1958), *Organizations*, New York: John Wiley.

Lawrence, P. R. and J. W. Lorsch (1967), Differentiation and integration in complex organizations, *Administrative Science Quarterly* 11, 1–47.

Lawrence, P. R. and J. W. Lorsch (1969), *Organization and Environment*, Homewood, IL: Irwin.

May, A. (1979), Concorde—bird of harmony or political albatross?, *International Organizations* 17, 481–508.

Koenig, C. and R.-A. Thietart (1988), Managers, engineers, and government: The emergence of the mutual organization in the European Aerospace Industry, *Technology in Society* 10, 45–69.

Gandz, J. and V. V. Murray (1980), Experiences of workplace politics, *Academy of Management Journal* 23, 237–251.

Hickson, D. J., C. R. Hinings, C. A. Lee, R. E. Schneck, and J. M. Pennings (1971), A strategic contingencies theory of intraorganizational power, *Administrative Sciences Quarterly* 16, 216–229.

Dill, D. D. and A. W. Pearson (1984), The effectiveness of project managers: Implications of a political model of influence, *IEEE Transactions on Engineering Management* EM-31, 138–146.

Talbott, G. M. (1994), Advance your career through networking, *Chemical Engineering Progress* 22, January 50–53.

Lovell, R. J. (1993), Power and the project manager, *International Journal of Project Management* 11(2), 73–78.

Payne, H. J. (1993), Introducing formal project management into a traditionally structured organization, *International Journal of Project Management* 11, 239–243.

## Chapter 4: Project Critical Success Factors

Haliburton, *The Nuttall Dictionary of Quotations*, compiled by J. Wood, London: Frederick Warne & Co., 1961 ed.

Baker, B. N., P. C. Murphy, and D. Fisher (1983), Factors affecting project success, in D. I. Cleland and W. R. King (eds.), *Project Management Handbook*, 2nd ed., New York: Van Nostrand Reinhold, pp. 902–919.

Pinto, J. K. and D. P. Slevin (1987), Critical factors in successful project implementation, *IEEE Transactions on Engineering Management* EM-34, 22–27.

Pinto, J. K. (1986), Project implementation: A determination of its critical success factors, moderators, and their relative importance across stages in the project life cycle, unpublished Ph.D. dissertation, University of Pittsburgh, Pittsburgh, PA.

Morris, P. W. G. (1988), Managing project interfaces—key points for project success, in D. I. Cleland and W. R. King (eds.), *Project Management Handbook*, 2nd ed., New York: Van Nostrand Reinhold, pp. 16–55.

Pinto, J. K. and D. P. Slevin (1988), Critical success factors across the project life cycle, *Project Management Journal* XIX(3), 67–75.

Beck, D. R. (1983), Implementing top management plans through project management, in D. I. Cleland and W. R. King (eds.), *Project Management Handbook*, New York: Van Nostrand Reinhold, pp. 166–184.

Manley, J. H. (1975), Implementation attitudes: A model and a measurement methodology, in R. L. Schultz and D. P. Slevin (eds.), *Implementing Operations Research/Management Science*, New York: Elsevier, pp. 183–202.

Hammond, J. S., III (1979), A practitioner-oriented framework for implementation, in R. Doktor, R. L. Schultz, and D. P. Slevin (eds.), *The Implementation of Management Science*, New York: North-Holland, pp. 35–62.

Bean, A. S. and M. Radnor (1979), The role of intermediaries in the implementation of management science, in R. Doktor, R. L. Schultz, and D. P. Slevin (eds.), *The Implementation of Management Science*, New York: North-Holland, pp. 121–138.

Pinto, J. K. and S. J. Mantel, Jr. (1990), The causes of project failure, *IEEE Transactions on Engineering Management* EM-37, 269–276.

## PART 2: LEADER PAR EXCELLENCE

*Chapter 5: Lead by Following*

Colvos, *The Nuttall Dictionary of Quotations,* compiled by J. Wood, London: Frederick Warne & Co., 1961 ed.

Slevin, D. P. and J. K. Pinto (1988), Leadership, motivation, and the project manager, in D. I. Cleland and W. R. King (eds.), *The Project Management Handbook,* 2nd ed., New York: Van Nostrand Reinhold, pp. 739–770.

Posner, B. Z. (1987), What it takes to be a good project manager, *Project Management Journal* XVIII(1), 51–54.

Gaddis, P. O. (1959), The project manager, *Harvard Business Review* 37, 89–97.

Hodgetts, R. M. (1968), Leadership techniques in the project organization, *Academy of Management Journal* 11, 211–219.

Blake, R. R. and J. Mouton (1964), *The Managerial Grid,* Houston, TX: Gulf Publishing.

Fiedler, F. E. (1978), Contingency models and the leadership process, in *Advances in Experimental Social Psychology,* Vol. 11, L. Berkowitz (ed.), New York: Academic Press, pp. 113–136.

Vroom, V. H. and P. W. Yetton (1973), *Leadership and Decision Making,* Pittsburgh, PA: University of Pittsburgh Press.

House, R. J. (1971), A path-goal theory of leadership effectiveness, *Administrative Science Quarterly* 16, 321–333.

Fleishman, E. A. (1973), Twenty years of consideration and structure, in E. A. Fleishman and J. G. Hunt (eds.), *Current Developments in the Study of Leadership,* Carbondale, IL: Southern Illinois University Press, pp. 79–101.

Fodor, E. M. (1976), Group stress, authoritarian style of control, and use of power, *Journal of Applied Psychology* 61, 313–318.

Tjosvold, D. (1984), Effects of leader warmth and directiveness on subordinate performance on a subsequent task, *Journal of Applied Psychology* 69, 422–427.

Heilman, M. E., H. A. Hornstein, J. H. Cage, and J. K. Herschlag (1984), Reactions to a prescribed leader behavior as a function of role perspective: The case of the Vroom–Yetton model, *Journal of Applied Psychology* 69, 50–60.

Stogdill, R. (1984), *Handbook of Leadership,* New York: Free Press.

Ghiselli, E. (1971), *Exploration of Managerial Talent,* Santa Monica, CA: Goodyear.

Dansereau, F., G. Graen, and B. Haga (1975), A vertical dyad linkage approach to leadership within formal organizations: A longitudinal investigation of role making process, *Organizational Behavior and Human Performance* 13, 45–78.

Salancik, G. R., B. J. Calder, K. M. Rowland, H. Leblibici, and M. Conway (1975), Leadership as an outcome of social structure and process: A multi-dimensional analysis, in J. G. Hunt and L. L. Larson (eds.), *Leadership Frontiers,* Kent, OH: Kent State University Press, pp. 133–161.

Kerr, S. and J. M. Jermier (1978), Substitutes for leadership: Their meaning and measurement, *Organizational Behavior and Human Performance* 22, 375–403.

Kouzes, J. M. and B. Z. Posner (1991), *The Leadership Challenge,* San Francisco, CA: Jossey-Bass.

Javidan, M. and A. Dastmachian (1993), Assessing senior executives: The impact of context on their roles, *Journal of Applied Behavioral Science* 29, 328–342.

Pettersen, N. (1991), What do we know about the effective project manager?, *International Journal of Project Management* 9, 99–104.

Einsiedel, A. A. (1987), Profile of effective project managers, *Project Management Journal* XVIII(5), 51–56.

Thamhain, H. J. and G. R. Gemmill (1974), Influence styles of project managers: Some project performance correlates, *Academy of Management Journal* 17, 216–224.

Keys, B. and T. Case (1990), How to become an influential manager, *Academy of Management Executive* IV(4), 38–51.

Gronn, P. (1993), Psychobiography on the couch: Character, biography, and the comparative study of leaders, *Journal of Applied Behavioral Science* 29, 343–358.

Leana, C. R. (1986), Predictors and consequences of delegation, *Academy of Management Journal* 29, 754–774.

Slevin, D. P. (1991), *The Whole Manager*, New York: AMACOM.

*Chapter 6: A Generalist, Not a Specialist*

Mikkelsen, H. and E. Folmann (1982), How to select managers for international projects, *Proceedings of the 7th (Internet) Congress on Project Management*, Copenhagen, September, pp. 909–916.

Gaddis, Paul O. (1959), The project manager, *Harvard Business Review* 37, 89–97.

Langley, R. A. and F. E. Meyer (1986), Managing a project, *Chemtech* 41, 402–403.

*AACE Transactions* (1988), Session 1, 3–7.

Randolph, W. A. and Barry Z. Posner (1988), What every manager needs to know about project management, *Sloan Management Review* 28, 65–73.

Toft, L. A. (1988), Project management—a personal view, *Proceedings of the Institution of Mechanical Engineers* 202(B1), 19–27.

Thornberry, N. E. (1987), Training the engineer as project manager, *Training and Development Journal* 41(10), 67–69.

Kharbanda, O. P. and E. A. Stallworthy (1990), *Management for Engineers*, Bradford, UK: MCB University Press.

Deeprose, D. (1992), Team leader or unit boss: Which do you want to be?, *Supervisory Management* 47, 3.

Larson, E. W. and D. H. Gobeli (1989), Significance of project management structure on development success, *IEEE Transactions on Engineering Management* EM-36, 119–125.

Kharbanda, O. P. and E. A. Stallworthy (1986), *Successful Projects— With a Moral for Management*, Aldershot, UK: Gower.

Lisberg, J. (1982), Selecting project managers, Paper presented at 7th Internet World Congress on Project Management, Copenhagen, September, pp. 909–916.

Lucas, C. L. (1981), A good project manager is hard to find, *Worldwide Projects* 8, 30.

*Engineering News Record* (1989), Construction manager's labor of love, March 2, 31.

*Engineering News Record* (1989), This is a lighter load? Project manager thinks so, August 10, 40.

*Engineering News Record* (1986), Women go underground, October 16, 27.

*Chapter 7: Project Managers' Duties: A to Z*

Kouzes, J. M. and B. Z. Posner, (1991), *The Leadership Challenge*, San Francisco, CA: Jossey-Bass.

Posner, B. Z. (1987), What it takes to be a good project manager, *Project Management Journal* XVIII(1), 51–54.

McClelland, D. C. (1961), *The Achieving Society*, New York: Van Nostrand.

Demming, W. E. (1986), *Out of the Crisis*, 2nd ed., Cambridge, MA: MIT Center for Advanced Engineering Study.

*Chapter 8: Motivation and the Project Manager*

McGregor, D. (1960), *The Human Side of Enterprise*, New York: McGraw-Hill.

Greenberg, J. and R. A. Baron (1993), *Behavior in Organizations*, 4th ed., Needham Heights, MA: Allyn and Bacon.

Graham, R. J. (1992), Private communication.

Maslow, A. H. (1943), A theory of human motive acquisition, *Psychological Review* 1, 370–396.

Herzberg, F. (1968), One more time: How do you motivate employees?, *Harvard Business Review* 46(1), 53–62.

Locke, E. A. and G. P. Latham (1990), *A Theory of Goal Setting and Task Performance*, Englewood Cliffs, NJ: Prentice Hall.

Tampoe, H. and L. Thurloway (1993), Project management—the use and abuse of techniques and teams (reflections from a motivation and environment study), *International Journal of Project Management* 11, 245–250.


*Chapter 9: Total Manager = Total Management*

Johnson, *The Nuttal Dictionary of Quotations*, compiled by J. Wood, London: Frederick Warne & Co., 1961 ed.

Stallworthy, E. A. and O. P. Kharbanda (1983), *Total Project Management*, Aldershot, Hampshire: Gower.

Merna, A. and N. J. Smith (1990), Project managers and the use of turn-key contracts, *Project Management* 8(3), 183–189.

Katz, R. and D. M. S. Lee (1992), Guest editorial—special issue on managing technical professionals, *IEEE Transactions on Engineering Management* EM-39, 201–202.

Kidder, T. (1981), *The Soul of a New Machine*, Boston, MA: Little, Brown.

Peters, T. (1989), *Thriving on Chaos: Handbook for a Management Revolution*, New Delhi, India: Tata-McGraw-Hill (reprint).

Zaleznick, A. (1977), Managers prefer working—managers and leaders: Are they different?, *Harvard Business Review* 55, 72.

Sweet, P. (1994), A planner's best friend, *Accountancy* 113(1206), 56–58.

Brine, W., M. Goddes, and C. Hastings (1990), *Project Leadership*, Aldershot, Hampshire: Gower.

Kharbanda, O. P. and E. A. Stallworthy (1990), *Project Teams: The Human Factor*, Oxford: Blackwell.

Cohen, A. R. (1993), *The Portable MBA in Management*, New York: John Wiley.

Kouzes, J. M. and B. Z. Posner (1993), *Credibility: How Leaders Gain and Lose It, Why People Demand It*, San Francisco, CA: Jossey-Bass.

Mancuso, J. (1993), *Winning with the Power of Persuasion: Mancuso's Secrets for Small Business Success*, Enterprise-Dearborn.

Alessandra, A. J. and P. Hunsaker (1993), *Communicating at Work*, New York: Simon & Schuster.

Wheatley, M. J. (1992), *Leadership and the New Science: Learning About Organizations from an Ordered Universe*, New York: Berrett-Koehler.

Chemers, M. M. and R. Ayman (1993), *Leadership Theory and Research: Perspectives and Directions*, New York: Academic Press.

Cleland, D. I. (1990), *Project Management: Strategic Design and Implementation*, Blue Ridge Summit, PA: Tab Books.

Elmes, M. and D. Wilemon (1988), Organizational culture and project leader effectiveness, *Project Management Journal* 19(4), 54–63.

## PART 3: TEAMS ACHIEVE WONDERS

*Chapter 10: "Excellence" Says So!*

Peters, T. and R. H. Waterman, Jr. (1982), *In Search of Excellence*, New York: HarperCollins.

Peters T. and N. Austin (1985), *A Passion for Excellence: The Leadership Difference*, New York: HarperCollins.

Waterman, R. H., Jr. (1987), *The Renewal Factor: How the Best Get and Keep the Competitive Edge*, New York: Bantam Books.

Peters, T. (1989), *Thriving on Chaos: Handbook for a Management Revolution*, New Delhi, India: Tata-McGraw-Hill (reprint).

Kharbanda, O. P. and E. A. Stallworthy (1988), *Project Teams—The Human Factor*, Oxford: Blackwell/NCC.

Barrett, F. D. (1987), Teamwork—how to expand its power and punch, *Business Quarterly*, Winter, 24–31.

Purokayastha, D. (1989), Teamwork responsible for current success, *Business India*, 177.

Vinton, G. (1989), Education, training and action learning, *Internal Auditing* 12, 3–7.

Foster Wheeler (1981), *Foster Wheeler Expertise*, Reading, Berkshire, UK.

Thamhain, J. H. and D. L. Wilemon (1987), Building high performance engineering project teams, *IEEE Transactions on Engineering Management* EM-34, 130–137.

Kernaghan, J. A. and R. A. Cooke (1990), Teamwork in planning innovative projects: Improving group performance by rational and interpersonal interventions in group process, *IEEE Transactions on Engineering Management* 37(2), 109–116.

Pinto, M. B. and J. K. Pinto (1990), Project team communication and cross-functional cooperation in new program development, *Journal of Product Innovation Management* 7 (3), 200–212.

## Chapter 11: 1 + 1 Can Equal 11!

Kharbanda, O. P. and E. A. Stallworthy (1990), *Project Teams: The Human Factor*, Oxford: Blackwell.

Sparks, D. B. (1982), *The Dynamics of Effective Negotiations*, Houston, TX: Gulf Publishing.

Woodstock, M. (1989), *Team Development Manual*, Oxford, UK: Gower.

Pinto, M. B., J. K. Pinto, and J. E. Prescott (1993), Antecedents and consequences of project team cross-functional cooperation, *Management Science* 39, 1281–1297.

Merrell, V. D. (1979), *Huddling—The Informal Way to Management Success*, New York: American Management Association.

Katzenbach, J. R. and D. K. Smith (1993), *The Wisdom of Teams: Creating the High Performance Organization*, Boston, MA: Harvard Business School.

Vincent, G. (1988), *Taming Technology—How to Manage a Development Project*, Corby: British Institute of Management.

Ballard, D. (1993), How to accomplish more, *Hydrocarbon Processing*, Part 1, 46, 189–194.

Covey, S. R., A. R. Merrill, and R. A. Merrill (1994), *First Things First —To Live, to Love, to Learn, to Leave a Legacy*, New York: Simon & Schuster.

Onken, W., Jr. and D. L. Wass (1974), Executive time management: Who's got the monkey?, *Harvard Business Review* 52, 75–80.

Adair, J. (1986), *Effective Teambuilding*, Aldershot, Hampshire: Gower.

*Chapter 12: Team Building*

Lippman, *The Nuttal Dictionary of Quotations*, compiled by J. Wood, London: Frederick Warne & Co., 1961 ed.

Wilemon, D. L. and H. J. Thamhain (1983), Team building in project management, *Project Management Quarterly* XIV, 21–33.

Pinto, J. K. and D. P. Slevin (1987), Critical factors in successful project implementation, *IEEE Transactions on Engineering Management* EM-34, 22–27.

Tuchman, B. W. and M. A. Jensen (1977), Stages in small group development revisited, *Group and Organizational Studies* 2, 419–427.

Graham, R. J. (1992), Personal communication.

Pinto, M. B., J. K. Pinto, and J. E. Prescott (1993), Antecedents and consequences of project team cross-functional cooperation, *Management Science* 39, 1281–1297.

Sherif, M. (1958), Superordinate goals in the reduction of intergroup conflict, *The American Journal of Sociology* 63(4), 349–356.

Galbraith, J. R. (1977), *Organization Design,* Reading, MA: Addison-Wesley.

Davis, T. E. (1984), The influence of the physical environment in offices, *Academy of Management Review* 9(2), 271–283.

Peters, M. P. (1986), Innovation for hospitals: An application of the product development process, *Journal of Health Care Marketing* 29, 182–191.

Leibson, D. E. (1981), How Corning designed a "talking" building to spur productivity, *Management Review* 70, 8–13.

## Chapter 13: Project Management and Conflict

Nietzche, *The Nuttall Dictionary of Quotations,* compiled by J. Wood, London: Frederick Warne & Co., 1961 ed.

Posner, B. Z. (1986), What's all the fighting about? Conflicts in project management, *IEEE Transactions on Engineering Management* EM-33, 207–211.

Thamhain, H. J. and D. L. Wilemon (1975), Conflict management in project life cycles, *Sloan Management Review* 16(3), 31–50.

Thamhain, H. J. and D. L. Wilemon (1977), Leadership, conflict, and program management effectiveness, *Sloan Management Review* 19(1), 69–89.

Thomas, K. W. and W. H. Schmidt (1976), A survey of managerial interests with respect to conflict, *Academy of Management Journal* 10, 315–318.

Thomas, K. W. (1992), Conflict and negotiation processes in organizations, in M. D. Dunnette (ed.), *Handbook of Industrial and Organizational Psychology,* 2nd ed., Palo Alto, CA: Consulting Psychologists Press, pp. 889–935.

Pondy, L. (1968), Organizational conflict: Concepts and models, *Administrative Science Quarterly* 12, 296–320.

Ruble, T. L. and K. W. Thomas (1976), Support for a two-dimensional model of conflict behavior, *Organizational Behavior and Human Performance* 16, 143–155.

Kilmann, R. H. and K. W. Thomas (1977), Developing a forced-choice measure of conflict-handling behavior: The MODE instrument, *Educational and Psychological Measurement* 37, 309–325.

Robbins, S. P. (1978), "Conflict management" and "conflict resolution" are not synonymous terms, *California Management Review* 21(2), 67–75.

Tjosvold, D. (1993), *Teamwork for Customers: Building Organizations That Take Pride in Serving*, San Francisco, CA: Jossey-Bass.

McCormack, M. H. (1989), *What They Still Don't Teach You at Harvard Business School*, New York: Bantam Books.

Adams, J. R. and S. E. Barndt (1988), Behavioral implications of the project life cycle, in D. I. Cleland and W. R. King (eds.), *Project Management Handbook*, 2nd ed., New York: Van Nostrand Reinhold, pp. 206–230.

Chan, M. (1989), Intergroup conflict and conflict management in the R&D divisions of four aerospace companies, *IEEE Transactions on Engineering Management* EM-36, 95–104.

*Chapter 14: Meeting Skills for Project Managers*

Burley-Allen, M. (1982), *Listening—The Forgotten Skill*, New York: John Wiley & Sons.

Kharbanda, O. P. (1983), Are you listening? *Swagat (Indian Airlines)*, 35–38.

Spiro, G. (1992), Are you listening comfortably?, *Business Age*, 110–111.

Shields, D. E. (1984), Listening—a small investment, a big payoff, *Supervisory Management* 29, 18–20.

Vining, J. W. and A. C. Yrle (1980), How do you rate as a listener?, *Supervisory Management* 25, 22–25.

Levin, D. M. (1989), *The Listening Self—Personal Growth, Social Change and the Closure of Metaphysics,* London: Routledge.

Anderson, A. and T. Lynch (1988), *Listening,* Oxford: Oxford University Press.

Sperry Corporation (1983), *How Important It Is to Listen,* New York: Sperry.

Prince, M. (1970), *The Practice of Creativity,* New York: Harper and Row.

Siegfried, D. and T. Englemann (1966), *Give Your Child a Superior Mind,* New York: Simon & Schuster.

*Economist* (1993), The melting pot bubbles less, Aug. 7, 69.

3M Meeting Management Team (1987), *How to Run Better Business Meetings—A Reference Guide for Managers,* New York: McGraw-Hill.

Brown, K. A., T. D. Klastorin, and J. L. Valluzzi (1990), Project performance and the liability of group harmony, *IEEE Transactions on Engineering Management* EM-37, 117–125.

Janis, I. L. (1982), *Groupthink: Psychological Studies of Policy Decisions and Fiascoes,* 2nd ed., Boston: Houghton-Mifflin.

## PART 4: SOME SUCCESS AND FAILURE STORIES

*Chapter 15: Case Studies*

Prior, *The Nuttall Dictionary of Quotations,* compiled by J. Wood, London: Frederick Warne & Co., 1961 ed.

Morris, P. W. G. and G. Hough (1987), *The Anatomy of Major Projects: The Realities of Managing Projects,* New York: John Wiley & Sons.

Morris, P. W. G. (1987), The everyday challenges of major projects, *Chartered Mechanical Engineer* 34(3), 33–38.

Kharbanda, O. P. and E. A. Stallworthy (1984), *How to Learn from Project Disasters,* Aldershot, UK: Gower.

Kharbanda, O. P. and E. A. Stallworthy (1992), *Lessons from Project Disasters,* Manchester, UK: MCB University Press.

Medley, J. (1991), *When AID Is No Help, How Projects Fail and How They Succeed,* New York: Intermediate Technological Publications.

Sobel, R. (1984), *IBM—Colossus in Transition,* New York: Sidgewick & Jackson.

Peters, T. J. and R. H. Waterman (1984), *In Search of Excellence—Lessons from America's Best-Run Companies,* New York: Sidgewick & Jackson.

Heller, R. (1994), *The Fate of IBM,* London: Little, Brown & Co.

Kharbanda, O. P. and E. A. Stallworthy (1990), *Project Teams: The Human Factor,* Manchester, UK: Blackwell.

Harris, M. (1985), IBM—more worlds to conquer, *BusinessWeek,* Feb. 18, 84–87.

Kharbanda, O. P. and E. A. Stallworthy (1987), *Company Rescue—How to Manage a Business Turnaround,* London, UK: Heinemann.

Peters, T. (1989), *Thriving on Chaos—Handbook for a Management Revolution,* New Delhi, India: Tata McGraw-Hill, India (reprint).

*Fortune* (1989), The U.S. must do as GM has done, 124(2), 70–79.

Adair, J. (1986), *Effective Teambuilding,* Aldershot, UK: Gower.

*Chapter 16: More Real-Life Examples*

Sen, *The Nuttall Dictionary of Quotations,* compiled by J. Wood, London: Frederick Warner & Co., 1961 ed.

Maude, B. (1978), *Leadership in Management,* New York: Business Books.

Peters, T. J. (1987), *Thriving on Chaos: Handbook for a Management Revolution,* New York: McGraw and Hill.

Mirchandani, H. V. (1983), Kudremukh—inception and implementation, in *Project Management in Public Enterprises,* Standing Conference of Public Enterprises, New Delhi, India (part of the proceedings of a National Workshop organized jointly by SCOPE and the Bureau of Public Enterprises), pp. 4.6.1–4.6.22, 9 annexes.

Kellogg, quoted in O. P. Kharbanda and E. A. Stallworthy (1990), *Project Teams*, Oxford, UK: Blackwell.

Seo, K. (1985), Asahan project—a shining example of economic cooperation, *Journal of Japanese Trade & Industry*, (2), 20–23.

Pintz, W. S. (1984), *Ok Tedi—Evolution of a Third World Mining Project*, London: Mining Journal Books.

Bechtel Civil and Minerals, Inc. (1985), *Ok Tedi*—Ready for the production of gold, quoted in O. P. Kharbanda and E. A. Stallworthy, (1990), *Project Teams*, Oxford, UK: Blackwell.

Kharbanda, O. P. and E. A. Stallworthy (1986), *Successful Projects— With a Moral for Management*, Aldershot, UK: Gower.

Taylor, R. (1989), Why Volvo is planning to go back to the future, *Financial Times*, June 9, A1.

*Bechtel Brief* (1979), Bechtel's project managers: Roger Elton directed the world's largest LNG project, Oct.

Kharbanda, O. P. and E. A. Stallworthy (1984), *How to Learn from Project Disasters*, Aldershot, UK: Gower.

Kharbanda, O. P. and E. A. Stallworthy (1987), *The Project Manager in the 1990's*, Bradford, UK: MCB University Press.

*Chapter 17: All Have One Goal*

Goethe, *The Nuttall Dictionary of Quotations*, compiled by J. Wood, London: Frederick Warne & Co., 1961 ed.

Nicholson, N. (1991), TQM—a contractor's perspective, *Process Engineering* 72(7), 31–32.

Kerzner, H. (1983), *Project Management—A Systems Approach to Planning, Scheduling and Controlling*, 5th ed., New York: Van Nostrand Reinhold.

Pinto, J. K. and S. J. Mantel, Jr. (1990), The causes of project failure, *IEEE Transactions on Engineering Management* EM-37, 269–276.

*Spaceflight* (1986), Shuttle enquiry—commission urges major changes, 292.

Kharbanda, O. P. and E. A. Stallworthy (1984), *How to Learn from Project Disasters*, Aldershot, UK: Gower.

Kharbanda, O. P. and E. A. Stallworthy (1992), *Lessons from Project Disasters*, Manchester, UK: MCB University Press.

Katz, R. and T. J. Allen (1985), Project performance and the locus of influence in the R&D matrix, *Academy of Management Journal* 28(1), 67–87.

McMorris, R. L. and R. J. Gravely (1993), Managing data from large-scale continuous monitoring projects, *Chemical Engineering Progress* 89, 111–115.

Gulliver, F. R. (1987), Post-project appraisals pay, *Harvard Business Review* 65(2), 128–132.

Price, F. (1984), *Right First Time—Using Quality Control for Profit*, Aldershot, UK: Gower.

Kharbanda, O. P. and E. A. Stallworthy (1991), Let's learn from Japan, *Management Accounting* 69(3), 26–30.

Munday, M. (1991) A case of Japanization?, *Management Accounting* 69(3), 32–33.

## PART 5: WHERE DO WE GO FROM HERE?

*Chapter 18: The Future Is Uncertain*

Drucker, P. (1992), Planning for uncertainty, *Wall Street Journal*, July 22, A12.

Cleland, D. I. (1991), The age of project management, *Project Management Journal* XXII(1), 19–24.

*Asian Review*, (1994), Construction industry remains buoyant, 131, 31.

Kharbanda, O. P. and E. A. Stallworthy (1992), *Lessons from Project Disasters*, Bradford, UK: MCB University Press.

Cooper, K. G. (1994), The $2,000 hour: How managers influence project performance through the rework cycle, *Project Management Journal* XXV(1), 11–24.

Barnes, N. M. L. and S. H. Wearne (1993), The future of major project management, *International Journal of Project Management* 11, 135–142.


Chapter 19: The New Breed

Carlyle, *The Nuttall Dictionary of Quotations*, compiled by J. Wood, London: Frederick Warne & Co., 1961 ed.

Aga, R. (1994), *Changing the Mindset: Reflections of a Chief Executive*, New Delhi, India: Tata McGraw-Hill.

Hawley, J. A. (1994), *Reawakening the Spirit in Work—The Power of Dharmic Management*, San Francisco, CA: Berrett-Koehler Publishers.

Obermeyer, N. J. and J. K. Pinto (1994), *Managing Geographical Information Systems*, New York: Guilford Press.

Adams, J. R. (1994), Project management: As a profession, in D. I. Cleland and R. Gareis (eds.), *Global Project Management Handbook*, New York: McGraw-Hill, Chap. 14, pp. 1–14.

Obradovitch, M. M. and S. E. Stephenou (1990), *Project Management: Risks and Productivity*, Bend, OR: Daniel Spencer.

Tampol, M. (1993), Motivating knowledge workers: The challenge of the 1990's, *Long Range Planning* 26(3), 49–55.

King, W. R. (1988), The role of projects in the implementation of business strategy, in D. I. Cleland and W. R. King (eds.), *Project Management Handbook*, 2nd ed., New York: Van Nostrand Reinhold, pp. 129–139.

Souder, W. (1988), Selecting projects that maximize profits, in D. I. Cleland and W. R. King (eds.), *Project Management Handbook*, 2nd ed., New York: Van Nostrand Reinhold, pp. 140–164.

Carr, C. (1992), *Smart Training: The Manager's Guide to Training for Improved Performance*, New York: McGraw-Hill.

Wearne, S. (1994), Training management for project success, *Professional Engineering* 7(3), 15.

Kharbanda, O. P. and E. A. Stallworthy (1990), *Management for Engineers*, Bradford, UK: MCB University Press.

Fayol, H. (1949), *General and Industrial Management*, London: Pitman.

Cleland, D. I. (1990), *Project Management: Strategic Design and Implementation*, Blue Ridge Summit, PA: Tab Books.

Larson, E. W. and D. H. Gobeli (1989), Significance of project management structure on development success, *IEEE Transactions on Engineering Management* EM-36, 119–125.

Pinto, M. B., J. K. Pinto, and J. E. Prescott (1993), Antecedents and consequences of project team cross-functional cooperation, *Management Science* 39, 1281–1297.

## Chapter 20: To a Successful End

Herrick, *The Nuttall Dictionary of Quotations*, compiled by J. Wood, London: Frederick Warne & co., 1961 ed.

Thamhain, H. J. (1991), Developing project management skills, *Project Management Journal* XXII(3), 39–53.

Lawrence, P. R. and J. W. Lorsch (1967), Differentiation and integration in complex organizations, *Administrative Science Quarterly* 11, 1–47.

Kaplan, R. E., W. H. Drath, and J. R. Kofodimos (1993), *Beyond Ambition: How Managers Can Lead Better and Live Better*, San Francisco, CA: Jossey-Bass.

O'Connor, L. (1993), Tunneling under the channel, *Mechanical Engineering* 115 (12), 60–66.

Gosselin, T. (1993), What to do with last-minute jobs, *World Executive Digest* 14, 70.

Turner, R. (1993), Editorial, *International Journal of Project Management* 11, 195.

Clarke, K. (1993), Survival skills for a new breed, *Management Today*, Dec., 5.

Horner, M. (1993), Review of "Managing people for project success," *International Journal of Project Management* 11(2), 125–126.

Nichols, M. (1994), Does new age business have a message for managers?, *Harvard Business Review* 72(2), 52–60.

Cleland, D. I. (1991), The age of project management, *Project Management Journal* XXII(1), 19–24.


## ADDITIONAL RESEARCH ON PROJECT CRITICAL SUCCESS FACTORS

Pinto, J. K. and J. G. Covin (1989), Critical factors in project implementation: A comparison of construction and R&D projects, *Technovation* 9, 49–62.

Pinto, J. K. and J. E. Prescott (1988), Variations in critical success factors over the stages in the project life cycle, *Journal of Management* 14, 5–18.

Pinto, J. K. and D. P. Slevin (1992), *The Project Implementation Profile*, Tuxedo, NY: Xicom, Inc.

# Index